S
Tr

G000298291

Luxor 80
TO 102

Contents

the magazine 5

Finding Your Feet 33

Cairo 45

Luxor 79

Written by Anthony Sattin and Sylvie Franquet

Copy edited by Maria Morgan
Page layout by Design 23
Magazine page layout by Nautilus Design (UK) Limited
Verified by Andrew Humphreys
Indexed by Marie Lorimer

Edited, designed and produced by AA Publishing.
© Automobile Association Developments Limited 2001
Maps © Automobile Association Developments Limited 2001

Automobile Association Developments Limited retains the copyright
in the original edition © 2001 and in all subsequent editions,
reprints and amendments.

All rights reserved. No part of this publication may be reproduced,
stored in a retrieval system, or transmitted in any form or by
any means – electronic, photocopying, recording or otherwise –
unless the written permission of the publishers has been obtained
beforehand.

The contents of this publication are believed correct at the time of
printing. Nevertheless, the publishers cannot be held responsible
for any errors or omissions or for changes in the details given in
this guide or for the consequences of any reliance on the information provided by the same.

Published in the United States by AAA Publishing, 1000 AAA Drive,
Heathrow, Florida 32746.
Published in the United Kingdom by AA Publishing.

ISBN 1–56251–501–2

Colour separation by Leo Reprographics
Printed and bound in China by Leo Paper Products

10 9 8 7 6 5 4 3 2 1

the magazine

The Best and Most of Egypt

but don't miss these...

Best Views
- **Of Cairo:** from a minaret, and there are plenty to choose from.
- **Of Luxor:** from the top of the Theban hills.
- **Of Sinai:** sunrise at Gebel St Catherine.
- **Of the Red Sea:** naturally from beneath the waves, where you'll also see blue, green and every other colour imaginable.
- **Of the Nile:** from the terrace of Aswan's Old Cataract Hotel (➤ 126).

Above: Tutankhamun's vibra enamelled jewellery

Pyramids at Giza, the only surviving Wonders of the Ancient World and still wonderful (➤ 62–6).

The Egyptian Museum of Antiquities in Cairo – for Tutankhamun's treasure, of course, but also to bring ancient Egypt to life, right down to the knitted socks (➤ 50–3).

Karnak Temple in Luxor, one of the world's greatest religious centres (➤ 84–7).

Valley of the Kings, for the beauty, awe and complexity of the pharaohs (➤ 91–3).

Sultan Hasan Mosque-Madrasa in Cairo, to appreciate the grandeur and harmony of Islamic architecture (➤ 69).

Above: Relax with a *sheesha*. Previous page: Woman in traditional costume

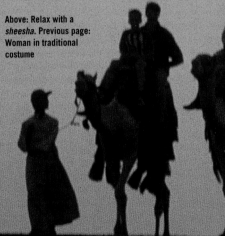

Best Buzzes
• Tea and *sheesha* – the tea comes strong and the tobacco rough – are quintessentially Egyptian.
• Joining a belly dancer may not be for everyone, but you'll never forget it.
• Being in an ancient temple alone – hard to do in high season, but there's nothing like it for sheer spookiness.
• Sunrise and sunset – a thrill wherever you are.

Best for Peace and Quiet
• The courtyards of mosques, but not during prayer time, or Friday at noon.
• The desert, though close to the cities it can be far from deserted.
• St Catherine's Monastery, but beware of tour groups (➤ 160–2).
• Downtown Cairo between 4 and 4:20am – it's almost worth staying up late for this (➤ 67).

A bird's eye view of Thebes

Best Mosques
• **Ibn Tulun**, simplicity and grandeur in harmony (➤ 68).
• **Al Azhar**, authority on Islam, and one of the world's oldest universities. (✚ 197 E4)
• **Abu Haggag**, built in the 13th century on the ruins of Luxor Temple, now hangs spectacularly over the excavated columns (➤ 89–90).
• **New Gurna**, Hassan Fathy's marvel in Luxor, shows just how far you can go with mudbrick (➤ 183).

Rest and watch the world go by over a glass of tea

• Hot-air ballooning over the desert (➤ 102).

Most Quirky
• The **Police Museum** at the Citadel, for a glimpse of crimes and corrective measures (➤ 69).
• The **chaplet of the Convent of St George** in Coptic Cairo (➤ 54–5), where you can wrap yourself in chains like the martyr .
• The **Cavafy Museum**, Alexandria, where you can sit by the poet's bed and read his more *risqué* works (➤ 137).
• **Fertility charms:** watch what you touch in temples and tombs – some statues and images are reputed to boost fertility.

The Desert

Nothing points out the delicate balance between the fertile and the barren better than a flight over Egypt. Thin strips of agricultural land line the ribbon of the Nile, and fan out into the delta. Beyond are the great deserts that form 90 per cent of the country: the Libyan Desert in the west, the mountainous Eastern Desert and, between the Mediterranean and Red Sea, the Sinai Desert.

Because of this stark contrast and the low rainfall, few countries are as dominated by their geography as Egypt. The

welcoming fertility of the Nile valley and the awesome wilderness of the all-encompassing deserts have had a huge influence on Egypt's history and culture. And one of ancient Egypt's most popular and enduring myths – the ongoing clash between desert and sown – is still relevant today.

Most camels in Egypt have come through the desert from Sudan, along the Forty Days Road

Top of the Pyramid

Aware of the need to work together to use the floodwater, early Egyptians created a hierarchy and bureaucracy as the basis for their civilisation. When the hierarchy and government were strong (for instance when the Pyramids were built), the Nile was harnessed and the area used for agriculture was increased. At times of a weaker government, the farmland quickly returned to desert.

Many Egyptian farmers still work the land like their ancestors

& the Sown

Order and Chaos

Osiris (▶ 12) brought order and civilisation to the Nile valley, making laws and teaching the Egyptians how to cultivate crops and produce wine. Along this generous if confined strip of land, the Egyptians thrived for thousands of years. It seemed such a wonderful place that ancient Egyptians hoped for its equal in their afterlife. Their idea of the perfect valley is echoed in many religions – in the Garden of Eden, for example, and in the Islamic shaded paradise cut through by running water, with food and drink in abundant supply.

Osiris's brother Seth, on the other hand, was associated with the desert, which was a constant threat to the sown. Perhaps

Intense farming occurs on the thin strip of fertile land along the Nile

not by chance the myth ties in with Egypt's early history, when global warming destroyed the forests on which the people of the Nile depended and the desert closed in on the river. Communities used to hunting and gathering then became reliant on the annual flooding of the Nile to irrigate their crops.

The Desert Was…

The desert wasn't seen in solely negative terms. Despite being the master of chaos, Seth was considered an essential part of the Egyptian world. Ancient Egyptians used the desert as a place to escape; it was where Moses and his people were tested and purified, and where Christianity's first monastic orders were founded in the 4th century. This spiritual place was also a place of wealth, for in spite of the challenging climate and land-scape, some of the pharaohs' gold was mined from the Red Sea mountains, while turquoise and lapis lazuli were found in Sinai. The desert also acted as a buffer against the wild Berber tribes of the Libyan Desert and the ambitious Bedouin Arabs to the west. Invasions, when they came, tended to arrive in the north or across the Sinai peninsula.

Disappearing Act

There was, perhaps, a moment when Egyptians blessed the desert. In the 6th century BC, after conquering Egypt and sacking Thebes, the great Persian emperor Cambyses sent an army to destroy the Oracle at Siwa Oasis.

Some 50,000 men marched into the sands.

None of them came out.

Like other temples along the Nile, Kom Ombo suffers from rising water caused by the Aswan Dam

Shifting Sands

Thebes was eulogised as 'hundred gated' by the Greek poet Homer and it was the epitome of the ancient city. Alexandria was the model of the classical city and Cairo was extolled as 'the Mother of the World' in *The Thousand and One Nights*. But despite this, Egyptian society has always been predominantly rural, until now...

Throughout history most Egyptians were farmers, tending their plots and bartering their produce. At the beginning of the 19th century Cairo was still mostly confined within its medieval walls and Alexandria was smaller than the Greek and Roman city from which it had grown. But since then, and particularly since the 1970s, when the Aswan High dam stopped the annual flooding of the Nile valley, more people are now living in cities than in the countryside. And there have been similarly dramatic changes in the desert.

'Egyptian society has always been predominantly rural, until now...'

The grass is green but the desert is never far away

The Desert Is...

Rather than threatening the stability of life in the Nile valley, the desert now seems to offer solutions. In 1869 the Suez Canal was cut across the desert that separated the Mediterranean and Red seas – it's currently the country's second-largest earner of foreign currency. Elsewhere in the desert, significant reserves of gas, oil, phosphates and fresh water boost Egypt's economy. New satellite cities have been established to ease the population squeeze in Cairo and are growing larger all the time. In the Libyan Desert mechanical diggers are at work on a project to divert water from the Nile along the new Toshka Canal and into a desert depression. It's hoped that this will create an alternative valley, a mirror image of the Nile. These exciting developments herald the start of a new era in the stormy yet inseparable relationship between the desert and the sown.

Often the only grass shepherds can find is on the side of the road

Whatever else you encounter in Egypt, there's no getting away from death. From the Great Pyramid and the fabulous golden mummy of Tutankhamun to the grandest of Cairo's mosques, many of the country's most memorable sights are connected to the cult of the dead.

Death on the Nile

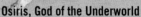

Osiris, God of the Underworld

Osiris was the archetypal good king and is credited with bringing civilisation to his people, teaching them how to farm and to honour their gods. Although he lived as a man, Osiris was born a god – the son of Geb, god of the earth, and Nut, the sky goddess. In true ancient Egyptian style, he married his sister Isis, while his brother Seth married their other sister Nephthys. But Seth was jealous of Osiris's success and, after inviting him to a feast, Seth presented Osiris with a beautiful box. Suddenly, he was bundled into it, thrown into the Nile and drowned.

According to the Greek writer Plutarch (c46–120), Isis found Osiris's body in Lebanon, where a tamarisk tree had grown round it. She returned her husband's corpse to Egypt, using magic to revive him for long enough to conceive a child: the falcon-headed god Horus. Later, Seth again found Osiris and this time cut him into 14 parts that were thrown into the Nile. The ever-resourceful Isis collected the parts, finding all of them except his penis, and bandaged them up before burying them. So, in addition to his many other distinctions, Osiris therefore became the first mummy.

Isis's lamentations were said to have been particularly beautiful and the tears she shed over her husband were believed to have caused the Nile to rise. Even today, the night in June when the Nile is seen to rise is known as the Night of the Drop.

Egyptian gods kept things running smoothly and could be petitioned in times of need. Myths developed to explain their origins and powers. Most had human bodies, but were often identified with animals.

Amun the ram
Anubis the jackal
Bastet the cat goddess
Edjo the cobra goddess
Horus the falcon-headed son of Isis and Osiris
Hapi the pot-bellied Nile god
Khepri the scarab beetle
Mut the vulture goddess
Ra the great sun god
Sekmet the lioness

Top left: Osiris, god of the underworld

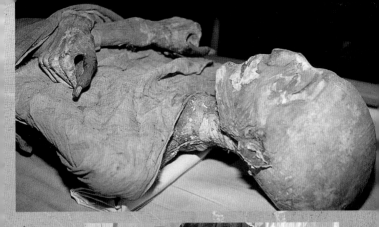

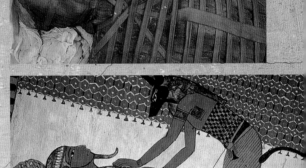

Above and right:
Corpses were
wrapped in
natron to dry out
for 70 days.
Below right:
Jackal-headed
Anubis, the god
associated with
funerary rites,
attends to the
mummy of King
Sennutem

Below: Child's
sarcophagus

Life After Death

Osiris's myth offered the promise of resurrection, so in the hope of joining him in the next life, Egyptians began to follow his style of burial by having themselves mummified. Isis kept the location of Osiris's tomb a secret, but it was believed that a part of his corpse was buried in each of Egypt's provinces. Temples were dedicated to him in each of these areas, but his main cult centres were at Bubastis in the Nile delta and Abydos on the Nile itself, where his head was believed to be buried and which Egyptians saw as the gateway to the afterlife (▶ 101). He was also held in reverence at Isis's temple on Philae (▶ 116–7).

Going Prepared

Ancient Egyptians believed that happiness in the afterlife depended on making the right preparations in this one.

As well as being well preserved, a dead person also needed help getting to the other side. The essential aids for this were spells and prayers; the Book of the Dead, for instance, was intended as a map to guide the deceased to the afterlife. The final barrier was Osiris's judgement, when the dead person's heart was weighed against the feather of truth. If the scales tipped in your favour, you were through to everlasting happiness. It's a common image on tomb walls and must have been a terrifying prospect, especially to those who had lived less than perfect lives.

Even if you were lucky enough to get through to paradise, your tomb still had to be kept in order, as it contained all the goods, treasures and models of workers that would be needed to provide for you. These, together with prayers and offerings made at your tomb, gave you a good chance of a sweet eternity.

At first corpses were kept intact by being buried in sand, but when tombs developed, bodies had to be mummified

Crossed arms and a beard symbolise the fact that the god Osiris is dead

Simple Muslim tombstones, facing Mecca, and splendid mausoleums in Cairo's City of the Dead

Top Three Movie Mummies
The Mummy (US, 1932) – Boris Karloff in bandages
The Mummy (UK, 1959) – Christopher Lee wreaks havok in England
The Mummy (US, 1999) – Brendan Fraser among state-of-the-art special effects (above)

Islamic Death Rites

Islam, which changed religious rituals, also changed burials. The prophet Muhammad announced that the best grave was one you could wipe away with your hand – a winding sheet and a hole in the desert were all that you needed. But before long the old ideas began to reassert themselves, especially the ancient cult of the dead and a belief in the ability of spirits to affect the living.

'Happiness in the afterlife depended on making the right preparations in this one'

When the Fatimid caliphs (▶ 24) established the city of al Qahira (Cairo), they brought the bones of their ancestors. And when the 15th-century sultan Qaytbay built his tomb, he added a school, monastery and *caravanserai* (lodgings). He wanted the tomb to be maintained after his death, and hoped that prayers would still be said for him long after he had gone. His name has certainly lived on – Qaytbay's tomb complex is one of the glories of Islamic architecture (▶ 179). Although it was built in a desert cemetery, outside the city limits, Cairo has since grown so dramatically that this City of the Dead is now well within Cairo – a city within the city. It's also where many ancient Egyptian funerary traditions are kept alive, from the regular offerings of the family to the spirit of the deceased, to people living in the cemetery alongside the dead.

Death on the Nile

The 1978 film of Agatha Christie's novel was a veritable travelogue, with a host of international stars attempting to baffle Peter Ustinov's detective Hercule Poirot. Pictured from left to right are some of the stars of the film: Angela Lansbury, Maggie Smith, Jack Warden, Bette Davis, Peter Ustinov, George Kennedy and David Niven.

The Land of Believers

T he Greek historian Herodotus, who visited Egypt in 450 BC, called the Egyptians 'religious to excess, beyond any other nation in the world.' Although much has changed over the past 2,000 years, religion still plays a key part in everyday life, and almost all Egyptians will identify themselves as much by their religion as by their city or region of birth. One reason for this is that Egypt has been important to the development of the region's three main religions: Islam, Christianity and Judaism.

Followers of Islam

The Muslim prophet Muhammad never visited Egypt, but several of his companions and close family members are buried there. Today, some 94 per cent of Egyptians are Muslims, or followers of Islam. The holy book of Islam, the Quran, is based on a series of revelations received by Muhammad in about AD 610 to 632. The new religion recognised the validity of Judaism and Christianity, but claimed to have superseded them.

Islam was brought to Egypt along with an army commanded by the great Arab general Amr ibn al As in AD 641, while the country was under the nominal rule of the Christian emperors

Friday noon prayers often block the traffic in the streets outside the mosques

of Constantinople (Istanbul). Radically, Islam abolished the priesthood that had dominated the older religions. In Egypt, where the ancient priests had often ruled the country, the idea of praying directly to God because all people were regarded as equal in His eyes, must have been especially popular.

After Muhammad's death in around 632, both his friend, Abu Bakr, and his son-in-law, Ali, claimed the title of leader of the faithful. The dispute caused a rift which continues today, with the followers of Ali known as Shi'a (Shi'ite) and the followers of Abu Bakr as Sunni. Most Egyptians are Sunni Muslims.

Five Rules of Islam

All Muslims must obey these rules:

◆ Declare 'that there is no God but Allah and that Muhammad is His Prophet'

◆ Pray five times a day

◆ Give alms

◆ Observe the daylight fast during the month of Ramadan

◆ Make the pilgrimage (*hajj*) to Mecca once in a lifetime

However, some aspects of Islam appear to be particularly Egyptian, for instance the annual saints' days, which have much in common with local festivities for ancient deities.

The Egyptian Christian Church

Egypt had links with Christianity from the very beginning, because the young Jesus is said to have been brought to Cairo by his parents. According to legend the Church in Egypt was founded after the evangelist St Mark

sailed into Alexandria in the 1st century AD. At the time of the Arab invasion most Egyptians belonged to the Coptic (Egyptian Christian) Church. Although Copts now make up less than 6 per cent of the population, they still exert a significant influence, perhaps because they claim to be the true heirs of Egypt's ancient civilisation. However, while Egyptians played an important part in establishing the rituals of the early Church, they were unable to accept an imperial ruling on the triple nature of God as Father, Son and Holy Ghost. To the Egyptians, they were all one. Refusing to toe the official line, they were condemned as heretics in AD 451 and since then, they have been isolated, their rituals and liturgy essentially uncorrupted by outside influences. Some scholars are now looking to the Egyptian Church to provide them with a glimpse of how the early Christian Church must have been.

Many aspects of Coptic rites seem to have preserved the world of the pharaohs. The Coptic language, still in use in churches and a few households, would be understood by the last of the ancients, while the liturgy and other prayers contain many phrases and images that seem to come from pagan texts. This idea is supported by the Jewish philosopher Philo of Alexandria (*c*15 BC–AD 50), who noted that Christians merely changed some of words of the ancient prayers. Many ancient gods seem also to find parallels in the new, from the holy mothers Mary and Isis, to Horus the Elder who is often depicted harpooning a hippo like St George fighting the dragon.

Religious tensions have led many young Coptic men to retire to desert monasteries

Common Ground

One thing Copts and Muslims share is a love of celebrations, in particular the annual saints' days, called *moulids*. These festivals often last over a week and take place all over the country. Some are small gatherings but others, such as the *moulids* of Huseyn in Cairo and Sayyid al Badawy in Tanta, attract millions. Their mixture of religion, social bonding and trade is similar to celebrations held in ancient Egypt. Whether the saint is Christian or Muslim, *moulids* tend to attract a mixed crowd who go for the saint's blessing and the chance to party.

The Jewish Community

The formative years of the early Jews were spent in Egypt, with Moses receiving the Ten Commandments on Gebel Musa in Sinai. Several thousand years later the Jewish holy book was first translated into Greek in Alexandria, making it accessible to a wider audience. Alexander the Great relocated Jews to his new city of Alexandria soon after it was founded in 331 BC and there's been a community in Egypt ever since. Most Jews emigrated or were expelled in the mid-20th century as a result of the creation of the State of Israel and the Arab-Israeli wars, although small and mostly elderly groups do survive in Alexandria and Cairo. Subsequently, the Jews are now the smallest religious group in Egypt.

Religious Tension

Always take off your shoes before entering a mosque or a tomb

There has always been tension between the different religions in Egypt. In 2nd- and 3rd-century Alexandria there was fighting between Christians, Jews and pagan sects, while medieval Cairo was a battleground for Copts, Sunni and Shi'a Muslims. In the 1950s and 60s, when Egypt was at war with Israel, the country's remaining Jewish population was discriminated

against. In the decades since then, particularly since the Afghan and Gulf wars (in which Egypt took part) there have been violent attacks on churches and Christian interests.

Recently, this has so embittered some of the Christian community that the Coptic Patriarch, Shenouda III, lifted his ban on Copts emigrating. Many young professional Coptic men have retreated to desert monasteries and created a monastic revival.

Often, there are not enough Jews in an Egyptian synagogue to perform a service

WHEN IN EGYPT

After thousands of years of invasions, floods, droughts, unreliable harvests, poverty and wars, Egyptians are used to taking what history throws at them. Stoicism has become part of the national character, and the first response to any calamity, whether it is big or small, might well be *maalesh*, *bukra* things will be better, *inshallah*.

Never Mind

Maalesh has a multitude of applications. You'll hear it after some mishap because even calamities are part of the grand scheme of things. If someone's pestering you to buy a plastic wallet or flashing sunglasses, *maalesh* shows you're not interested.

Talk Like an Egyptian

If you speak Egyptian Arabic in another Arab country, chances are you'll get a laugh – and not just for your accent. Egyptians are notorious in the Arab world for their irrepressible sense of humour and love of play and drama. They are the masters of Arab soap opera, which is seen from Morocco on the Atlantic coast to Dubai on the Indian Ocean and beyond.

God Willing

Step into a taxi and tell the driver where you want to go and he'll invariably reply, '*Inshallah*'. He means 'yes' but is actually saying 'God willing'. To assume that this is just a hackneyed saying is to underestimate the importance of Allah in everyday life, and to dismiss the fundamental belief in divine intervention.

■ ■ ■

Tomorrow

'*Bukra*' used to be the standard reply for whatever service you were requesting, whether you wanted a train ticket or collect your laundry. 'Come back tomorrow', or 'not ready till tomorrow' showed that Egyptians had a different sense of time and priorities from many foreigners visiting their country. But it's now a sign of the changing ethos in Egyptian society – particularly in the cities – that people resort less and less to this line of defence.

Exchanging Greetings

Wherever they are and whatever pressing business they have, Egyptians always make time for an elaborate exchange of greetings. A simple version might be a rally of blessings such as *sabah al ishtar* ('morning of cream') and *sabah al yasmin* ('morning of jasmine'). Between men there's also likely to be handshaking, kissing, hugging and an insistence that they visit the nearest café there and then. Among women there will be an extended series of questions and answers about every member of each other's family.

Family Life

Most Egyptians are passionately patriotic and, if you meet an Egyptian abroad, it doesn't take much to bring on a bout of nostalgia for their homeland and their family. In a country with no social security system, families support out-of-work men and will provide a son with a home for his wife and children until they can afford a place of their own. They will also look after the sick and elderly. Sons are especially important and the birth of a male is greeted with particular joy, while young girls are often treated as dolls. But attitudes to daughters (at least in public) tend to change after puberty, when many of them are hidden behind veils and voluminous dresses for reasons of modesty, often dictated as much by a desire for social conformity as religious zeal.

c5000 BC

Neolithic farming communities are already well established in the Nile valley area.

King Menes may have been a composite of several kings

c3000 BC

King Menes (or Narmer) unites the two lands of Upper and Lower Egypt (the Nile delta), establishing its capital at Memphis. Menes is now generally regarded as the first pharaoh of the 1st Dynasty in Egypt.

c2600 BC

Imhotep, architect to the 3rd-Dynasty King Zoser (2667–48 BC), creates the world's first pyramid, at Saqqara (▶ 61–3). The ancients were suitably impressed and later deified him. He became the god of medicine, son of the god Ptah and his consort Sekhmet.

1352–1336 BC

The ruling pharaoh Amenhotep IV tries to free his administration from the influence of the priesthood of Thebes by moving the capital to Amarna, some 370km miles north. To promote the worship of a single god, the sun god Aton, he changed his own name from 'Amun is pleased' to Akhenaton ('Servant of Aton'). Akhenaton is most famous today for being depicted in art with his beautiful wife Nefertiti and his children (▶ 51).

1336–1327 BC

After Amenhotep's death, his nine-year-old son-in-law Tutankhaten becomes ruler. Within a short time, he restores the old order, moves the capital back to Thebes and reinstates Amun as the state god, changing his name to Tutankhamun. He dies at the age of 18 with no heirs, the last male of the 18th Dynasty.

The Saqqara step pyramid was the world's first large stone monument

1279–1213 BC

Ramses II rules for more than 60 years – time enough to build grand monuments, marry many wives and father over 100 children, helping to guarantee his name in posterity. He leaves his mark on almost every significant monument in Egypt, adding huge colossi in his image and decorating temple walls with scenes of his greatest victories. He deifies himself in the

Prolific pharaoh, Ramses II

eighth year of his reign and the two temples that bear his name, at Abu Simbel and in Thebes, are as monumental as his self-esteem. Many of his 50 sons are buried in KV5, the princely gallery tomb that is now being excavated in the Valley of the Kings (► 93).

8th–7th century BC

Egypt is ruled for a time by kings from Nubia, the area of southern Egypt and northern Sudan.

332 BC

Alexander the Great (356–23) conquers Egypt, which passes to a general, Ptolemy, and into the Macedonian era.

General Alexander the Great

c270 BC

In Alexandria, the Greek architect Sostratos builds one of the seven wonders of the world – the marble lighthouse on the island of Pharos in the harbour.

Cleopatra VII's tomb in Alexandria has disappeared

47–30 BC

At the beginning of her reign, at the age of 21, Cleopatra VII flees Egypt to escape her murderous brother-husband Ptolemy XIII, but is restored to the throne by Julius Caesar. In return she bears his only son, Caesarion. Five years later, with Caesar dead, Cleopatra falls for his successor Mark Antony, by whom she has three more children. But in 30 BC Octavian, the future Emperor Augustus, defeats the lovers' army and captures Alexandria. When Mark Antony commits suicide, Cleopatra causes her own death soon after by the bite of an asp, thus sealing one of the greatest love stories. Cleopatra is the last ruler, until the modern era, of an independent Egypt. The country falls under Roman and Byzantine rule.

The Pharos was said to contain 300 rooms for its mechanics and builders

St Anthony of Egypt lived to the wise old age of 105

AD 251–356

At the age of 18 the future St Anthony, a wealthy young man from the town of Beni Suef, is inspired to become a hermit after hearing the gospel of Matthew. He retreats to an isolated cave on Mount Qalah, where he lives until the age of 105. His followers, settling at the foot of the mountain, found the world's first monastery (➤ 164).

639–641

When Amr ibn al As visits Alexandria as a young man he is struck by the capital's wealth. He returns in 639 with a 4,000-strong Arab army and meets little opposition from the ruling Byzantines. The Arabs take Heliopolis and then besiege Babylon-in-Egypt. By 641 Egypt is an Arab province. Amr establishes his capital in Fustat (later Cairo), where he builds his mosque and replaces Christianity with Islam.

973–1171

During the Fatimid Dynasty, al Hakim, who rules from 996 to 1021 is the maddest and most capricious of the caliphs (literally, 'Successor to Muhammad'). He persecutes the Jewish and Christian minorities and destroys countless churches. He forbids women to go out, outlawing the manufacture of their shoes. He also hates daylight, decreeing that all work should be done at night. He even declares himself divine as the pharoahs did before him. After mysteriously disappearing while out riding, he is commonly presumed dead, but according to the Druze, a political and religious Islamic sect for whom he becomes a cult figure, he's actually escaped to Lebanon.

Muhammad Ali's mosque now crowns the citadel built by Saladin

1171–1193

Legacies of the reign of the Kurdish general Salah ad Din (Saladin) include Cairo's Citadel and the ending of the Shi'a caliphate rule. He establishes the Ayyubid Dynasty after becoming sultan, and is also notable for uniting Egyptian Muslims in a common cause. For most of his rule he is away fighting a *jihad* ('holy war') to free the Holy Land from the Crusaders. He succeeds in recapturing Syria and Jerusalem, but dies in Damascus, where he is buried. His legendary qualities turn him into a hero throughout Europe and the Arab world.

1250–1517

The Mamelukes – soldiers descended from slaves who made up the Ayyubid army – overthrow the Ayyubids with their highly professional army, led by amirs. Their Muslim dynasties lasts until their conquest by the Ottoman Turks.

The Mamelukes proved their fighting abilities in the Crusades

1517

Egypt comes under the control of the Ottoman Empire, which had been founded in the 13th century by Osman I, but the Mamelukes continue to rule. With increasing trade between the East and Europe, the important route between Alexandria, Cairo and Suez prompts British and French attempts to control it.

Below: Cairo was always an important trading post

1798–1801

Napoleon Bonaparte leads scholars and troops into Egypt to study and to remove antiquities, creating the first systematic record of Egypt's treasures.

1805–1848

Muhammad Ali, an Albanian officer whose army arrived in Egypt with the French, is regarded as the founder of modern Egypt. After the French leave, Ali supports Egypt's rulers against the Mamelukes and becomes viceroy. Influenced by advances in Europe, he modernises the country's infrastructure, building roads and Africa's first railway. He reorganises the army, reformes agriculture with improved irrigation and establishes industry. His dynasty rules Egypt under the title of Khedive and later King, until the revolution in 1952.

1869

After ten years of problematic construction, the Suez Canal is finally opened, linking the Mediterranean at the newly created Port Said with the Red Sea at Suez (► 168–9). The new towns of Port Said and Ismailiya grow as the area becomes wealthy. Port Said is named after Egypt's ruler (although he dies before the project was completed) and Ismailiya receives its name from the subsequent ruler, Khedive Ismail, who opens the canal.

Napoleon defeated the Mamelukes at the Battle of the Pyramids in 1798

1882

Riots begin after an army faction objects to the British and French control of Egypt's finances. As a result, British troops

bombard Alexandria and occupy Egypt under the pretext of restoring peace to the country. They remain as a colonial presence until 1952.

Muhammad Ali laid the foundations for modern Egypt

1952

A military coup by the 'Free Officers' overthrows King Farouk and declares a republic. The army officer and politician Gamal Abd al Nasser (1918–70), becomes Egypt's prime minister in 1954 and later president (1956–70). His Arab nationalism and socialism makes him popular in Egypt and the Arab world.

The charismatic Nasser

Scottish troops at the Sphinx in 1882

When he nationalises the Suez Canal in 1956 Britain, France and Israel invade Egypt, but Nasser stands up to them, adding to his cult status.

Above: In 1973 Sinai became a battlefield in the Arab–Israeli war

1970s

Both Egypt and Israel claim victory after several Arab-Israeli wars. Anwar al Sadat (1918–81) becomes president in 1970 and sets about restructuring the political system (founding the National Democratic Party) and diversifying the economy. After some initial aggression, his work towards peace in the Middle East leads to talks with the Israeli Prime Minister Menachem Begin (1913–92). This culminates in the 1978 Camp David Peace Accord, for which the two leaders share the Nobel Peace Prize. Although Egypt becomes somewhat isolated from other Arab countries, the agreement encourages foreign investment and strengthens the economy. However, only a minority become wealthy and the decade ends in social unrest and a general feeling of dissatisfaction.

1981 to present

On 6 October 1981, President Sadat is assassinated by the radical group Muslim Brotherhood. Hosni Mubarak (born 1928), a fellow member of the Free Officers group, succeeds him as president, with the support of the armed forces. Mubarak has continued Sadat's policy of liberalisation of trade, helping to create the conditions for a boom in the Egyptian Stock Market. He's also been energetic in regional politics, chairing pan-African organisations, encouraging Arab solidarity and acting as a mediator in Arab-Israeli peace talks. Egypt is now seen as a moderating influence in the region.

Current president, Mubarak

كُل، كُل... يّاللَّا كُل!

Kul, kul... yallah kul

The phrase means 'eat, eat... come on eat', and you'll hear it often if you dine with Egyptians, who love to eat, to talk about food and to share a meal.

It's always been this way – their forefathers are depicted on the walls of tombs attending lavish banquets. Some dishes are still favourites today, particularly *faseekh*, roast goose and *meloukhia* (see panel).

Modern meals include as many dishes as the host can afford, and the tastiest morsels will be put in your mouth at what can be an alarming rate. In restaurants Egyptians continue the habit of sharing by ordering vast amounts of *mezze*, hot or cold starters, dips and salads.

Left: Street food is available everywhere

Sweetness Delight

If you've seen Egyptians piling sugar into their tea, then you'll have noticed their sweet tooth. That's why the country's numerous pâtisseries sell a wide variety of cream-filled Western pastries and finger-licking good Oriental pastries, usually dripping in honey. The 'queen' of Egyptian desserts is *Umm Ali*, which some sources suggest was introduced into Egypt by an Irish woman, Miss O'Malley, who was mistress to the 19th-century leader, Khedive Ismail.

The Egyptian Staple

Fuul (fava beans) is one of the basics of the national diet and, while some poorer Egyptians live on them, even wealthy Cairenes have them for breakfast. The dried beans are simmered for about six hours, and then sold in the morning from carts on street corners. The stew is often eaten with more beans crushed and fried into little patties (*taamiya*).

'The tastiest morsels will be put in your mouth at an alarming rate'

Some Dishes to Sample

Faseekh: salted dried fish

Meloukhia: thick green soup made with a leafy vegetable similar to spinach, served with chicken or rabbit

Kushari: a delicious mixture of macaroni, rice, fried onions, chickpeas and lentils, topped with a spicy tomato sauce

Qawaria: a clear cows' feet soup, said to enhance sexual potency

Lambs' testicles: found in sandwiches or stews, said to have similar properties to *qawaria*

Umm Ali: crisp pitta bread, coconut, cream, nuts, raisins and sugar, soaked in hot milk

Below: Smoking a *sheesha* is the best way to digest a platter of *mezze* (right)

Absence Makes the Heart Grow Fonder

During the lunar month of Ramadan Muslims abstain from eating, drinking, smoking and making love between sunrise and sunset. Perversely, although this is a month of fasting, more food is consumed during the nights of Ramadan than at any other time. Ramadan also brings its social obligations, as it's traditionally when people visit friends and relatives for an evening breakfast. They then splurge on meat and more luxurious ingredients than usual to make up for the hardship of the day's fasting.

Bakers' boys carry big trays of hot, fresh pitta bread on their heads at all times of the day

Café Pleasures

The best thirst-quencher in a hot climate is tea, and there's no shortage of it in Egypt. Tea is drunk black or with milk and lots of sugar at the local *ahwa* (coffee house). The other ubiquitous drink is syrupy Turkish coffee, which soon becomes a compulsion and has the bonus of being the medium for fortune-telling (it's like reading tea leaves). Cafés are also places to relax, chat or ponder while drawing on a *sheesha* (water pipe or hookah), which can usually be ordered with normal tobacco, *ma'assal* (tobacco sweetened with molasses) or *tuffah* (sweetened with apple). Traditional cafés also serve herbal infusions such as *yansoon* (anis), *helba* (fenugreek), *karkadeh* (hibiscus) and *irfa* (cinnamon). Warm yourself in winter with a delicious, custardy *sahlab* – made of arrowroot and cinnamon topped with coconut and other nuts.

Juicy Delights

'Once you drink water from the Nile, you will always return to Egypt' goes the old saying. But ignoring that advice is the best way to ensure you're able to come back. Avoid tap water and river water – look for bottled mineral water or head for the colourful juice bars behind piles of oranges or strawberries and indulge in the delights of the season.

Some cafés serve *shay bin naana* or tea with mint

Above: Freshly brewed herbal infusions are excellent thirst-quenchers

---

Authentic Restaurants

For a taste of real Egyptian food, try one of these:
- In Alexandria, Muhammad Ahmed, Kadoura
- In Cairo, Felfella (➤ 75), Andrea's (➤ 74), Alfi Bey (➤ 74)
- In Luxor, Cafeteria Muhammad (➤ 104), Peace Abouzeid (➤ 105)
- In Aswan, al Masry (➤ 126)

Undulations & Gyrations

From Salome's dance of the seven veils in return for the head of John the Baptist, to modern-day sell-out shows at 2am, belly dancing has always pulled the crowds.

Raqs sharqi, or more properly Oriental dance, is a social phenomenon in Egypt. From its origins in the Middle East it stretches back in time, through ancient tomb paintings of women apparently belly dancing, and cuts through social barriers. Everyone, from the haughtiest society princess to the poorest rag-picker, will have a go at some time.

Professional dancers claim it's in the genes and that every Egyptian is born with the ability to dance in this way. But it's not all in the belly. The dance also demands great control of the hips, expression of the hands and (if you can afford it) the backing of a 30-piece band.

As they get older not all Egyptian belly dancers continue to perform in public, except perhaps at weddings and big family parties. There's a growing social stigma about dancing, linked to increasing religious conservatism, which has led to some very public retirements by famous dancers. Foreign girls have arrived in their wake, but the biggest stars, such as Dina, Lucy and Fifi Abdou, remain Egyptian.

These days it's not even confined to Egypt, as the energy required and effort involved has made belly dancing a popular way of keeping fit in the West.

In the Egyptian music world one voice is heard above all others: that of Umm Kalthoum (1898–1975), known as *Sitt al Kull* (The Lady of All) and *Kawkab al Sharq* (The Star of the East).

Star of the East:
Umm Kalthoum

Umm Kalthoum was born in the village of Tumay al Zahayra in the delta's Gharbiya province. Talented from an early age, she starred in six films from 1936. But it was for her extraordinary voice that she stood out, and she gave up films in 1947 to concentrate on singing. She was a social phenomenon. At a time when Egyptians didn't talk about love, emotions or sexual pleasure, she provided them with a vocabulary to do so, using ambiguous lyrics to avoid offending public morals. In the process she liberated both men and women.

On the first Thursday of each month Umm Kalthoum would give concerts that became an institution, attracting dignitaries from around the Arab world. They were also broadcast live to millions on radio.

Like western celebrities, Umm Kalthoum's life was often controversial. Her success aroused the jealousy of singers and critics, who accused her of being domineering and of stifling younger talent. Her passionate songs also provoked rumours about her love life and she was romantically linked to several people, but she married a doctor and university professor called Dr Hassan Hefnawy in 1953.

Umm Kalthoum was fêted around the world, but attained the status of a guru in Egypt. A firm supporter of the 1952 revolution, she influenced public opinion and had the ear of Presidents Nasser and Sadat.

Millions of fans attended her funeral in 1975, one of the largest and most dramatic ever seen in modern Egypt.

Many of Umm Kulthoum's songs are now available on tape and CD, and sales rose by 40 per cent after a TV series about her life, shown during Ramadan, 1999.

Among her best live recordings are:
- *Alf Layla wa Layla* (The Thousand and One Nights)
- *Enta Omri* (You Are My Life)
- *Al Atlaa* (The Ruins), which was voted one of the top 100 songs of the 20th century by French newspaper *Le Monde*.

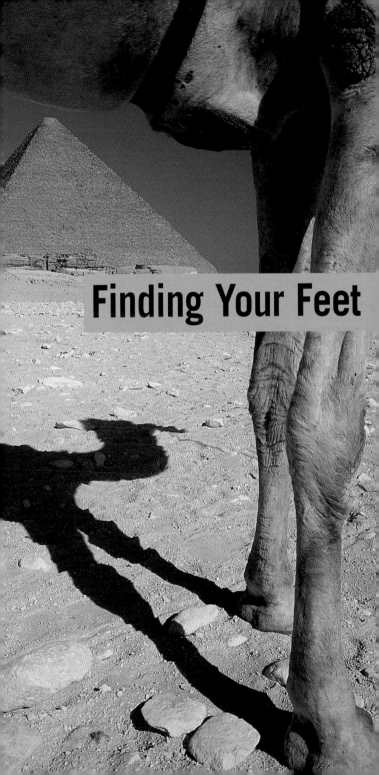

Finding Your Feet

First Two Hours

Cairo is traditionally the main point of entry for visitors to Egypt, but there are now a growing number of international flights direct to Luxor, and also charter flights to Hurghada on the Red Sea and to Sharm al Sheikh in Sinai.

Cairo International Airport

- The main airport is **25km from the city centre**, or 35–45 minutes by car.
- There are **two main terminals** connected by a free Egypt Air shuttle-bus that runs through the day and night. **Terminal 1** is used by Egyptian and other Arab airlines and El Al, while **Terminal 2** serves Western carriers.
- Both have **24-hour currency exchange** and automatic cash machines accepting Visa, Cirrus and Mastercard.
- **Taxis** are generally cheaper than in Europe and America, but beyond customs you'll be accosted by taxi drivers, some of whom may overcharge. If you've already booked a hotel they may tell you it has closed down and offer to take you to another hotel where they will earn a commission.
- To avoid the hassle you can book a **limousine** in the arrival hall. These are slightly more expensive, but you fix a price and pay before you ride. However, the driver will expect a tip on arrival. If you do take a taxi, check out limousine prices first and make sure you pay less.
- There are also extremely cheap **buses** (24 hours) and more comfortable **minibuses** into the centre. No 948 bus runs to Midan Ataba from Terminals 1 and 2, and Nos 400 and 949 go to Midan Tahrir in Downtown (all run 24 hours). Minibus No 27 also runs to Midan Tahrir until midnight.
- The **tourist office** at Terminal 1 is open daily from 8am to 9pm (tel: 02-291 4255, ext 2223) and the tourist office at Terminal 2 is open for 24 hours every day (tel: 02-291 4277).

Luxor International Airport

- The airport is about 12km out of town and there's **no public transport** into town, so try to arrange to be met by a travel agent. Otherwise, you'll have to deal with Luxor's taxi drivers, who are notorious for overcharging, so agree the fare before getting in.
- Beyond the airport run, **taxi fares** in Luxor, as elsewhere in Egypt, are generally relatively cheap.
- The airport **tourist office** is open 24 hours in winter peak season (tel: 095-372 306)

Hurghada Airport

- There's **no public transport** from the airport into the town centre so independent travellers must rely on taxis, which charge reasonable fares into town.

Sharm al Sheikh

- Ras Nasrani airport is about 15km north of the tourist centre at Naama Bay, and again there's **no public transport**. Most visitors are met by a travel agent, but if you're arriving independently you'll have to take a cab into town.

Tourist Information Offices

- Most tourist offices in Egypt are **rather limited** in the services they provide and the brochures they hand out. They can be useful for official prices of *calèches* (horse-drawn carriages), taxis and *feluccas* (boats), or for a city map, but they are not always as accurate as maps in this and other guidebooks.
- Tourist offices will rarely help with **accommodation**, except those at airports, which might make suggestions. However, Shukri Saad at the Aswan Tourist Office, one of the most helpful tourist officials in Egypt, also assists in booking accommodation.

Cairo Tourist Office
✚ 196 C4 ✉ 5 Sharia Adly, Downtown
☎ 02-391 3454
⏰ Daily 9–8
Try visiting in the afternoon and asking for Mr Laboudi, an experienced officer with wide knowledge and a helpful manner.

Egyptian Tourist Authority, Luxor
✚ 202 B4 ✉ Corniche, just south of Luxor Temple
☎ 095-372 215/373 294
⏰ Daily 8–8
Provides a useful list of official rates for *calèches*, taxis, *feluccas* and guides.

Hurghada Tourist Information
✚ 201 E1 ✉ Opposite the Grand Hotel in New Hurghada
☎ 065-444 420
⏰ Sat–Thu 8–2

Aswan Tourist Office
✚ 202 C3 ✉ Beside the train station
☎ 097-312 811
⏰ Daily 9–3, 6–8 in winter; 7–9pm in summer; 10–2 during Ramadan
Very helpful staff, who can point you towards the trustworthy *felucca* captains.

Alexandria Tourist Office
✚ 200 A5 ✉ Midan Saad Zaghloul, Downtown
☎ 03-484 3380
⏰ Daily 8–6 (8pm mid-Jul to mid-Aug); 9–4 during Ramadan

Local Issues
In a country troubled by religious tension, a recent spate of anti-Christian and anti-governmental violence coincided with the emergence of a small Islamic group, the Gamaiyat al Islamiya, which has carried out attacks not only on governmental institutions but also on tourists in an attempt to force the government to agree to their demands for an Islamic state. Their campaign of attacks against trains, cruise boats and tourist buses culminated in the attack in 1997 at Deir al Bahari in Luxor, in which 58 foreigners and 10 Egyptians were killed. But the government was determined in its response, arresting many suspects and introducing the death penalty for terrorists. Tourists are protected by police and soldiers at the main sites, and must travel through Upper Egypt in an armed convoy.

However, the subsequent discussion of the role of religion in the state has led to a new wave of religious conservatism. The most obvious sign of this trend is the growing number of middle-class women wearing the veil, the ever-greater numbers who spread prayer mats in the street for Friday's midday prayers and men with 'raisins' or bruises on their forehead caused by praying.

Visitors should respect the culture when visiting more traditional areas and mosques by dressing modestly (women should cover their hair, upper arms and legs) and behaving discreetly. Men and women should not show affection in public.

Admission Charges
The cost of admission for museums and other sites of interest mentioned in the text is indicated by price categories:

Inexpensive under 15LE   **Moderate** 15–30LE   **Expensive** over 30LE

Getting Around

On the whole the public transport system in Egypt works well, with regular buses and trains to most major destinations, and service taxis (*beejous*) covering the rest.

Urban Transport
Cairo

- Cairo has a whole fleet of **buses**, but they're usually packed, and women often get hassled. You might be happier sticking to the smaller **mini-** and **microbuses**, which are slightly more expensive but only take as many passengers as there are seats. Minibuses are orange and white, and follow the usual bus routes. Microbuses are more like a shared taxi.
- Taxis are cheap and more comfortable than buses.
- The **metro** is clean and easy to use, especially from Downtown Cairo to Coptic Cairo. Tickets are cheap (£) and there are special carriages for women only (at the back or front). Women getting in a mixed carriage will be stared at.
- **River buses** are becoming scarce, but are still a good way to avoid the traffic jams and dangerous driving.
- Private **motorboats** (launches) and *feluccas* make excursions on the river.

Elsewhere

- Outside Cairo it's a different story. In most other cities, except perhaps Alexandria, you may prefer taxis to the **scant public transport** service.

Buses

- **Intercity buses** are cheap and often faster and more reliable than trains, and they serve areas not covered by the rail network, such as Sinai and the oases. Buses tend to fill up quickly, so buy tickets for long-haul or air-conditioned services at least a day in advance and you will often be assigned a particular seat. However, expect to stand when buses are crowded, and be aware that air-conditioning does not always function.
- The different bus companies all run both **cheaper non-air-conditioned buses** and **faster, modern air-conditioned vehicles**. The four main operators are all based in Cairo, operating from **Turgoman Garage**, 600m southwest of Ramses Station, in Bulaq.
- The **West Delta Bus Company** (tel: 02-431 6742) runs services to Alexandria, Marsa Matruh, Siwa Oasis and the Nile delta from the Turgoman Garage.
- The **East Delta Bus Company** (tel: 02-431 6723) operates to Sinai and the Canal zone.
- The **Upper Egypt Bus Company** serves all cities south of Cairo along the Nile, the Fayoum, the Western Desert oases and the Red Sea coast up to al Quseyr. Most buses for Middle Egypt, from Cairo to Qena leave from the Aboud Bus Station, on Sharia Shubra, 500m north of Ramses Station. Buses for Luxor, Aswan, the Western Desert oases and the Red Sea coast leave from the Turgoman Garage.
- **Superjet** runs more luxurious air-conditioned buses (with video, snacks and toilet) from Cairo to Alexandria, Luxor, Aswan and Hurghada. There are also five fast buses daily to Sharm al Sheikh from the Turgoman Garage.

Taxis

- Taxis are **black and white** and tend to be four-seater cars.

- Taxis are **much cheaper** than in Europe, but rarely use their meters. Even if they do, the amount shown will probably bear little resemblance to the fare charged by the driver.
- Cairenes usually **hail a taxi** by shouting out their destination as it drives past. They don't discuss the fare as they know roughly what to pay, but as a visitor it may be best to agree a fare and ask someone in your hotel for the going rate before you travel. Be prepared to haggle for a reasonable price.
- **Estate-car cabs**, known as **service taxis**, usually charge limousine rates if they're working as normal taxis. These serve everywhere in Egypt and can be the fastest way of getting around. As they're usually Peugeots, they're known as **beejous**. The drivers announce their destination and leave as soon as there are six or seven passengers. The fares charged are similar to buses (again, check that you are not charged tourist rates).
- Due to **travel restrictions** for foreigners, it can be difficult to take a service taxi. Often you have to pay for all seven seats and use the car as a private taxi in an armed convoy.
- **Beware:** beejous have been nicknamed **'flying coffins'** as they tend to be driven fast and recklessly. Accidents are common, especially at night.

Trains

- The government-owned **Egyptian State Railway** operates services through the Nile Valley to Aswan, Alexandria, Suez, Port Said and Marsa Matruh. The line from Safaga on the Red Sea coast to Qena, Kharga and Paris is expected to be connected to the Toshka region in the Western Desert in the coming years.
- Egyptian State Railway tickets are inexpensive and must be **bought in advance** from the railway station.
- The privately owned **Wagon-Lits** operates a rather worn sleeper train from Cairo to Luxor and Aswan, and several fast and comfortable turbo trains a day to Alexandria (2 hours). In summer there are three sleeper trains a week to Marsa Matruh.
- Wagon-Lits tickets must be booked in advance from **Ramses Station** in Cairo (tel: 02-574 9474).

Domestic Flights

- As **Egypt Air** almost has a monopoly on domestic flights, fares are uncompetitive and have become quite expensive. If you are flying into Egypt with Egypt Air, book your internal flights at the same time to save up to 50 per cent on published fares. Egypt Air flies **daily** from Cairo to most of Egypt's main cities (tel: 02-579 3049; www.egyptair.com.eg).
- **Book well in advance**, especially during the busy winter season, and be aware that overbooking is unfortunately quite common. To minimise the risk of being 'bumped', always reconfirm bookings well in advance, and turn up earlier than the recommended check-in time at the airport,
- All domestic flights leave from **Terminal 1** of Cairo airport, also known as the Old Airport (al matar al qadima).
- You can also book **Air Sinai** flights to Hurghada, Sinai and Tel Aviv.
- **Orascom** (tel: 02-301 5632), a private airline, operates regular flights from Cairo and Luxor to Gouna.

Driving

- Driving in Cairo can be nerve-wracking, and in rural areas it's often dangerous, so consider **renting a car with a driver** if you are nervous.
- Since the terrorist attack in Luxor in 1997 **security** is tight along Egypt's roads and it's almost impossible for foreigners to pass the many roadblocks along the Nile without the protection of an armed convoy.

Driving Essentials

- Speed limits on **motorways:** 120km/h (75mph)
- On other **roads:** 90km/h (56mph)
- In **urban centres:** 50km/h (31mph)
- **Seat belts** are compulsory.
- Driving is on the **right**-hand side of the road.
- Avoid driving in the **dark** outside cities as most people drive without headlights, saving them for the moment before collision, when they use full beam. In the countryside, remember that villagers walk their animals home just after dusk and that people often sit on the side of the road.
- Many roads have **checkpoints**, where the police may ask for your papers, so be prepared for delays.
- Always carry your **passport and driving licence**. Failing to do so makes you liable to an instant fine, and onward travelling may be prevented.
- If you hit someone in the countryside, **report it** immediately at the nearest police station, and be aware that you may be attacked by angry villagers.

Car Rental

- **Car-rental agencies** operate in most major hotels.
- **Credit cards** are accepted.
- Drivers must be at least **25 years old** and hold an International Driving Licence.
- Car-rental contracts must be sold with a **third-party liability insurance**, but check if **accident and damage insurance** is included. If you're involved in an accident, you'll need to provide the insurance company with a written report from the police and from the doctor who first treats the injuries.

Upkeep

- Main towns and cities will have many **petrol** (*benzene*) stations, but there are fewer in the countryside. To be safe, always fill the tank to the limit, and clean the oil filter regularly because dust and impurities in the petrol tend to clog up the engine.
- Larger **petrol stations** are often open until late at night.
- Petrol is much **less expensive** than in Europe.
- The cheapest petrol is **normal** (*tamaneen*), but **super** (*tisaeen*) is better quality. Lead-free petrol is only available from a few petrol stations in more afflluent areas of Cairo and Alexandria.
- Egyptian car **mechanics** are often masters of invention and can usually fix a breakdown.
- Most large garages stock a good range of **spare parts**.
- If you run into trouble, **people will often gladly help** you push your car to the next garage or to the side of the road.

Motoring Club

Automobile and Touring Club of Egypt
10 Sharia Kasr al Nil, Downtown Cairo
✚ 196 C4 ☎ 02-574 3355

Travel Restrictions

- Incidences of terrorist violence against tourists has led to **tight security** and travel restrictions for visitors on certain overland routes, notably between Luxor and Aswan, with travel only possible in armed convoys.
- Officially, tourists are also only allowed on two guarded air-conditioned **trains** between Cairo, Luxor and Aswan.
- The **situation changes frequently** so check with the tourist office before travelling, or use river transport where possible.

Accommodation

There's a large choice of accommodation in Egypt's main tourist centres, but elsewhere it's often down to the very basic. This guide includes a selected cross-section of places to stay, from luxury hotels in palaces to good inexpensive pensions.

Hotels

- Hotels are rated from **deluxe to budget**, with a few unclassified hotels geared mainly towards backpackers and Egyptian families.
- **Deluxe** hotels, almost always part of international chains, usually have international facilities, but service may not always be up to standard.
- **Mid-range hotels** include some of the more characterful old hotels, such as the Cecil in Alexandria, and also more modern concrete resort hotels on the Red Sea.
- **Budget hotels** are rarely air-conditioned, but some will have cooling fans. A few are real gems, old art-deco buildings with high ceilings, old-fashioned furniture and unreliable plumbing. The less said about others, the better.

Pensions

Pensions are similar to budget hotels but, as they're often run by one family, the atmosphere tends to be much friendlier and relaxed, and the rooms better maintained.

Hostels

- Egypt has **15 cheap hostels** in the main towns, recognised by Hostelling International. Rooms are cheaper if you have a HI membership, but it is not strictly necessary.
- More information is available from **Egyptian Youth Hostel Association**, 1 Sharia Ibrahimy, Garden City, Cairo (tel: 02-354 0527; fax: 355 0329)

Camping

- Camping is **not popular** in Egypt and the country's few campsites are mostly along the coast and in the oases, where they're generally a long way from the sights and poorly equipped. Campsites attached to hotels are usually slightly better.
- Camping outside designated sites along the coast is not advisable as some empty beaches are still **mined**. This is less of a problem in the desert.

Booking Accommodation

- Rooms at more expensive hotels are often cheaper when booked either through the chain's international reservation system or when bought as part of a package. Other places recommended here should preferably be **booked in advance**, particularly in high season when hotels fill up fast.
- Check the website **www.tourism.egnet.net** for hotels, reservation services, travel agents and other related services.

Accommodation Prices

In many hotels, it is possible to bargain over the advertised room rate, particularly in off-peak periods and if you are staying for a few days. The set price of accommodation featured in the guide is indicated below. The prices are for a double room per night.

£ = under 200LE   **££** = 200–500LE   **£££** = over 500LE

Food and Drink

You can eat well in Egypt, but don't expect to find gourmet food. Egyptian cuisine is peasant food, a lot less sophisticated, for instance, than its Lebanese neighbour (➤ 28–30).

The Egyptian Way of Eating

■ **Lunch** is usually from 12:30 to 3pm and dinner from 8 to 10:30pm, but many places in tourist areas stay open all day.

■ At a **restaurant**, local people tend to start a meal with a good selection of cold and/or hot *mezze* (small dishes) with drinks. If the spread is big enough, this can sometimes make a whole meal.

■ **Flat pitta bread** is often used in place of a fork to scoop up food.

■ An important point of etiquette to remember: only use the **right hand** while eating this way, because the left hand is traditionally used for ablutions.

On the Street

Everywhere in Egypt you will come across street stalls selling everything from cheese sandwiches and delicious *shawarma* to cow's-feet soup and lamb-testicle sandwiches. However tempting these may look and smell, street food is only recommended for the adventurous or those with a strong stomach, as hygiene conditions on these stalls are usually quite poor and very few have running water.

International Cuisine

■ You can now find most styles of cooking in **Cairo** and, unlike in Europe, ethnic restaurants are usually more upmarket.

■ **Outside Cairo** the choice is more limited. Most international restaurants are in the luxury hotels, with prices to match. Hotel food can often be bland, especially set menus or open buffets, but some restaurants are excellent.

■ International **fast-food** chains are a relatively recent arrival in Egypt, but have proved to be immensely popular and just about every tourist resort now boasts McDonalds, PizzaExpress and so on.

■ In spite of this success, Egyptians have not entirely abandoned their own interesting varieties of fast food. Examples include *kushari* (a spicy mix of pulses, pasta and rice) and *falafel* (deep-fried, spiced, mashed chickpeas) or *fuul* sandwiches.

Vegetarians

Although most Egyptians can't afford to eat meat more than once a week and many Christians go through periods of abstention, there is little understanding of why a foreigner should choose to live off vegetables alone. Having said that, there are usually plenty of vegetable stews or other vegetarian dishes on restaurant menus and fish, usually from the Nile or the Red Sea, is available for those that eat it.

Eating Out

■ If you have a **sensitive stomach**, try to avoid raw vegetables, unpeeled fruit, ice-cream, open buffets and food that has been stewing for a while, such as *shawarma*.

■ Drink plenty of **water and fresh juices** to replace fluids, but avoid heavily chilled drinks in the midday sun, particularly alcohol.

■ Egyptians love to **dress up** to go to a fancy restaurant, but other places are fairly casual about clothes.

Useful Reading

- The *Egypt Today Restaurant Guide*, available from local bookshops, has reviews of a wide selection of restaurants and watering holes.
- The monthly magazine *Egypt Today*, which also has a restaurant selection, reviews new places in Cairo.

Best for Fresh Fish
Fish restaurant next to the Hilton Fayrouz, Sharm al Sheikh (➤ 173)
George's, Ismailiya (➤ 173)
Samakmak, Cairo (➤ 76) and Alexandria (➤ 147)
Zephyrion, Abu Qir beach, Alexandria suburbs (➤ 148)

Drinks

- **Tap-water** and ice made from it is heavily chlorinated but can still cause problems.
- **Bottled mineral water** (*maaya maadaniya*) is widely available.
- Most Egyptians drink a lot of tea, coffee, herbal drinks, cold drinks and juice (➤ 30). Everywhere you'll find stalls making cheap, **fresh juices** from whatever is in season: orange, pomegranate, strawberry, carrot and mango, as well as bananas in milk. Fresh lime juice is a perfect thirst-quencher, but it's often served with lots of sugar. If you want drinks without sugar, be sure to mention it when ordering.

Alcohol

- Egypt is officially a Muslim country and, although alcohol is widely available in tourist centres, it's **prohibited** in some parts of the country, particularly away from the main towns. Even where it is available, show your respect for the culture by drinking it only in moderation.
- Hotels and some restaurants usually sell **local beer and wine**, but imported alcoholic drinks are often only available in the luxury hotels and at hugely inflated prices.
- **Locally made liquors**, with names such as Johnny Talker and Good Gin, are best avoided; there have been several cases of serious illness resulting from bootleg liquor. Zbib, quite similar to Greek ouzo, is the exception.
- Several varieties of **beer**, including Stella, are brewed in Egypt.
- The long-established and recently privatised **Gianaclis Vineyards** in the delta region produce drinkable red, white and rosé wines, although you may not want to take any home.
- The other local wine, red and white **Obelisque**, is made in Gouna from good-quality grape concentrates from Sicily.

Best Watering Holes
Absolut, Cairo (➤ 74)
Cairo Jazz Club (➤ 75)
Marriott Garden, Cairo (➤ 75)
Windsor Hotel Bar, Cairo (➤ 76)
Cap d'Or, Alexandria (➤ 147)
Spitfire Bar, Alexandria (➤ 148)

Restaurant Prices

Below is the price of establishments featured in this guide, based on the amount you should expect to pay per person for a three-course meal, excluding alcoholic drinks and tips.

£ up to 50LE   **££** 50–100LE   **£££** over 100LE
Note that some hotels charge an extra service tax of 22 per cent.

Shopping

Wherever you go in Egypt, there will be no shortage of shopping opportunities. Egyptians are traders at heart and they also love to shop, so it often seems as if most of the country is one big bazaar. Shopping can be a lengthy process involving exchanging greetings, drinking tea, choosing the items you want to buy and then, eventually, discussing and agreeing on the price.

Shopping Hours

- **Department stores**, often state run, are usually open Monday to Saturday from 9am to 1pm and again from 5 to 8pm, while smaller shops tend to be open all day, and often until 8pm or later in tourist areas.
- Most **bazaars** are closed on Sundays, but some tourist shops might still be open.
- Some Muslim shopkeepers close during the **Friday noon prayers**, but will reopen as soon as they come back from the mosque. At the regular prayer times you may find the shopkeeper performing his prayers behind the counter. Just hang around, as these will not take very long.
- Major **credit cards and travellers' cheques** are now widely accepted in tourist areas, but many smaller shops still only accept cash or will add a surcharge for using credit cards.

Bargaining

Western visitors are often too embarrassed or impatient to haggle over a price, but for Egyptians this is the normal state of affairs: when Egyptians go shopping they expect to bargain for everything. You may prefer the few shops with fixed prices, but they are often more expensive and tourists who cannot read Arabic numerals are still likely to be overcharged. Just remember that bargaining can be fun once you understand the rules. Window-shop at the fixed-price stores to get an idea of prices before venturing into the bazaars, where haggling is the norm. As a general rule, try halving the asking price and watching the trader's reaction. If he's quick to accept, you're still offering too much. If he's not interested, you could offer a little more, or try walking away: if your price was fair he will call you back.

Handicrafts

- The **variety** of Egyptian handicrafts is endless and prices are very good, but the quality of the work has deteriorated as Egyptian tastes have changed; most crafts are now produced for the tourist trade. Typical souvenirs are mostly cheap reproductions of pharaonic art. Papyrus, for example, is often made of banana leaves, painted with scenes copied from original papyri and tomb paintings. Also look out for poorly executed reproductions of ancient statues.
- Several **aid organisations** are trying hard to revive old crafts, such as embroidery, pottery and weaving, particularly as a way of making the women in rural areas who produce them more financially independent. A sign of their success is the appearance of a few new shops selling better-quality products, such as Marketing Link (apt 8, 27 Sharia Yehia Ibrahim, Zamalek, Cairo, tel: 02-735 5123), a fair-trade shop selling quality products from projects all over Egypt.
- The cheapest place to buy crafts is in **Khan al Khalili** in Cairo (➤ 70), or in the bazaars at Luxor and Aswan. The best buys are painted papyrus, hand-blown recycled glass, mother-of-pearl inlay work, brass and copper work, woven tablecloths and alabaster.

Antiques and Antiquities

Genuine pharaonic, Islamic and Coptic antiques can only be exported with a licence from the Department of Antiquities, best obtained by the dealer. Be aware that most antiquities on offer are fakes, although there is still an important and damaging trade in stolen antiquities.

Cotton and Other Fabrics

■ Good-quality **Egyptian cotton** is hard to come by in Egypt as most of it is exported, but it's still possible to find inexpensive cotton casual clothes almost everywhere.

■ For traditional **Egyptian clothes** it's best to try looking in the markets in the main towns.

■ The small town of **Akhmim** in Upper Egypt is famous for its superb woven textiles, available from better fabric shops in Cairo and Luxor.

■ Bedouin women produce beautifully **embroidered shawls** and clothes.

■ Cairo is probably the best and the cheapest place to buy **belly dance outfits**. You can either buy ready made clothes or have them tailored to your whims with as much beading, glitter, bells and sequins as your heart desires. The best place is the Haberdashery emporium in Khan al Khalili (➤ 70).

Jewellery

■ Many Egyptian women still prefer to put their money in **jewellery**, preferably gold, rather than in a bank, so jewellery is readily available.

■ Bedouin and rural women prefer 21-carat gold, but most Western-style jewellery is 18 carat. **Gold and silver jewellery** is sold by the gram, with an additional fee for the workmanship. Bullion prices are printed daily in the *Egyptian Gazette*.

■ Jewellery is **relatively cheap** in Egypt, as wages are still very low.

■ Gold or silver **cartouches** with names written in hieroglyphics are probably the most popular jewellery buy for tourists. These usually take the form of pendants on chains.

Perfumes and Spices

■ Cairo has long been the **largest perfume and spice market** in the Middle East. Try Khan al Khalili (➤ 70) for the best stalls.

■ Essences are sold by the **ounce** (28g), to be diluted in alcohol for perfume.

■ Take care when buying **scents**. Egypt produces many pure essences that are used in Western perfumes, and several shops offer close copies of famous brands. Some shops offer the real thing, but overcharging and diluting pure essences is a common scam.

■ **Spices** such as black pepper (*filfil*), cumin (*kamum*), red pepper (*shatta*) and cinnamon (*irfa*) make inexpensive and welcome souvenirs, useful for recreating Egyptian cuisine back home.

■ **Stick to the spices used locally** as more exotic spices such as saffron (*zaafaran*) or green pepper (*filfil ahdar*) may be considerably cheaper than back home, but since they are often artificially dyed and have no taste whatsoever, are of inferior quality.

■ In Aswan look out for the red **hibiscus** flower (*karkadeh*), which makes a delicious hot or cold drink.

Best Markets...

...**souvenirs:** Khan al Khalili, Cairo (➤ 70; 77)
...**antiques and junk:** Attarin Market, Alexandria (➤ 149)
...**camels:** Birqash (➤ 71) and Daraw (➤ 122)
...**spices:** *souk*, Luxor (➤ 105)
...**Nubian baskets, silk shawls:** *souk*, Aswan (➤ 127)

Entertainment

Most visitors to Egypt have such a full schedule that they have very little energy left for sports or nightlife. But if you have the time and the inclination, you can find information about what's on in the *Egyptian Mail* (Saturday), the daily *Egyptian Gazette*, *Al Ahram Weekly*, and the monthly magazines *Egypt Today* and *Insight*. If you have access to a computer or internet café, also try the websites www.ecroc.com and www.egypttoday.com.

Bars and Clubs

- Cairo has a wide variety of bars and clubs, but elsewhere in the country most of the nightlife happens in the hotels. The **music** on offer is partly Western and partly Egyptian, with the occasional Sudanese or Greek song thrown in.
- Some places will refuse you entry if you are dressed too **casually** or in jeans, and others have a couples-only policy to avoid trouble, although single foreign women will invariably be let in.
- **Pavement cafés** are a great place to watch the world, but this is usually done over tea, coffee or cold drinks and a *sheeshas* (water pipe), as alcohol is rarely served.

Belly Dancing

Belly dancing has become less popular in recent years as many younger Egyptians and Arabs opt for Western-style entertainment. When religious leaders condemned belly dancing as sinful, many Egyptian dancers took early retirement, and their places were filled by foreign dancers. You'll find the best shows in the nightclubs of the upmarket hotels, which charge a flat fee for the show and a four-course meal. The dancers to look out for are Fifi Abdou, Lucy, Dina and the British-born Yasmina. Less salubrious clubs can be rather sleazy but fascinating, where beer flows at a price and where men shower dancers with paper money. (See also Undulations and Gyrations, ► 31.)

Nile-side Entertainment

On hot summer nights many Egyptians like to go down to the Nile to catch the cooler breeze. Many towns have casinos, or café terraces on the banks of the Nile where families come for cold drinks and a snack, and where lovers meet to discuss their future. At almost any time of the year it's possible to rent a *felucca* (sailing boat) or a motorboat to watch the sunset or to spend a pleasant evening with drinks and a picnic.

Spectator Sports

Egyptians are crazy about football and the adventurous can attend matches during the season (September–May). Cairo has two premier league teams. Ahli's stadium is in Zamalek and, rather confusingly, Zamalek Club plays at Muhandiseen. The national stadium is in Madinet Nasr. Another popular spectator sport is horse-racing, which is held at Cairo's Gezira or Heliopolis hippodromes, between October and May.

Festivals

October: Pharoah's Rally, a desert 4WD race attracting an international field.
November: Arab Music Festival at Cairo Opera House, featuring classical and traditional Arabic music.
December: Cairo International Film Festival held in several Downtown cinemas.

Cairo

Getting Your Bearings

In a tale from *The Thousand and One Nights*, a man who is talking of wondrous cities claims:

'He who has not seen Cairo has not seen the World. Its dust is gold; its Nile is a wonder; its women are like the black-eyed virgins of paradise: and how could it not be otherwise, when she is the Mother of the World?'

The Nile still runs like a mirage through the city and some of the women are indeed beauties, but the dust is more concrete than gold, and the Mother of the World now nurses a population of more than 15 million.

Cairo is full of extremes: poverty and wealth, widespread illiteracy and internet cafés, mudbrick buildings beneath skyscrapers. There's always a surprise around the corner, but somehow the city continues to function, and even to flourish.

★ Don't Miss

At Your Leisure

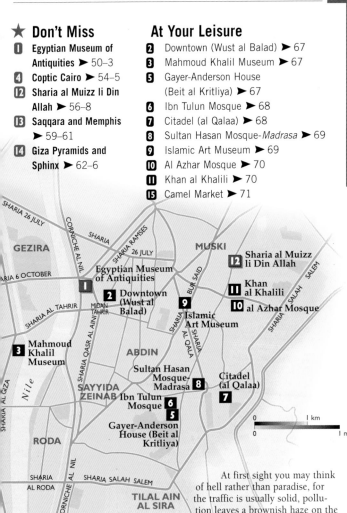

Far left: View from Gezira Island. Left: Herbalists in Khan al Khalili bazaar

At first sight you may think of hell rather than paradise, for the traffic is usually solid, pollution leaves a brownish haze on the horizon and the cacophony of noises produces instant headaches. Less than 200 years of urban and industrial sprawl is now threatening to engulf monuments that have stood for 5,000 years. Yet in the face of turmoil, Cairenes merely go about their business. You may lose patience – some people hate the city, but most are exhilarated by the chaotic overdose of humanity, and its unpredictability.

The secret of enjoying Cairo is perhaps to do as the Cairenes and take it as it comes, with humour and heaps of patience. The reward is instant and you'll soon discover one of the most fascinating cities in the world, where history is just another part of everyday life.

It would take months to explore all of Cairo's treasures, but in three days you can get a sense of the many facets of this fascinating city.

Cairo in Three Days

Day One

Morning
Start with a long morning visit to the **Egyptian Museum of Antiquities** (left, ➤ 50–3), then stroll over to **Downtown Cairo** (➤ 67) for lunch in one of the numerous restaurants. Try either the upmarket Arabesque (➤ 74) or the cheaper Felfella (➤ 75).

Afternoon
Walk back to Midan Tahrir (Liberation Square), cross the Nile over Kasr al Nil Bridge, passing the modern Opera House and walk to the **Mahmoud Khalil Museum** (➤ 67). Walk back towards the Nile and take a *felucca* to watch the sun setting over Cairo.

Day Two

Morning
Start early and take a taxi or the metro to **Coptic Cairo** (➤ 54–5) to visit the Coptic Museum and old churches. Take a taxi to the **Sultan Hasan Mosque-Madrasa** (➤ 69) and from there another cab to **Khan al Khalili** (below, ➤ 70) where you can have a quick lunch at the Egyptian Pancake House (➤ 75).

Afternoon

After lunch, stroll through **Khan al Khalili** (➤ 70) towards the Barquq Mausoleum and on to the superbly preserved merchant's house, **Beit al Suhaymi** (➤ 57). Afterwards, return along **Sharia al Muizz li Din Allah** (➤ 56–8) up to the Tentmakers Bazaar. Return to Khan al Khalili for a restoring cup of mint tea and water pipe at the renowned al Fishawi café (right, ➤ 75).

Evening

Finish the evening watching a belly dance show at one of the upmarket hotels (➤ 78).

Day Three

Morning

Take a taxi to Memphis, and continue from there to the Step Pyramid and tombs at **Saqqara** (➤ 59–61). Have a late lunch at Andrea's (➤ 74) or in the garden of the Mena House Oberoi (➤ 73).

Afternoon

Take another cab or walk over to the **Giza Pyramids, the Sphinx** and the **Solar Boat Museum** (➤ 62–6) for a leisurely visit. Head for the stables and rent a horse or camel to go for a sunset trip in the desert.

Evening

Have dinner near by and watch the *son et lumière* show at the pyramids (above, ➤ 66).

🚹

The Egyptian Museum of Antiquities

The Egyptian Museum in Cairo houses the world's most exquisite and extensive collection of ancient Egyptian artefacts, covering more than 3,000 years, from the Old Kingdom to the Roman period. It's said that if you allowed one minute for each exhibit, it would take nine months to see everything here. But if that's a little too long, take at least a morning (or better still two) to see the museum's many highlights, even though the exhibits are often badly lit and displayed. The ground floor is arranged chronologically, moving clockwise from the entrance hall (pictured below), while exhibits on the first floor are grouped thematically.

Ground Floor Highlights

The beginnings of Egyptian art are marked by the **Narmer Palette** in Room 47, which records the unification of Egypt by King Menes (► 22), and by the museum's oldest **statues** – that of the seated King Zoser was found near his step pyramid at Saqqara. The smooth black statue of the pyramid builder

---

➕ 196 B4
✉ Midan Tahrir, Downtown
☎ 02-575 4319
🕐 Daily 9–4:30.
🍽 Museum cafeteria (£); Abu Ali's café (£);

Italian restaurant with terrace (££);
coffee shop (££)
🚇 Sadat station
💰 Moderate; extra charge for the Mummy
Room from its first-floor entrance (expensive)

A New Museum

This is the fifth building that has been used to house the ever-growing collection of Egyptian antiquities but, like its predecessors, it has become too small and outdated. It's long been a running joke in Cairo that the basement is so full of

uncatalogued artefacts sinking into the earth that archaeologists will soon need to excavate. There are plans to build a new Egyptian Museum within sight of the pyramids at Giza, which will relieve the current building of some of its burden and create more space for better displays.

Above: The statue of Chephren radiates a sense of his power

Below: Taking time to look at the smaller details can be rewarding

Chephren is a masterpiece, as is the striking wooden man known as the Sheikh al Balad or Village Chief (both Room 42).

Room 32 is dominated by the striking double statue of the harmonious couple Rahotep and Nofret, which has exceptionally well-preserved colours. Rather more bizarre is the statue of the dwarf Seneb and his wife, with his children placed to hide his short legs. The remarkably colourful chapel of Hathor, with a life-size statue of the cow goddess (Room 12), was found at Hatshepsut's Temple, Deir al Bahari, in Luxor (► 94–5).

One of the museum's most fascinating collections, in Room 3, shows the ground-breaking realistic art from the time of the rebellious pharaoh Akhenaton (► 22). In four large statues here Akhneton is shown with a long face, a gorgeous mouth, and over-sized hips and belly. He's seen with his famously beautiful wife Nefertiti, and playing with their children.

Now walk along the eastern wing to the southeast staircase leading to the first floor.

Left: Tutankhamun probably died before the age of 20 from a brain tumour and a lung disease. Below: This gold jewel from his tomb is inlaid with semi-precious stones

The First Floor

The biggest crowd-puller among the museum's many world-class treasures is undoubtedly **Tutankhamun's treasure**. Akhenaton's son-in-law only ruled for nine years, but he became famous when the English archaeologist Howard Carter (1874–1939) discovered his intact tomb in 1922 in the Valley of the Kings, packed to the roof with the dazzling objects that were intended to see him through the afterlife.

Tutankhamun's splendid mask is made of solid gold with decorations in lapis lazuli, turquoise, carnelian and glass paste

By walking up the southeast stairs you encounter the items more or less as they were placed in the tomb. Room 45 starts with two life-size statues of the pharaoh that guarded his burial chamber, and the next galleries show the vast amount of refined furniture, often gold-plated, that was placed in this modest tomb. Rooms 7 and 8 are filled with the gilded wooden shrines that fitted into each other and contained the pharaoh's sarcophagus. You may have to queue in Room 3 to see the biggest treasure of all, Tutankhamun's solid-gold death mask, encrusted with semi-precious stones, his golden sarcophagus and his jewellery.

In Room 2 you'll find more gold and glittering jewellery, all of which came from Tanis in the Nile delta.

The Royal Mummy Room

Room 56 houses the **mummies** of 11 of Egypt's most illustrious pharaohs, including Seti I, his son Ramses II (► 23) and Tuthmosis II.

Former President Sadat had the room closed in 1981, considering it disrespectful to the dead. But since it partly reopened in 1995, visitors are asked to keep respectfully quiet and tour groups are not allowed. A further 16 mummies are also expected to go on display here.

TAKING A BREAK

There's no café inside the museum and the one in the garden is a bit dull. For something a little more exciting try the **Nile Hilton** next door, where Abu Ali's terrace café offers drinks, water pipes and tasty snacks. Alternatively, a neighbouring Italian restaurant, called **Da Mario**, serves pasta and pizzas, while the coffee shop has excellent coffee and pastries on sale.

The Aten sun-disc shines on the intimacy of the royal couple

THE EGYPTIAN MUSEUM OF ANTIQUITIES: INSIDE INFO

Top tips Most tour buses get to the museum around 10am, so avoid the crowds by going earlier for an hour of peace and quiet, or in the afternoon.
• The amount of things to see is staggering so try to spread your visit over at least two half days, maybe exploring one floor at a time.

Ones to miss The eastern wing of the ground floor, mostly devoted to the Late Period, is badly labelled and less interesting than the rest, except for the Graeco-Roman art in Room 34.
• You could also skip the western outer galleries of sarcophagi on the first floor and the eastern inner galleries (except Room 14) for the same reasons.

Hidden gems Room 14 on the first floor is rather poorly presented but has a superb collection of Graeco-Roman mummies with beautifully painted face masks, known as the Fayoum portraits.
• Also on the first floor (in Rooms 32 and 27) are some amazingly detailed, lifelike models of fishing boats, butchers, cattle with herdsmen and a villa with garden that give a fascinating insight into life in the Middle Kingdom.

In more depth For more details check out the museum's bookshop. *Egyptian Museum Cairo* by Dr Eduard Lambelet is a good descriptive guide with many illustrations of the star attractions. The guide by Muhammad Saleh, the museum's ex-director, focuses on the 50 most important exhibits. A wonderful illustrated book by Francesco Tiradritti is *The Cairo Museum Masterpieces of Egyptian Art* (AUC).

❹

Coptic Cairo

One of the oldest-inhabited parts of the city is Masr al Qadima (Old Cairo), the Coptic neighbourhood that provides a fascinating link between Egypt's pharaonic and Islamic civilisations. In the 6th century BC a fortified garrison known as Babylon-in-Egypt guarded a river crossing here. Some of the Roman fortifications have survived, but the area's real attraction is its narrow lanes lined with early churches, and Egypt's oldest synagogue. Cairo's first mosque is also near by.

The first thing you'll see when you get here are two Roman towers, which were part of the fortifications built by Emperor Trajan in AD 130, and some fragments of the walls of Babylon-in-Egypt. Behind these lies the fascinating **Coptic Museum**, which clearly illustrates the development of Coptic art from

Enthusiastic Coptic volunteers may show you around the Muallaqa Church

Coptic Museum
✚ 196 B1
✉ Masr al Qadima (Old Cairo)
☎ 02-362 8766
🕐 Daily 9–4
🍽 Cafeteria in garden (£)
Ⓜ Mari Girgis (from Midan Tahrir)
🚤 Water buses from Maspero Dock to Mari Girgis, not Friday or during Ramadan
💰 Moderate

Coptic Churches
✉ Masr al Qadima (Old Cairo)
🕐 Churches and synagogue daily 9–4 and during services
Ⓜ Mari Girgis (from Midan Tahrir)
🚤 Water buses from Maspero Dock to Mari Girgis, not Friday or during Ramadan
💰 Free; donations welcome

the Graeco-Roman period well into the early Islamic era (from about AD 300 to 1000). Here you can see how some Christian symbols may have evolved from pharaonic ones, including the cross and the image of the Virgin and Child.

The Copts were excellent weavers and the upper floor contains a collection of beautiful early textile fragments.

A passage near the cafeteria leads to the **al Muallaqa Church** (Hanging Church), built over one of the Roman bastions, which can still be seen at the back of the church. The building is reached via a steep staircase and a vestibule where Coptic souvenirs are on sale. The church probably dates from the 7th century, although most Copts claim it's older. Its dark interior is magnificent, with cedar panelling, a wooden Ark-like ceiling, a fine carved marble pulpit supported by 12 pillars representing the Apostles, and superb 13th-century panels inlaid with bone and ivory hiding the three *haikals* (altars).

Probably the oldest church here is the 5th-century **Abu Sarga (St Sergius)**, where you can see the steps that lead to an older crypt where the Holy Family is said to have rested during their exile in Egypt. The nearby 11th-century **Church of St Barbara** replaced an earlier one dedicated to St Cyrus and St John.

The Jewish community has long gone but the **Ben Ezra Synagogue**, at the other end of the street, has been restored to its former glory. Originally a Coptic church, the building was transformed in the 11th century and the decoration remained very similar to that of the nearby churches. According to Jewish tradition, this is where the prophet Jeremiah preached in the 6th century BC, while the Copts believe that it marks the site where baby Moses was found in a basket.

The Holy Family in Egypt

'The angel of the Lord appeared to Joseph in a dream, saying, "Arise, and take the young child and his mother, and flee into Egypt... for Herod will seek the young child to destroy him" ... He took the young child and his mother by night, and departed into Egypt.' Matthew 2:13–14.

It's believed that the Holy Family – Mary, the infant Jesus and Mary's husband Joseph – spent four years on the move, crossing Sinai and then travelling along the Nile to Asyut. Coptic churches and monasteries were built in many of the places they are believed to have rested.

TAKING A BREAK

The **cafeteria** in the museum garden is a peaceful place.

COPTIC CAIRO: INSIDE INFO

Top tip Attend a **Coptic Mass** at the Hanging Church (Friday 8–11am and Sunday 7–10am) and hear the sound of the pharaohs, as the Copts claim to be their direct descendants. The instruments, music and language you hear are similar to those in ancient Egypt. On 1 June, a festival commemorates the Holy Family's stay in the area.

Hidden gems To the right of the entrance of the Hanging Church is a beautiful 10th-century **icon of the Virgin and Child** with obvious Egyptian facial features.
• Walk along the alleys behind St Barbara's church to discover a hidden Christian cemetery.

⑫

Sharia al Muizz li Din Allah

This is the main thoroughfare of the original Fatimid city of al Qahira (Cairo), and is lined with some of the city's most glorious mosques and palaces. As it was customary to build shops outside mosques, it's also home to some of Cairo's less touristy bazaars.

✚ 197 E4
⊙ Most monuments daily 9–4; mosques may close for Fri noon prayers; less-visited monuments such as the ramparts and Qasr Bashtak may appear closed, but a custodian is usually on duty near by
💲 Inexpensive or free but remember to tip the custodian

The 11th-century **Fatimid walls** and the gate called **Bab al Futuh** mark the northern end of Sharia al Muizz. Built before the Crusades by Armenians (using stones from pharaonic structures), they were reinforced by Saladin (➤ 25) a century later. To appreciate the architectural and military genius, take a torch and walk the ramparts to **Bab al Nasr**, and back for marvellous views over the Northern Cemetery and Cairo.

Adjacent is the **mosque of al Hakim** (➤ 24), with a marble courtyard and huge minarets that are among the oldest in the city. You may guess from the smell that this part of the street is also home to the onion and garlic market.

Further to the right, the **mosque and sabil-kuttab of Sulayman Agha al Silahdar** is built in a mixture of Turkish and Cairene styles, and has a slim pencil minaret. Opposite is **Darb al Asfar**, a narrow side street with several renovated merchant houses, a sign of the government's plans for the entire old city. The finest mansion is **Beit al Suhaymi**, two 17th- and 18th-century houses knocked together. Its rooms are decorated with inlaid marble and *mashrabia* woodwork, and a fabulous shaded courtyard is filled with birdsong.

Back along Sharia al Muizz to the left is the elegant mosque of **al Aqmar** ('the moonlit'), a rare surviving Fatimid monument. On the next left corner is the prominent **sabil-kuttab of Abd al Rahman Katkhuda**, which has a fountain downstairs and Quranic school upstairs, with a beautiful carved ceiling. Here, Sharia Muizz opens out to **Bayn al Qasrayn** ('Between the Two Palaces'), after the long-gone Fatimid palaces at the core of the original city. Only two of the original five storeys of the 14th-century palace of Qasr Amir Bashtak have survived (on the left of the street), but this is one of Cairo's most impressive secular medieval buildings.

Opposite is the 185m façade of the epitomy of Mameluke architecture. This complex includes the cruciform **madrasa-khanqah of Sultan Barquq** (1384), the **madrasa-mausoleum of al Nasir** (1304) with a marble Gothic doorway, and the **madrasa-mausoleum and maristan of Sultan Qalawun**, al Nasir's father. The *maristan* functioned as a medical centre until the 19th century.

Top: Courtyard of al Hakim Mosque. Above: The Northern Cemetery

Enjoy the peacefulness of the delightful shady courtyard of Beit al Suhaymi

Opposite Qalawun's complex, **Sultan Ayyub's** *madrasa-mausoleum* was built in 1242 as Cairo's first Quranic school. Lined with coppersmith shops, the street turns into the Gold Bazaar, where a small alley to the left leads into **Khan al Khalili** (▶ 70). Past the busy shopping street of al Muski is the imposing *madrasa* **of Sultan Barsbay** (1425), and at its southern end an alley leads into the **Perfume and Spice Market**. Across Sharia al Azhar is the impressive **Ghuriya complex** of the Mameluke Sultan al Ghuri, with its mausoleum on the left and *madrasa* on the right.

Beyond the city's last two *tarboush* (fez) shops, the street ends at Bab Zuwayla, the southern city gate, former place of execution. Beside the gate is the **mosque of Sultan al Muayyad** (1415) with a splendid raised façade and twin minarets on top of the gate.

TAKING A BREAK

For a sumptuous street café with drinks, snacks and water pipes head for the **Naguib Mahfouz café** (▶ 76) or the more authentic **al Fishawi** (▶ 75), both in Khan al Khalili bazaar.

SHARIA AL MUIZZ LI DIN ALLAH: INSIDE INFO

Top tips Explore the street in the **morning or late afternoon** when it's cooler.
• **Dress modestly**, covering arms and legs, as this is a socially traditional part of town. Women should take a scarf to cover their heads and everyone should remove their shoes before entering a mosque.
• Climb up one of the **minarets** for a view over the historic centre and then stop for a rest in one of the mosque courtyards, which are often oases of calm.

Hidden gems Stroll around in the area between al Azhar Mosque and Sharia al Muizz to discover several workshops and fine mansions.

13

Saqqara and Memphis

Saqqara was one of the largest burial grounds in Egypt and in use for over 3,000 years. Most of it remains unexcavated, but among the wonders on show is the impressive Step Pyramid of Zoser. The tomb was built by the innovative architect Imhotep for King Zoser in the 27th century BC. But instead of the king's traditional mudbrick *mastaba* grave, Imhotep built in stone and stacked several *mastabas* on top of each other to create the first pyramid and the first large stone building.

Originally the Step Pyramid complex was enclosed in a limestone wall, which had fake doors to confuse intruders

A narrow portal leads through a Hypostyle Hall into the impressive complex at Saqqara

Some tomb decorations at Saqqara are among the finest of the Old Kingdom period

With its original shiny limestone casing, Zoser's pyramid stood 62m high and 118m by 140m around its base. A 28m deep shaft leads into the burial chamber. Part of the original limestone enclosure wall has been rebuilt near the entrance in the south-eastern corner. Enter the complex via a pillared corridor, and on the right is the Heb Sed Court, where the king's vitality was symbolically renewed at a festival held every seven years. Further on are the Houses of the South and the North, thought to represent older shrines of Upper and Lower Egypt, and the Serdab, with a copy of Zoser's statue (the original is in the Egyptian Museum of Antiquities in Cairo, ► 50–3). Across the Great Court is the deep shaft of the South Tomb that probably contained the king's internal organs.

Other Tombs

To the south rises the ruined and less impressive **pyramid of Unas**, built 350 years after Zoser's. Its interest stems from the walls inside the burial

Saqqara	Memphis
✚ 200 C4	✚ 200 C4
✉ 21km south of Giza pyramids; 32km from Cairo	✉ Mit Rahina, 3km from Saqqara
⊙ Daily 8–5	⊙ Daily 8–5
🍴 Cafeteria (£)	🍴 Cafeteria across the road (£££)
🚌 Bus from Downtown to Pyramids Road (Sharia al Haram); from the Maryuteyya Canal (1km before the pyramids) get a microbus to Saqqara	🚌 No public transport
♿ Step Pyramid moderate; separate charge for other tombs	♿ Moderate

chamber, which are covered with the Pyramid Texts. The
Book of the Dead is derived from these, the earliest-known
examples of decorative writing in a tomb.

Northeast of Zoser's complex you can see the magnificent
6th-Dynasty *mastabas* of the viziers Mereruka, Ankh-Ma-Hor
and Kagemni, containing the finest reliefs of the Old
Kingdom. The double *mastaba* of Akhti-Hotep and Ptah-
Hotep shows the different stages of tomb decoration and also
has some superb reliefs. The walls of the *mastaba* of the royal
hairdresser Ti are covered with wonderful scenes of daily life
in ancient Egypt. But the strangest place in Saqqara is the
Serapeum, where mummified sacred bulls were buried like
pharaohs in underground, rock-hewn galleries.

Memphis

Just a short way from Saqqara
lie the remains of Memphis,
the world's first imperial city,
founded in about 3100 BC by
King Menes (➤ 22). Old
Kingdom pharaohs and nobil-
ity were buried in its
necropolis at Saqqara.

As the first capital of a
united Egypt, Memphis was
symbolically built at the place
where the delta met the south-
ern valley. Even after the 5th century BC, when Thebes had
long taken over as the capital of Egypt, it was a splendid city,
a thriving commercial centre and an important cult centre
dedicated to the God Ptah. It's hard to imagine such splendour today, as the mudbrick palaces have dissolved and the
stones of its temples, including the grand temple of Ptah,
were plundered centuries ago for other buildings.

The sleepy village of Mit Rahina has a few minor statues.
Its tiny museum has a fine limestone colossus of Ramses II as
a young man, and a beautiful alabaster sphinx in the garden.

The lush green
area around
Saqqara and
Memphis ends
abruptly at the
necropolis

TAKING A BREAK

Saqqara has a small **café** selling cold drinks and tea, but
Egyptian families like to picnic in the shade of the ruined
6th-century Monastery of Jeremiah, near the car-park. If the
weather's not too hot you could also **picnic in North
Saqqara**, with Imhotep's masterpiece as a backdrop.

SAQQARA AND MEMPHIS: INSIDE INFO

Top tips The most spectacular approach to the Step Pyramid is on horseback
across the desert. You can rent a horse from the stables in Giza (➤ 78).
• It gets hot in Saqqara, so make sure you take enough liquids.

Ones to miss The *mastabas* beyond the pyramid of Unas have some fine
reliefs, but can be skipped if time is short.

🔟

Giza Pyramids and Sphinx

The Pyramids of Giza, sole survivors of the seven wonders of the ancient world, embody the mystery and magic of antiquity. Along with the Sphinx, they have attracted more speculation and explanation than any other monument. Despite their enduring fascination, countless questions remain that may never be answered.

Many people dream of seeing these pyramids once in their lives but, strangely enough, the first sight can be disappointing. Perhaps because they are so familiar, the pyramids seem smaller than you might expect and the mystique often disappears in the face of relentless hassle from touts and camel drivers. But if you take time to walk around them, preferably

Above: The pyramids and the Sphinx remain mysterious

✚ 200 B4
✉ Giza, 18km southwest of Cairo
☎ 02-383 8823 (tourist office)
🕐 Daily 7am–7:30pm; Great Pyramid 8:30–4:30
🍴 Cafeteria (£)
🚌 Bus 913 to Nazlat al Samaan near the Sphinx, 900 to Mena House, and minibus 83, all from Midan Tahrir
🚗 To walk on the plateau and visit Sphinx moderate; extra charges for Solar Boat Museum (inexpensive), Cheops's pyramid (moderate), Chephren's and Mycerinus's pyramids (inexpensive)

Right: The Muslim cemetery of Nazlet al Semaan overlooks the pyramids' plateau

Right:
Exploring the
inside of the
pyramids is
not for the
claustrophobic

early in the morning, it's still possible to sense their over-whelming grandeur and to evoke the 45 centuries of history they represent.

The **Great Pyramid of Cheops** (Khufu, second king of the 4th Dynasty, 2589–66 BC) is the oldest and largest of the three main pyramids. Built out of 2.3 million blocks weighing an average of 2.5 tonnes each (but sometimes up to 15 tonnes), with its original casing it reached a height of 146.6m but is now 10m lower than that.

Since it was first reopened in the 9th century, three chambers have been found inside the pyramid, all empty except for Cheops's sarcophagus. But some archaeologists believe there's a fourth chamber, containing the king's treasure. From the entrance a claustrophobic corridor descends steeply into an unfinished chamber. Alternatively, an ascending corridor leads left into the Queen's Chamber or right into the spectacular

Above: The pyramids are spectacular when seen from the desert at sunrise or sunset
Right: The area can get crowded during the day

47m long Great Gallery and, beyond it, the King's Chamber with the sarcophagus. East of the pyramid are the remains of the king's funerary temple and causeway, and the three smaller Queens' Pyramids.

The King's Guardian

Cheops's son **Chephren** (Khafre, fourth king of the 4th Dynasty, 2558–32 BC) built the second pyramid, which is 136.4m high – but the higher ground makes it appear taller than his father's. This pyramid has two chambers, one of which houses the king's sarcophagus. To the east are the remains of Chephren's Funerary Temple and of the causeway leading to his Valley Temple, guarded by the legendary **Sphinx**, which was carved out of the hillside.

Known as *Abu al Hol* ('the Father of Terror') in Arabic, this massive statue remains a mystery: the face is clearly

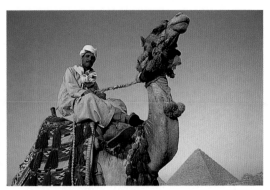

Camel and horse drivers around the pyramids can be annoying. Try to ignore them and concentrate on the grandeur of the monuments

Chephren's, but the lionesque body appears to be as much as 2,600 years older. The Sphinx is in a poor condition – the old story goes that its nose fell off after apparently being used as a target by Mameluke and Napoleonic soldiers, while its beard is in the British Museum in London. The soft limestone has not stood the test of time but recent restorations have added thousands of hand-cut limestone blocks to support the legs and haunches.

Chephren's son **Mycerinus** (Menkaure, 2532–04 BC) built the third pyramid, which is only 70m high but surrounded by the smaller pyramids of the royal family.

TAKING A BREAK

There are a few small restaurants in Nazlat al Samaan, but for a more sumptuous lunch with a view of the pyramids, head for the poolside restaurant of the **Mena House Oberoi** hotel (➤ 73), or relax in the garden of **Andrea's** (➤ 74).

GIZA PYRAMIDS AND SPHINX: INSIDE INFO

Top tips Visit the pyramids in the **early morning or late afternoon** to avoid the crowds. Follow the road past the pyramids to reach a plateau for a panoramic view of all three, but souvenir stalls and touts may disturb your enjoyment.
• A great way to view the pyramids is on **horseback** from the desert beyond. Before hiring a horse, camel or horse-drawn cart agree the price (per animal or cart) and specify the time you wish to ride. To avoid problems, use the stables near the Sphinx (➤ 78), or check the official price at the tourist office opposite the Mena House Oberoi hotel. If you have any trouble at all contact the on-site tourist police immediately.
• A *son et lumière* show is held several times daily at a theatre beside the Sphinx. For infomation tel: 02-386 3469 or check online at www.sound-light.egypt.com.

Hidden gem The **Solar Boat Museum** behind the Great Pyramid contains a superb 43m boat that was intended to carry the king through the underworld. The vessel was found in 1,200 pieces which restorers spent a total of 124 years putting back together. Another well-preserved boat was found near by, but it remains unexcavated.

At Your Leisure

2 Downtown (Wust al Balad)

Midan Tahrir (Liberation Square) is the centre of modern Cairo. Landmarks to look out for include the Egyptian Museum of Antiquities (➤ 50–3); the Nile Hilton (built over the British barracks after the 1952 revolution); the Mugamma, a Soviet-inspired 'temple' of bureaucracy;

Umar Makram Mosque and the American University.

Khedive Ismail developed the downtown area in the 1860s as part of a modernisation drive connected to the opening of the Suez Canal. The scheme was heavily influenced by Hausmann's plans for Paris boulevards. The main streets of Talaat Harb and Kasr al Nil are lined with elegant buildings that now house offices, shops and banks. The famous but dilapidated Groppi Café graces Midan Talaat Harb, while the picturesque food market of Tawfiqiya sits at the north end of Sharia Talaat Harb, a road lined with shoe shops. With its seedy nightclubs and back-street bars, 26th-of-July Street leads to the once-grand Ezbekiya Gardens.

➕ 196 C4

Men's reception room at the Beit al Kritliya

3 Mahmoud Khalil Museum

This splendid museum houses Egypt's finest collection of Western art. The works of French Impressionist and Post-Impressionist artists, including Rodin, Monet, Gauguin, Renoir, Van Gogh and Delacroix, belonged to the prewar minister Mahmoud Khalil and his French wife, who bequeathed them to the State on condition that they were exhibited in their elegant former residence.

➕ 196 A3 ✉ 1 Sharia Kafour, near the Cairo Sheraton, Giza ☎ 02-336 2358 🕐 Tue–Sun 10–5 🚌 Bus 30, 108, 200 and 356 from Midan Tahrir 🎟 Moderate (passport required)

5 Gayer-Anderson House (Beit al Kritliya)

The Beit al Kritliya gives a fascinating insight into the life of stylish and wealthy medieval Cairenes. Englishman Major Gayer-Anderson, a doctor to the royal family from 1935 to 1942, joined two houses together and lovingly restored and furnished them with Oriental *objets d'art* and paintings picked up on his travels. The ornate reception room on the ground floor featured in the James Bond movie *The Spy Who Loved Me* (1977). The museum is

by a rolled-up piece of paper.

The vast courtyard, strewn with pebbles, has a peaceful quality and is surrounded by elegant arcades. A 2km long sycamore frieze below the ceiling is inscribed with about one-fifth of the Quran.

🕇 197 D3 ⊠ Sharia Saliba, Midan Ahmed Ibn Tulun 🕐 Daily 8–5 in winter, 8–6 in summer 🚌 Bus 174 and minibus 54 from Midan Tahrir 🎫 Inexpensive

🔟 Citadel (al Qalaa)

The largest fortification in the Middle East and still dominating Cairo's skyline, al Qalaa stands on a spur of the al Muqattam hills. It was the royal residence for over 700 years. The citadel was built in 1176 by Salah ad Din (Saladin, ➤ 25) as part of his programme of fortifications against the Crusaders. The impressive walls still remain, but the original buildings were torn down first by Sultan al Nasir, whose striped mosque with faïence minaret is the only reminder of that period. In the 19th century Muhammad Ali (➤ 26)

Above: Fine plasterwork at the Mosque of Ibn Tulun

administered by the Islamic Art Museum but is adjacent to, and entered via, the Ibn Tulun Mosque.

🕇 197 D3 ⊠ Midan Ahmed Ibn Tulun ☎ 02-364 7822 🕐 Sat–Thu 9–4, Fri 9–11, 1:30–3:30 🚌 Bus 174 and minibus 54 from Midan Tahrir 🎫 Inexpensive; free with a ticket to the Islamic Art Museum (➤ 69)

🔟 Ibn Tulun Mosque

A masterpiece of classical Islamic architecture, and the largest and oldest intact mosque in Cairo, Ibn Tulun's mosque impresses with its vast scale and elegant simplicity. It was built in AD 879 by the Abbasid sultan Ahmed Ibn Tulun, who was clearly influenced by the mosques in his native Iraq. The spiral minaret was probably based on the mosque in Samarra (Iraq), although legend has it that Ibn Tulun was in fact inspired

tore down more to build his mosque and palaces. The Muhammad Ali Mosque, built between 1824 and 1848 and modelled on Istanbul's Sultanahmet Mosque, is more striking from a distance than close up. The interior is disappointing, but the views from the terrace are impressive. The clock in the courtyard was a gift from King Louis Philippe of France (1773–1850), given in return for the obelisk that now stands in Paris.

The Gawhara Palace houses a small museum of Muhammad Ali's family belongings. Of the other museums, only the Carriage Museum and the bizarre National Police Museum are interesting.

➕ 197 E3 ✉ Midan Salah ad Din
🕐 Daily 9–5 in winter, 9–6 in summer; mosques closed Fri 🍴 Cafeteria (£)
🚌 Bus 174, 194, 609, 811 and minibus 54 from Midan Tahrir 💷 Moderate

8 Sultan Hasan Mosque-Madrasa

One of the finest Islamic monuments in Egypt, this was built between 1356 and 1363 on an unprecedented grand scale, as it included shops, schools and apartments. The first mosque to have a cruciform plan, it has four *iwans* (vaulted spaces around a courtyard), and within each corner is a *madrasa* (Quranic school)

Left: Muhammad Ali's mosque is a Cairo landmark. Right: Spectacular view from the citadel over the mosque of Sultan Hasan

Five Best Viewpoints
• **Top of Cairo Tower at Gezira Island:** terrace, cafeteria and revolving restaurant
• **Citadel terrace** before sunset
• **Windows on the World** (36th floor, Ramses Hilton, Downtown): bar with wonderful views over Cairo by night
• **Top of the minaret of al Muayyad Mosque**, Bab Zuwayla
• **Virginian Bar** on top of the al Muqattam hills – turn right at the little mosque

dedicated to the four main legal rites of Sunni Islam.

The entrance to this splendid building is through a dark corridor leading into the dazzling courtyard, with its sense of overwhelming peacefulness and monumental simplicity. The light is most beautiful in the morning. Huge portals on either side of the *mihrab* (niche indicating the direction of Mecca) lead into a sombre mausoleum. There's some confusion as to whether anyone is buried here – some sources say the Sultan's sons are interred inside, while others say that the grave is empty.

➕ 197 D3 ✉ Midan Salah ad Din
🕐 Daily 8–5 in winter, 8–6 in summer
🍴 Pleasant café next door (£) 🚌 Bus 174, 194, 609, 811 and minibus 54 from Midan Tahrir 💷 Inexpensive

9 Islamic Art Museum

A visit to this rich collection is essential for a clearer understanding of the Islamic monuments in Cairo, as most of the objects were salvaged from local mosques, *madrasas* and palaces. The exhibits may look rather dusty and are sometimes arranged quite confusingly (by period and medium), but the collection contains some masterpieces. Highlights include an elegant Mameluke fountain and mosque lights (Room 5), some unusual woodwork decorated with birds and animals from the

Tulunid period (Room 6), and some fine Egyptian glass (Room 21).

➕ 197 D3 ✉ Sharia Bur Said, Bab al Khalq ☎ 02-390 1520 🕐 Daily 9–4. Closed Fri 11–2 🍴 Cafeteria (£) 🖐 Moderate

⑩ Al Azhar Mosque

Al Azhar ('the blooming' or 'the radiant'), was built in AD 971 as the first mosque in Fatimid Cairo. It is often claimed to be the oldest university in the world, and is also Egypt's supreme theological authority, presided over by the influential Sheikh of al Azhar. The entrance to this splendid mosque is the ornate 15th-century Barber's Gate, where students traditionally had their heads shaved. The *sahn* (courtyard), part

Al Azhar has been a great conservator of Islamic traditions for the past 1,000 years

of the original Fatimid design, is overlooked by three minarets and flanked on the right by a Mameluke *madrasa* with rooms for the students. The university itself, which offers religious studies to students from all over the Muslim world, is now housed in modern buildings behind the mosque.

➕ 197 E4 ✉ Sharia al Azhar 🕐 Daily 8–5. Closed during prayer times, particularly Fri noon 🚌 Bus 186, 815, 904 and minibus 77 and 102 from Midan Tahrir 🖐 Inexpensive

⑪ Khan al Khalili

The Khan, a confusing maze of alleys and bazaars that are mostly organised by trade, has been the bustling commercial soul of Cairo's old city since the Middle Ages. The main street, al Badestan, is now mostly devoted to souvenirs, but for more interesting buys stroll into the

The cafés around al Husayn Mosque serve endless *sheeshas*, tea and juices

Five Places for Children

- **Cairo Zoo**, Sharia al-Gamia, Giza (daily 8:30–4:30, inexpensive)
- **Camel Market**
- **Dr Ragab's Pharaonic Village** (St Jacob's Island, 2km south of Giza Bridge on the Corniche, Giza; tel: 02-571 8675; daily 9–5 in winter, 9–9 in summer). A kitsch but fun two-hour boat tour taking in scenes of ancient Egypt, all performed by costumed Egyptians.
- **Horse- or camel-riding** at the pyramids (▶ 78)
- **Dream Park**, Oasis Road, near 6 October City, Giza (tel: 011-400 561; daily 9am–midnight). A Western-style amusement park with hair-raising attractions.

smaller alleys to find out where the locals shop. The gold market around Sharia al Muizz li Din Allah (▶ 56–8) is big and busy, as the amount of gold given by a groom to his bride is still an important part of the marriage contract. The spice and perfume bazaar in an alley to the side of the Barsbay mosque, on Sharia al Muizz li Din Allah (just follow your nose), still has an authentic medieval atmosphere. Near the mosque of al Husayn is al Fishawi (▶ 75), a café that claims to have been serving continuously since it opened in 1773 – perhaps something of an exaggeration but still worth a visit.

🔲 197 E4 ✉ Between Midan al Husayn and Sharia al Muski 🕐 Mon–Sat 9–6 🍴 Al Fishawi and Naguib Mahfouz café and restaurant (£–££) 🚌 Bus 186, 815, 904 and minibus 77 and 102 from Midan Tahrir 🎫 Free

15 Camel Market

The camel market is exotic, but it's not for the faint-hearted. Most of the camels you'll see there have walked the Forty Days Road with Bishari herdsmen through the

desert from Sudan to Daraw (▶ 122), and are then put on a truck or train to Cairo. Here they spring around, exhausted but nervous, while Sudanese traders shout at each other to conclude their deals. Some camels are bought by Egyptian peasants and farmers as beasts of burden, while the remainder eventually end up in a Cairene abattoir.

Most camels from the market end up working the fields

Livestock and bric-à-brac markets are held in a compound near by.

🔲 200 B4 ✉ Birqash, 35km north-west of Cairo 📞 02-578 1786 for organised tour by Sun Hotel 🕐 Fri dawn–early afternoon (best between 6 and 9am) 🍴 Cafés (£) 🚌 Bus 214 from Nile Hilton terminal on Tahrir to Nile Barrage at Qanatir, then a service taxi or microbus but a private taxi is quicker 🎫 Inexpensive

Where to... Stay

Prices
The prices are for a double room per night.
£ under 200LE ££ 200–500LE £££ over 500LE

As Egypt's main city, Cairo has a huge range of accommodation, from the sleazy fleapits near Ataba market to sumptuous palaces with spectacular views of the Nile or the pyramids. Whatever your priorities might be, in summer try to get a room with air-conditioning, as it can get incredibly hot and sticky even at night. Try to book ahead during high season and you'll be lucky to find a bed anywhere.

Cairo Marriott £££

The 19th-century ruler Khedive Ismail built this superb palace on the Nile to house the French empress, Eugenie, and other foreign guests attending the opening of the Suez Canal in 1869. The palace and garden now form the central part of the hotel, and the bedrooms are in two modern towers. Many of the well-equipped rooms have splendid views over the Nile and the city, but they lack the pomp and grandeur of the palace. The *khedival* garden (▶ 75) with its swimming pool is an oasis of calm in busy Cairo, while you can drink cocktails in Empress Eugenie's impressive bedroom. There's also a casino for those seeking extra excitement.

🕂 196 B5 ⊠ Sharia Saray al Gezira, Zamalek ☎ 02-735 8888; fax 02-735 6667; email: marr-resv@link.com.eg

Cosmopolitan ££

Downtown Cairo is one of the noisiest places on earth, but the Cosmopolitan is tucked away in a surprisingly quiet back street in a heart of the area, its magnificent art-nouveau building a reminder of Cairo's *belle époque*. The hotel has been carefully renovated and has spacious and comfortable rooms, full of character. The service can be slow at times, but somehow that's all part of the charm.

🕂 196 C4 ⊠ 1 Sharia Ibn Tahlab, Downtown ☎ 02-392 3845; fax 02-393 3531

Four Seasons £££

This is the newest and most impressive of Cairo's luxury hotels. The stylish rooms are spacious, with large marble bathrooms and views of the pyramids, Cairo's zoo and the Nile. But what sets the Four Seasons apart is the unmatched level of service. The hotel also offers Cairo's first Spa and Wellness Centre, with a wide range of treatments, sauna, exercise room and outdoor swimming pool.

🕂 196 A2 ⊠ 35 Sharia al Giza, Giza ☎ 02-573 1212; fax 02-568 1616; website: www.fourseasons.com

Gezira Sheraton £££

It's one of the ugliest luxury hotels, a round tower on the tip of Gezira Island, but all rooms have stunning views over the Nile and the city. Rooms are comfortable and well equipped, but not particularly characterful. There are several good restaurants and bars and it's lively, particularly in the evening. Zamalek, Downtown Cairo and the Opera House are a short walk away.

🕂 196 B3 ⊠ 3 Sharia Maglis Quadet al Thawra, Gezira Island ☎ 02-736 1333; fax: 02-735 5056; email: gzher@rite.com

Horus House ££

Small, friendly hotels are in short supply in Cairo, which is why the Horus House is such a well-kept secret by regular visitors. Located in the quiet heart of the residential area of Zamalek, it's close to many shops, restaurants and bars. Book well in advance because enthusiasts tend to stay for a while. The restaurant offers a good-value lunch and counts among its regulars some older couples who have lived on the island for years.

➕ 196 A5 ☒ 21 Sharia Ismail Muhammad, Zamalek ☎ 02-735 3977; fax: 02-735 3182

Mena House Oberoi £££

Here, you can be one of the lucky few with a view of the pyramids from their room. The beautifully decorated, Oriental-Moorish rooms in the 19th-century wing of this former *khedival* hunting lodge sit right beside the Great Pyramid. Standard rooms in the modern garden annexe are spacious and comfortable and, although they lack the grandeur and immediacy of the palace rooms, you might still get a glimpse of the ancient wonders. Even the swimming pool has a view. Eat breakfast on the garden terrace, and the garden restaurant is perfect for lunch or afternoon tea, while the Moghul Room (▶ 75) is the best Indian restaurant in town.

➕ 196, off A2 ☒ Sharia al Ahram, near the pyramids ☎ 02-383 3222; fax 02-383 7777; email: obmhosm@oberoi.com.eg

Pensione Roma £

Madame Cressaty's diligence has maintained this 1940s hotel as one of the best budget options downtown. Behind the Moorish façade, the clean rooms have polished wooden floors, high ceilings and comfortable old furniture. Book ahead as the hotel is extremely popular with travellers and students.

➕ 196 C4 ☒ 169 Sharia Muhammad Farid ☎ 02-391 1088; fax: 02-579 6243

Saqqara Palm Club ££

There's plenty of accommodation around the pyramids at Giza, but Saqqara is another matter, which makes this small comfortable hotel all the more appealing. Set in lush and tranquil gardens in the middle of the Egyptian countryside, this is the perfect escape from Cairo's crowded and polluted streets. The large lagoon-style swimming pool is an attractive proposition at the end of a long day spent sightseeing at nearby Memphis, Saqqara and Giza.

➕ 200 C4 ☒ Saqqara Road, Badrshein ☎ 02-200 791; fax 02-201 187

Umm Kalthoum ££

Egypt's greatest singer, Umm Kalthoum (▶ 32), lived in a villa on this site, and a hotel dedicated to her has been opened in a tower that replaced her home. Its elegant lobby is filled with memorabilia, and her music is played constantly. Rooms are comfortable, and some have a view of the Nile, although

for most people the attraction here is of sleeping 'in the company' of the legendary Umm Kalthoum.

➕ 196, off A5 ☒ 5 Sharia Abu al Feda, Zamalek ☎ 02-736 5304; fax: 02-735 5304

Windsor £–££

The Windsor is one of a kind. A well-run family affair, it's one of Cairo's most popular budget hotels, although it's more expensive than most and the decoration and furnishings are worn. The spacious rooms in the colonial-style Moorish building have arched windows and high ceilings, and most have private bathrooms. The bar on the first floor is a particular treat – it's old-fashioned and wonderful for a refreshing drink, although the food should be avoided. Book in advance as the hotel is often used by tour groups and may be block-booked at the time you want to stay.

➕ 196 C4 ☒ 19 Sharia al Alfi, Downtown ☎ 02-591 5277; fax 02-592 1621; email: wdoss@link.com.eg

Where to...
Eat and Drink

Prices

Expect to pay per person for a meal, excluding drinks and tips.
£ up to 50LE ££ 50–100LE £££ over 100LE

Cairo's wide variety of restaurants reflects the city's cosmopolitan character. National dishes such as *fuul*, *koshari* and kebabs are inexpensive and widely available from food stalls and eateries on many street corners, but most of these places don't serve alcohol. Restaurants serving ethnic or international cuisine, often part of a hotel, are more upmarket. Note that wealthy Cairenes like to dress up for dinner in the trendier restaurants.

Absolut ££

One of Lebanese restaurateur Nischa Sursock's many successes, this fashionable hangout is popular with a beautiful young crowd. Come early in the evening for a quick bite from a good selection of Mediterranean dishes, or later on just to drink and listen to the latest Western and Egyptian music, played amazingly loudly.

🕂 196, off A4 ⊠ 10 Midan Amman, Muhandiseen ☎ 02-749 7326 🕙 Daily from 7pm

Alfi Bey ££

Alfi Bey is an unashamedly old-fashioned Cairo institution, where the cooking is simple Egyptian, the decoration and paper table-coverings are without complications and service comes with a smile. Start with a plate of *mezze*, followed by one of the house specialities: pigeons stuffed with *firik* (crushed wheat) or a lamb kebab. Traditional desserts are made without thought to calories or waistlines – the ice pudding and *mahalabeya* (dessert made of rice flour) are particularly good. No alcohol.

🕂 196 C4 ⊠ 3 Sharia al Alfi, Downtown ☎ 02-577 1888/577 4999 🕙 Daily 1pm–1am

Andrea's £–££

The real pleasure here is to be had outdoors, sitting at tables covered in red-and-white checked cloths, in a garden of bougainvillea and shady trees. Start with a selection of *mezze* and fresh salads that are presented on a large tray, and scooped up with delicious pitta bread (made by women working at the entrance). Main courses are limited to grilled meat and poultry, with the roast chicken coming particularly recommended. Andrea's is perfect after a visit to the pyramids, though it does sometimes suffer from an influx of tour groups.

🕂 200 B4 ⊠ 59–60 Marioutiya Canal, near the Giza pyramids ☎ 02-383 1133 🕙 Noon–midnight

Arabesque ££

A decade ago this was about as good as food got in Cairo and, although it hasn't quite kept up with the latest trends, Egyptian movie stars and French ex-pats have remained faithful. The menu offers excellent continental classics such as steaks in sauces and a legendary scampi thermidor, as well as some excellent local specialities, including pigeon stuffed with wheat and fenugreek and a wonderful *meloukhiya* (a soup or stew of a spinach-like vegetable with chicken, served with bread, onion and condiments). A must from the attractive dessert list is *Umm Ali*, a hot pudding of bread cooked in milk, with nuts, raisins and spices.

➕ 196 C4 ⊠ 6 Sharia Qasr an Nil, Downtown ☎ 02-574 7898 ⏰ Daily 12:30–3:30, 7:30–12:30

Cairo Jazz Club £–££

Another Nischa Sursock venture (see Absolut ▶ 75), Cairo's only live jazz venue gets particularly crowded late in the evening. The sound switches between jazz, reggae and rock and there's also the occasional classical night. It serves good *mezze*, salads and simple pastas, but the real attraction is the music and the intriguing dark, smokey, lively atmosphere.

➕ 196 A5 ⊠ 197 Sharia 26 July, Agouza, opposite the Balloon Theatre ☎ 02-345 9939 ⏰ Daily 7pm till the last person leaves (around 3am)

Egyptian Pancake House £

Places to eat in and around Khan al

Khalili bazaar are limited, but this one has long been reliable. Egyptian pancakes (*fteers* in Arabic) are a cross between a pizza and a crêpe. *Fteers* can come sweet with nuts and honey, or savoury with cheese, tomatoes and chilli. Inside the restaurant is calmer, but outside you get to sit still and see the endless fascination provided by Islamic Cairo.

➕ 197 E4 ⊠ Between Sharia al Azhar and Midan al Husayn, Khan al Khalili ⏰ Daily from morning until the last customer leaves late evening

Felfella £–££

If you know nothing about Egyptian food but are keen to find out, then this is as good a place to start as any. The clientele is predominantly foreign, but locals come here as well for the traditional dishes, if not the wacky décor of stuffed animals and Egyptian artefacts. Try a selection of salads and *mezze* to start, followed by a kebab or grilled pigeon. However,

the desserts are less exciting (you won't often see Egyptians eating them here) and the tea is better at the café around the corner. Felfella has now become a chain, but this is the original and best.

➕ 196 C4 ⊠ 15 Sharia Hoda Shaarawi, Downtown ☎ 02-392 2833 ⏰ Daily 7am–midnight

Al Fishawi £

The claim that they have never closed at Fishawi since 1773 may be a slight exaggeration, but this is the oldest teahouse in Cairo. It's also one of the few cafés where you'll find Egyptian women and families sitting with their men. It's a great place to sip mint tea or smoke a sweet water pipe and watch the world go by. During the day it's a good place to stop while visiting the old city, and at night it gets very lively with locals. As it's close to the mosque of al Husayn no alcohol is served.

➕ 197 E4 ⊠ Khan al Khalili, just off Midan al Husayn ⏰ Daily 24 hours

Marriott Garden ££

Cairo doesn't have many secluded outdoor spaces where you can have a drink or a meal in relative peace. However, the Marriott Garden, all that remains of the original 1869 design, is a perfect place to restore your spirits after sightseeing. Beyond the tourists, it's also a great place to watch wealthy Cairenes or young Gulf Arabs relaxing. It serves drinks and ice-creams as well as some tasty sandwiches, good pizzas and several excellent grilled Egyptian specialities.

➕ 196 B5 ⊠ Cairo Marriott Hotel, Sharia Saray al Gezira, Zamalek ☎ 02-735 8888 ⏰ Daily 9am–1am

Moghul Room £££

A wonderful spot to recover from a hectic day, this elegant and beautifully decorated restaurant serves the best Indian cuisine in town. The curries are subtly spiced, the tandooris are excellent and the array of breads is amazing, while the *kulfi* (Indian ice-cream) is a dessert institution in Cairo. In addition, there's live, soothing sitar music and accompanying singing to add to the calming and authentic atmosphere.

✚ 196, off A2 ✉ Mena House Oberoi Hotel, Sharia al Ahram ☎ 02-383 3222 ⏰ Daily 12–3, 7.30–12.30

Naguib Mahfouz Coffee Shop £ & Khan al Khalili Restaurant ££

This combination is the only 'upmarket' place to eat in the bazaar area and, just as important, has the only decent toilets. The coffee shop serves traditional Egyptian hot drinks, fresh juices, water pipes and sweets in an Oriental décor. The more expensive restaurant serves *mezze* and a wide selection of Egyptian or Middle Eastern main courses. Although the clientele are almost exclusively tourists, it's still a cosy and quiet place off a very busy street.

✚ 197 E4 ✉ 5 Sikket al Badestan, an alley in Khan al Khalili ☎ 02-590 3788 ⏰ Daily 10am–2am

La Piazza ££

Of the several restaurants in this complex, La Piazza has remained the most popular. A stylish Italian restaurant, it serves delectable fresh pastas with the standard sauces as well as more inventive Italian main courses. Unsurprisingly, it's a favourite meeting place for the Zamalek 'ladies who lunch'.

✚ 196 B5 ✉ Four Corners, 4 Sharia Hassan Sabry, Zamalek ☎ 02-736 2961 ⏰ Daily 12:30pm–12:30am

Samakmak ££

Getting fresh fish in a Cairene restaurant can sometimes be a problem, but the highly recommended Samakmak has proved to be reliable. It's a casual place, with tables on the pavement in summer, the sort of restaurant where you select fish or seafood from the display and then discuss whether to have it fried or grilled, and served with Oriental rice or bread. The fresh salads and dips are superb and, even better, there's no hurrying you out when you've finished. Instead, do as the locals do and finish with a digestive sweet *sheesha* (water pipe) while watching the Cairo traffic roar past outside.

✚ 196, off A4 ✉ 92 Sharia Ahmed Orabi, Muhandiseen ☎ 02-347 8232 ⏰ Daily 24 hours

Sushiyama £££

Egypt has long enjoyed cordial relations with Japan (the Japanese built the Opera House), so it should come as no surprise to find an excellent Japanese restaurant in town. Sushiyama serves a wide range of sushi, *sashimi* and *tempura*. The food grilled on the personal barbecues at the table is excellent and fun to watch.

✚ 196 B5 ✉ World Trade Centre, 1191 Corniche al Nil, Boulaq ☎ 02-578 5161 ⏰ Daily lunch, dinner and takeaway

Le Tabasco ££

Another Nischa Sursock success, beautiful young Egyptians flock to this funky bar-restaurant to see and be seen against a cool, Oriental backdrop that was arranged by a trendy Egyptian designer. You can eat here too, from a menu of good Mediterranean dishes. But forget about cosy dinner *à deux* later in the evening when the contemporary music is turned up and the smoke starts to thicken.

✚ 196, off A4 ✉ 8 Midan Amman, Muhandiseen ☎ 02-336 5583 ⏰ Daily dinner only

Windsor Hotel Bar £

Several places in Cairo have adopted a latter-day colonial look, but this one is original. The building is beautifully Moorish, the bar is dusty, the whole place smells of intrigue, the animals are stuffed and some of the waiters seem to be as ancient as the furniture. It's a perfect place for a discreet assignation or quiet drink.

✚ 196 C4 ✉ 19 Sharia al Alfi, Downtown ☎ 02-591 5277 ⏰ Daily noon–1am

Where to... Shop

Cairo often seems like one big bazaar, so there should be no shortage of shopping opportunities, from exotic spices to cotton clothing and silver Bedouin jewellery.

Books and Music

Downtown Cairo has some excellent bookshops with titles in several foreign languages on Egypt and the Middle East. The most extensive range, many published by the American University in Cairo (AUC) Press, is available at AUC bookshop (Hill House on the main campus of the American University, 113 Sharia Qasr al Aini). Lehnert and Landrock (44 Sharia Sherif) also has a great selection of books on Egypt and sells old postcards and photographs of Cairo in the past. For valuable antiquarian Oriental books and maps take a look in l'Orientaliste (15 Sharia Qasr al Nil), but prices here are high and it only opens sporadically.

One of the best places to buy good-quality CDs and tapes, including recordings of local greats such as Umm Kalthoum, Farid al Atrash and Abdel Wahaab, is Sono Cairo (Downtown, on the corner of Sikket Ali Labib Gabr and the pedestrian street Sharia Shawarbi). Abdullah, in the alley behind l'Americaine on Sharia Talaat Harb, sells funky new-wave Arab music.

Craft Shops

Khan al Khalili (▶70) sells a selection of souvenirs, but the better crafts are in more specialised shops. Ring the doorbell at Senouhi (54 Sharia Abdel Khalek Sarwat, 5th floor, apt 51, Downtown; tel: 02-391 0955) to find a treasure trove filled with carpets, jewellery, embroidered clothes, old books and hand-made felt puppets. Khan Misr Touloun (opposite Ibn Tulun Mosque; tel: 02-365 2227) and Marketing Link (27 Sharia Yahia Ibrahim, 1st floor, apt 8, Zamalek; tel: 02-736 5123) both promote high-quality Egyptian crafts, including pottery, tablecloths, embroidery and carpets at fixed prices. Zaki Sherif sells a fascinating mixture of Ottoman art and his own funky designs inspired by the country's past in his Zamalek shop Beit Sherif (3 Boghat Aly; tel: 02-736 5689). Dr Ragab, who reinstated the making of papyrus, sells top-quality papyri with matching prices at Dr Ragab's Papyrus Institute (Corniche al Nil, near Cairo Sheraton, Giza). Nagada (8 Sharia Dar al Shefa, 3rd floor, Garden City, by appointment; tel: 02-736 4500) sells superb hand-woven cotton and pottery made in Fayoum Oasis. Crafts from Siwa oasis are on sale in the elegant Nomad Gallery (14 Saray al Gezira, 1st floor, Zamalek; tel: 02-341 1917), or at the Cairo Marriott shopping arcade. Shops in al Khiyamiya ('Tentmakers' Bazaar'), outside Bab Zuwayla, sell traditional appliqué work for tents, cushion covers or wallhangings.

Egyptians had mastered the art of glass-blowing by 1500 BC, and Muski glass is still produced in the time-honoured way, using recycled glass. It's available from a tiny shop in Khan al Khalili, just off Sharia al Muizz li Din Allah before the madrasa of Sultan Ayyub.

Clothes

The World Trade Centre (1191 Corniche al Nil, Boulaq) is Cairo's most upmarket shopping mall, where chains sell casual cotton clothing. However, the new mall at the First Residence (35 Sharia al Gamea, Giza) provides some competition. For belly dance outfits go to Haberdashery, reached via a dark stairway signposted 'Everything a Belly Dancer Needs', on Sharia Gawhar al Qayed near al Fishawi Café in Khan al Khalili.

Where to...
Be Entertained

Cairo is as alive at night as it is during the day. Check the daily *Egyptian Gazette*, the weekly *Cairo Times* and *al Ahram Weekly* and the monthly *Egypt Today*.

Ahwas (Coffee Houses)

Egyptian men love to spend the evening in their local *ahwa* or café, chatting over a water pipe and coffee or tea – no alcohol is served (▶ 28–30). **Al Fishawi** (▶ 75) and the area near the mosque of al Husayn in the old city are particularly lively at night.

Music

Most classical concerts are performed at the **Cairo Opera House** on Gezira Island (tel: 02-737

0598), where men are obliged to wear a jacket and tie. The **Umm Kalthoum Classical Arabic Music Troupe** performs twice a month on Thursdays or Sundays, from October to April at the Sayyid Darwish Concert Hall on Sharia Gamal ad Din al Afghani, off Sharia al Ahram, Giza (tel: 02-560 2473). For less formal live music there's the **Cairo Jazz Club** (▶ 75).

Belly Dancing

The best dancers perform at clubs in expensive hotels, at an 8pm performance for tourists and a 1am show for Egyptians. Shows at **Le Meridien** (tel: 02-362 1717) and **Semiramis InterContinental** (tel: 02-795 7171) are the most popular. Downtown nightclubs such as **Palmyra**, in the alley beside the

Chemla store on Sharia 26 July, are sleazier – better dancers only arrive when enough money has been thrown on to the stage. It's especially fun when audience members are taken up on stage. Be sure to ask the price of things before you order.

Sufi Performances

The **Mawlawiyya** are an Egyptian Sufi sect also known as the **Whirling Dervishes**. When they're in town they do an enthralling performance of whirling on Wednesdays and Saturdays at 9pm at the al Ghuri Mausoleum, on the corner of Sharia al Azhar and Sharia al Muizz li Din Allah.

Discos

The big night out in Cairo is Thursday, and the trendiest venue is **Gato Negro** (32 Sharia Jeddah in Dokki; tel: 02-761 6888). Discos in luxury hotels are often for residents only, but they will let other foreigners in on a quiet night; others may ask for a hefty minimum charge.

The most popular venue is **Jackie's** at the Nile Hilton on Midan Tahrir (tel: 02-578 0444). **Tamango** in the Atlas Zamalek Hotel (Sharia Gamaa ad Duwal al Arabiya, Muhandiseen; tel: 02-346 4157) admits couples only but has a good atmosphere. **Pharaoh's Hotel** (12 Sharia Lutfi Hassouna, Dokki; tel: 02-761 0871) is the only place that plays hip hop and rap. The **Crazy House Disco** in the Cairo Land complex (1 Sharia Salah Salem; tel: 02-366 1082) has three huge dance floors and is open from midnight to 6am.

Horse-riding

Only hire horses from one of the renowned stables. Try **AA Stables** (tel: 02-385 0531), which are excellent for children, **MG Stables** (tel: 02-385 1241) or **Eurostables** (tel: 02-385 5849), all in **Nazlat as-Samaan** near the Sphinx. The **Saqqara Country Club Hotel** (Saqqara road to Abu al Nomros; tel: 02-384 6115) has good facilities and offers temporary membership.

Luxor

Getting Your Bearings

It was the capital of the New Kingdom for more than 500 years, and Luxor boasts some of the world's most extraordinary monuments, many of which have defied the passing of time. As a provincial Egyptian town it also offers relative peace and quiet, especially on the West Bank.

Luxor is a bustling town, with the Temple of Luxor at its centre surrounded by a crowded *souk* and hotels. By day the Corniche is busy with locals coming off the ferry, tourists getting off their boats and buses touring the sights. But at night, when people come to catch the breeze along the Nile after a hot day, it's calm.

There were settlements here from an early age, but the town (then known as Waset and later as Thebes) only became important when the princes of Thebes established the New Kingdom (1550–1069 BC). Successive pharaohs vied to build ever-greater additions to the state temple of Amun in Karnak and its sister temple in Luxor. As secular buildings were made of mudbrick, little else remains of the fabled city that Homer described as 'hundred-gated'.

Luxor Temple and its god Amun were popular even after the Romans camped in the sacred precinct. Previous page: The Court of Ramses II at Luxor Temple

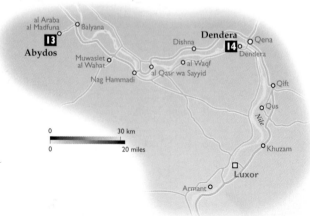

9 Valley of the Kings

10 Deir al Bahari   DRA ABU AL NAGA

Valley of the Queens

7
6

Deir al Madina
8

11 Tombs of the Nobles

AL GURNA

mb of fertari

Ticket Office ▣

12 Ramesseum

Colossi of Memnon

NEW GURNA

at Fadliya Canal

GEZIRAT SAAD

Nile

1 Karnak

5

Madinat Habu

2 km
1 mile

GEZIRAT

2 Luxor Museum

3 Mummification Museum

4 Luxor Temple

LUXOR

The dead were buried on the west bank of the Nile, and the kings hid extraordinary treasures in a secluded valley in the Theban mountains, although their security measures failed to foil the tomb robbers. The queens and nobles had less secretive burial grounds, facing the pharaohs' mortuary temples. Until recently the only way to cross to the West Bank was by ferry, but there's now a bridge to the south of the city.

In 1997 Luxor suffered Egypt's worst act of terrorism, when 58 tourists were shot at Deir al Bahari. Since then it has been peaceful, but security remains tight and visitors leaving town by road do so as part of an armed convoy.

The mosque of Luxor's patron saint Abu al Haggag sits atop Luxor Temple

This is where the ancient Egyptians were most prolific, where great temples stand as testimony to their creators' wealth and imagination, and where monuments slowly crumble into dust.

Luxor in Three Days

Day One

Morning
Start early, before it gets hot, by taking a *calèche* (horse-drawn carriage) to **Karnak Temple** (left, ➤ 84–7), where you can easily spend a morning. Have lunch beside the Nile at the Peace Abouzeid Restaurant (➤ 105), a short taxi ride away.

Afternoon
After lunch take another cab to **Luxor Temple** (➤ 88–90) for a leisurely stroll around the ruins. It's then a short walk to the **Sofitel Old Winter Palace** (➤ 103) for a touch of grandeur and tea on the terrace. That will take you to early evening, and time for shopping in the *souk*.

Day Two

Morning
Make another early start, especially in the summer. Take a taxi to the ticket booth on the West Bank, where you must buy tickets for all West Bank sites you want to visit. Back in the cab, head first for the exposed **Valley of the Kings** (right, ➤ 91–3), which gets very hot by noon. Ask the driver to wait for you, as there's little other transport back. The Marsam Hotel (➤ 103) is good for a simple lunch.

Afternoon

Walk next door for a visit to the **Ramesseum** (➤ 100). There's no problem getting a cab here, but for some local flavour flag down a passing pick-up truck, most of which go to the ferry terminal (*al mina*). Once across the river, walk to the small, but beautifully arranged **Luxor Museum** (Coptic relief carving pictured left, ➤ 98) for a short visit. Afterwards, rent a *felucca* and, wind permitting, sail into the sunset.

Day Three

Morning

Rent a bicycle (➤ 182–3) or take a taxi (first agree a price that includes all your chosen sights) and then take the ferry to the West Bank, stopping again at the ticket booth as tickets are only valid for the day they're purchased. Carry on to the temple of **Deir al Bahari** (below; ➤ 94–5), passing the two **Memnon Colossi** (➤ 183). From Deir al Bahari retrace your steps to the **Tombs of the Nobles** (➤ 96–7), with their realistic depictions of daily life. Have a late lunch in the garden of Cafeteria Muhammad (➤ 104), near the ticket office.

Afternoon

After lunch, walk or cycle to the **Temple of Madinet Habu** (➤ 98), which is at its best in the softer afternoon light. Take time to walk around the temple precinct and watch the sunset from one of the cafés opposite, or head back to the stables near the ferry (➤ 106) for a ride through the countryside. La Mamma, the garden restaurant of the Sheraton Hotel (➤ 104) is a good place for dinner.

Evening

After dinner, cross back to the East Bank to Luxor Temple, which is perhaps even more striking when floodlit.

❶

Karnak

The ancient Egyptians called Karnak 'Ipet-Isut' ('The Most Perfect of Places'), and for 1,500 years this was the most important place of worship in the country, dedicated to their great god Amun. Much more than just a temple, it was also an important intellectual centre, a spectacular complex of temples, chapels, pylons, obelisks and sanctuaries, covering more than 400 hectares – enough space for 10 cathedrals. Every pharaoh of note built, destroyed, enlarged, embellished or restored part of the complex to express his devotion to Amun. In the process, Karnak became one of the largest and most magnificent temple complexes in the ancient world.

Take a *calèche* along the Corniche to get to Karnak which, with all its splendour and history, can be a confusing place to visit. The complex consists of several temple compounds and many additions by different kings. But, as Egyptologist T G H James put it, 'Karnak is an archaeological department store containing something for everyone.' One rule to remember is that the monuments mostly get older the deeper inside you go.

The temple, and particularly the Great Hypostyle Hall in Karnak never fail to impress the visitor with their overwhelming grandeur

✚ 202 B4
✉ 2.5km north of Luxor
🕐 Daily 6–5:30 (6am–6:30pm in summer)
🍴 Café by the Sacred Lake (£)
🚌 Minibuses from Luxor centre
👜 Complex moderate; museum inexpensive

The Triad of Thebes

The temples of Luxor and Karnak are both dedicated to the Theban triad of the gods Amun, Mut and Khonsu. Amun, the most important of these, later became a state deity as the Supreme Creator Amun-Ra, the fusion of Amun with the sun-god Ra. Mut, the Mistress of Heaven, was his wife or consort and Khonsu, also known as 'the traveller' or the moon-god, was their son.

The most accessible part of Karnak is the **Precinct of Amun**, which seems like an endless succession of massive pylons (temple gateways), monumental statues and grand hypostyle halls. The precinct is approached from the **Processional Way** of ram-headed sphinxes (Amun was often represented as a human wearing ram horns), which connected with the temple of Luxor (► 88–90). This leads to the **First Pylon** which, at 43m high and 130m wide is the largest in Egypt, even though it was never finished. In the forecourt you'll find **Seti II's shrine**, which

Every day, water birds were led through a stone tunnel from the fowl-yard to the Sacred Lake

housed the sacred boats of the triad and, in the south corner, the superb **Temple of Ramses III** (20th Dynasty), also thought to be a way station for the sacred boats. The walls of this small temple, which follows the perfect plan of the classical temple, are decorated with scenes of the annual Opet festival. In front of the **Second Pylon** rises the granite colossus of the ubiquitous Ramses II with one of his many daughters beside him.

Behind the Second Pylon lies the most spectacular sight of all, the 13th-century BC **Great Hypostyle Hall** – an amazing 'forest' of over 140 tall papyrus pillars covering 5,500sq m, built by Seti I and his son Ramses II. Beyond the Hypostyle Hall lies a rather larger and more confusing section of the temple, built during the 18th Dynasty (1550–1295 BC). In the courtyards beyond the Third and Fourth Pylons are the finely carved **obelisks** of Tuthmosis II and, further on, of the only female pharaoh, Queen Hatshepsut (1473–58 BC, ► 94–5). The tip of her second fallen obelisk lies on the way to the Sacred Lake.

Past the Sixth Pylon stand two elegant pillars carved with lotus and papyrus flowers, symbolic of Upper and Lower Egypt, and the granite **Sanctuary of Amun**, built by Philip Arrhidaeus,

An avenue of ram-headed sphinxes connected Karnak Temple to Luxor Temple

the half-brother of Alexander the Great. This is where Amun's effigy was kept and where, as the images on the walls show, daily offerings were made in his honour. Beyond lies a large **Central Court** and the **Jubilee Temple of Tuthmosis**, where the king's vitality and authority was symbolically renewed during his jubilee. It's interesting that this huge temple complex was only entered by the powerful priesthood; lay Egyptians were excluded and used intermediary deities, whose shrines they built against the temple's enclosure wall. One such series of chapels, known as the **Chapels of the Hearing Ear**, lies at the back of the Jubilee Temple.

Between the Third and Fourth Pylons the temple spreads southwards along the side of the **Sacred Lake**. In 1903, in the Cachette Court in front of the lake, some 17,000 bronze and 800 stone statues were uncovered. The finest of them are now in the Egyptian Museum of Antiquities in Cairo (► 50–3).

The **Open Air Museum** houses a few reconstructions of earlier buildings, two fine barque shrines and an elegant 12th-Dynasty white chapel with fine carvings.

Two monumental colossi of Ramses II guard the Second Pylon

TAKING A BREAK

The **café** near the Sacred Lake is a relaxing place to have a drink or two under the trees. For lunch leave the site and head for the **Peace Abouzeid Restaurant** on the Corniche (► 105), or the coffee shop of the quiet **Luxor Hilton Hotel** near by.

KARNAK: INSIDE INFO

Top tips The temple **can get very crowded** with tour groups from 10am to 3pm, but earlier or later, when the light is at its best, you could have the place more or less to yourself.
• A splendid 90-minute *son et lumière show* is held three or four times each evening. The first part of the show is a walk through the floodlit temple, the other part is viewed from a theatre beyond the Sacred Lake. Buy your ticket at the site. For information check the ticket booth (tel: 02-386 3469) or website: www.sound-light.egypt.com.

Hidden gems The **bas-reliefs** on the northern side of the Hypostyle Hall, representing Seti I's victories and battles, are exquisite – much better than the crudely executed sunk reliefs from the reign of his son Ramses II on the other side.

Ones to miss The badly ruined **Precincts of Mut** to the south and of Mont to the north are rarely visited, as are the courts beyond the 7th Pylon.

4

Luxor Temple

This magnificent structure, known in ancient times as the 'Harem of the South', is connected to the Temple of Karnak (► 84–7) by a 3km processional Avenue of Sphinxes. Like Karnak, Luxor's temple was dedicated to the Theban triad of Amun, Mut and Khonsu, whose statues stood here during the Opet festival.

Even though Luxor Temple was expanded several times throughout the ages, it's much more compact and coherent than Karnak, perhaps because its core was built by just one pharaoh, Amenophis III (1390–52 BC). The walls are decorated with some of the finest (and often best-preserved) carvings in Egypt, protected because much of the temple was buried until 1885. Before excavations, only the heads of the Ramses II (1279–13 BC, ► 23) colossi and the tips of the obelisks stuck out above the pile of debris on which Luxor village was built. The village was removed bit by bit as the excavations started, but when it came to destroying the tomb and mosque of Luxor's patron saint, Youssef Abu al Haggag, the people refused. As a result, the little mosque now perches awkwardly on top of the excavated temple.

Abu al Haggag

The patron *sheikh* of Luxor, Abu al Haggag, was born in Baghdad in around AD 1150, moved to Mecca and later made his way to Luxor where he founded a Sufi school. Every year during the saint's *moulid* (festival), huge floats move slowly through the streets and a few *feluccas* are dragged around his mosque by local people. These represent the boats that were pulled around the temple during the ancient Opet festival.

✚ 202 B4
✉ Corniche, East Bank
🕐 Daily 7am–10pm in summer, 7am–9pm in winter
💲 Expensive

The **Avenue of Sphinxes** leads to the monumental **First Pylon** built by Ramses II, which was once fronted by two obelisks and six colossi of the man himself. One obelisk and two of the statues were taken to France in the 19th century, but the remaining ones are still very impressive. The pylon is decorated, as so many other Egyptian temples, with Ramses II's favourite story, the Battle of Qadesh. Beyond the pylon, the large Court of **Ramses II** is surrounded by two rows of papyrus-bud columns, interspersed with more statues of the king.

To the left of the court, the **Mosque of Abu al Haggag** hangs over the temple, while to the right is the *barque* shrine that was used for the three statues that came from Karnak during the annual Opet festival (see panel). Also of interest on this side are

Top left: Luxor Temple is dramatically illuminated at night

Above: Luxor Temple suffers from humidity caused by the rising water tables

reliefs of the temple itself and of a funerary procession led by Ramses II's sons. Beyond the Second Pylon the impressive **Processional Colonnade** of Amenophis III, with huge papyrus columns, was the model for the Great Hypostyle Hall at Karnak. The carvings on the walls were added by Tutankhamun and give a picture of the Opet celebrations: one wall shows the outward journey, the other the return of the procession.

At the end of the colonnade is perhaps the temple's most impressive part, the **Great Sun Court**, also built by Amenophis III, its fine decorations developed over the millennium between the reigns of Amenophis and Alexander the Great. Unfortunately this court has suffered badly from the rising water level and a major restoration project is underway. A large cache of statues unearthed here in 1989 can now be seen in Luxor Museum (► 98).

Behind a columned portico, used as a chapel by Roman soldiers, lies the temple's **inner sanctuary**, with Alexander the Great's Sanctuary of Amun's Barge and Amenophis III's Birth Room, which has images of the king's divine conception and birth, and his nurturing by goddesses. The bedrock on which this part of the temple was built was believed to be the site where Amun was born.

TAKING A BREAK

Enjoy Nile views with your tea at the splendid colonial **Sofitel Old Winter Palace** (► 103).

The late afternoon sun gives the monuments a warm pinkish glow

The Opet Festival

During the splendid annual Opet (fertility festival) priests would bring the statues of the gods Amun, Mut and Khonsu in a procession of holy barges up the Nile from Karnak to Luxor, where they would spend a symbolic honeymoon. This festival, held during the second month of the Nile flood, was intended to ensure a good harvest for the coming season.

LUXOR TEMPLE: INSIDE INFO

Top tips It's best to explore Luxor Temple during the day, but return at night when floodlights add to the mysterious atmosphere and accentuate the fine carvings.
• Ask the tourist office when the *moulid* happens, as it's quite spectacular.

Hidden gem Study the reliefs on the walls carefully to understand the **rituals of the Opet festival**.

9

Valley of the Kings

Ever since Howard Carter discovered Tutankhamun's tomb in 1922, filled to the brim with untold wonders (► 52), the Valley of the Kings (Wadi al Muluk) has excited, intrigued and fuelled the imagination of the world. For over 500 years this barren and secluded valley, also known as 'The Place of Truth', was the last abode of the mighty New Kingdom pharaohs. Their elaborate tombs were carved into the mountain, their mummies covered with gold and jewels, and surrounded with treasure and everything else they would need in their afterlife.

Top: The barren hills contrast with the richly decorated tomb interiors

✚ 202 B4
✉ West Bank, beyond al Gurna
🕐 Daily 7–5 in winter, 7–6 in summer
🍴 Cafeteria (£)
💰 Expensive

These tombs were intended to be secure places where the mummies could rest eternally, ensuring the deceased pharaohs a happy afterlife. But the prize was too great – treasure hunters and tomb raiders were not easily deterred and most tombs had been raided before much time had passed. But even without the mummies and their treasure, the massive scale of some of these tombs and the magnificence of their wall paintings allows you to imagine the original splendour, particularly if you can get away from the crowds.

Keeping Mum

As the pyramids had proved relatively easy to break into, pharaohs of the New Kingdom chose to be buried with less ostentation. The architecture of the tomb in some way reflected the journey the dead pharaoh was making, so rock-hewn

The Royal Mummies

In 1876 the greatest cache of mummies was discovered near the Temple of Hatshepsut. The mummies of 40 pharaohs, queens and nobles including Amenophis I, Tuthmosis III, Seti I and Ramses II, were found in a huge burial pit (tomb No 320). It's believed that New Kingdom priests, realising the mummies' allure to robbers, moved them to this secret communal tomb. Some are now on display in the Mummy Room of the Egyptian Museum of Antiquities in Cairo (➤ 50–3).

tombs with long corridors leading down into antechambers and finally into the burial chamber represented the underworld. Artists and workers from Deir al Madina (➤ 99–100) decorated the tomb walls with mysterious and complicated inscriptions and images from the Book of the Dead, to help guide the pharaoh to the underworld.

It's All Relative

Tutankhamun's tomb may be famous for the treasure it contained, but as the king died young and insignificant, his tomb is small and the decorations hastily executed. Just try to imagine the amount of gold and wealth that would have been buried with more powerful pharaohs such as Ramses II or Tuthmosis III. Tuthmosis (1479–1425 BC) was one of the first to be buried in the valley; his is a very secretive space, high up in the cliffs past a ravine. That the Tomb of Ramses VI was already a tourist attraction in antiquity is obvious from the centuries of graffiti near the entrance.

The 100m long tomb of Seti I (1294–1279 BC) is the most beautiful in the valley, with carvings even finer than those in the pharaoh's temple in Abydos (➤ 101). Seti's tomb, closed for years, is due to reopen soon. Alternatively, the Tomb of

More Discoveries

Some 80 tombs have been discovered to date, and the latest are almost as spectacular as Carter's find. In 1995 the American archaeologist Kent Weeks announced that KV5, dismissed for centuries as uninteresting, was the largest tomb ever found in Egypt. With perhaps another 10 years' work in front of him, Weeks and his team have so far found more than 110 rooms, believed to be the tomb of more than 50 of Ramses II's sons. You can follow his progress online at www.kv5.com.

Ramses III is almost as grand, or there's Horemheb's tomb, which is similar in design if not décor.

TAKING A BREAK

The only place open for refreshments in the valley is at the **resthouse** near the entrance, which serves expensive cold drinks and meals.

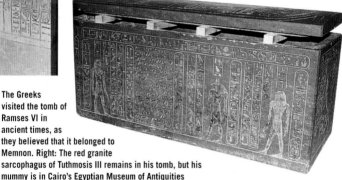

The Greeks visited the tomb of Ramses VI in ancient times, as they believed that it belonged to Memnon. Right: The red granite sarcophagus of Tuthmosis III remains in his tomb, but his mummy is in Cairo's Egyptian Museum of Antiquities

VALLEY OF THE KINGS: INSIDE INFO

Top tips Tomb openings are rotated to protect paintings from damage caused by human sweat. Check which tombs are open with the ticket office near Deir al Madina before you go.
• Tickets are sold per three tombs, with a separate ticket for Tutankhamun's tomb.
• To avoid the crowds head for the tombs further away from the entrance.
• Don't use flash photography or touch the walls inside the tombs as they are very easily damaged.

Ones to miss Tutankhamun's tomb is small and often disappointing because the treasure is in the Egyptian Museum of Antiquities in Cairo, and the poor decorations have been blackened by a fungus caused by the humidity created by the crowds.
• If you're short of time skip the tombs of Yuya and Thuya, Seti II, Smenkhare and Thawsert.

⑩

Deir al Bahari

The magnificent Mortuary Temple of Hatshepsut is set dramatically against the cliff face of the Theban hills. The imposing terraces look surprisingly stark and modern, but you have to imagine them in Hatshepsut's days, when they were filled with exotic perfumed trees, and fountains to cool the air. Hatshepsut called her temple Djeser Djeseru ('the Sacred of Sacreds'). It was a ruin when excavated in 1891, but it's been carefully restored over many years.

In ancient times the temple was connected to the Nile by a wide avenue of sphinxes. The Lower Terrace would have been lined with sweet-smelling myrrh trees and refreshing fountains. The pylons have disappeared and the colonnades were defaced by Tuthmosis III, but you can still see the stumps of a few 3,500-year-old trees, the massive ramp that connects the terraces and the fabulous reliefs on the portico of the Second Terrace. On the north side is the Birth Colonnade, with scenes confirming the queen's divine parentage and her right to rule. To the south is the Punt Colonnade, depicting the expedition to Punt (probably in present-day Somalia) sent by Queen Hatshepsut to bring back myrrh trees, ebony, ivory and spices.

Beyond lies the Chapel of Hathor, with a hidden representation of the queen's favourite, and architect of the temple, Senenmut. The Third Terrace had a portico with Osirian statues of the queen in front of each pillar, but unfortunately it's closed to the public at the moment.

TAKING A BREAK

Several stalls sell cold drinks, but for a rest head for one of the **cafés at al Gurna**, or to the **Marsam Hotel** (► 103).'

✚ 202 B4
✉ Al Gurna, West Bank
🕐 Daily 7–5 in winter, 7–6 in summer
💷 Moderate

The Female Pharaoh

Tuthmosis I's daughter, Queen Hatshepsut, was Egypt's first female ruler and her life was full of intrigue. Her husband Tuthmosis II died before she produced a son, so she usurped Tuthmosis III, son of another wife, and became the absolute ruler of Egypt from 1473 to 1458 BC. She is often represented as a man. After her death Tuthmosis III tried to obliterate her name from history, defacing her images and cartouches.

The setting of Hatshepsut's mortuary temple against the pink Theban hills is spectacular

DEIR AL BAHARI: INSIDE INFO

Top tips Tickets for this temple, as for every monument on the West Bank, are only available from the ticket office near the crossroads before Deir al Madina. You must buy your ticket on the day you intend to visit.
• Two paths lead up the mountain near Deir al Bahari. Climb to the top for some fabulous views, or walk across the hill to the Valley of the Kings (➤ 91–3).

Tombs of the Nobles

The nobles – local rulers, ministers and governors under the pharaohs – enjoyed a good life and were keen for pleasures to continue after their death. As a result, their tombs are not decorated with cryptic texts from the Book of the Dead, but with realistic and vividly coloured depictions of their lives. The work is inferior to that of the royal tombs, but it provides a wonderful insight into ancient Egyptian society and the daily life of wealthy Egyptians and their servants.

Whereas the pharaohs' tombs were hidden in the Theban hills, the nobles built theirs ostentatiously on the frontline, facing the mortuary temples of their masters. There are many tombs in this necropolis, but only seven are open to the public. The furthest two are the tombs of **Rekhmire** and **Sennofer**. The first

has scenes of the vizier Rekhmire receiving tributes from foreign lands and overseeing the agricultural revenue, while the second is known as the 'tomb of the vines' for its ceiling of beautifully painted vines. The decorative style of the nearby tomb of **Ramose** reflects that he was a vizier immediately before and after the Amarna revolution (➤ 22). The superb carvings along the entrance wall are all in the classical style, showing Ramose making offerings, but on the opposite side they also reveal the more naturalistic Amarna style. Immediately south, the tomb of **Khaemhat**, a royal scribe, contains a variety of fishing, family and funerary scenes and has exceptionally well-preserved colours.

Further north lies another beautiful group of tombs. The Tomb of **Nakht** has fascinating scenes of a banquet with dancers and a blind harpist, with a cat

Above: Entrance to the tomb of the supervisor Menna.
Right: Sennofer's tomb, decorated with vines, is one of the most pleasing tombs in this valley

eating fish under his chair, while that of **Menna**, an inspector of estates, depicts scenes of rural life and of Menna and his wife performing ceremonies for the gods.

TAKING A BREAK

Two cafés in **al Gurna** sell cold drinks or tea. The **Marsam Hotel** restaurant (➤ 103), opposite the tombs, is good for lunch.

➕ 202 B4
✉ Old Gurna
🕐 Daily 6–5, but smaller tombs often close around 3pm
🍴 Cafés (£)
🎟 Tickets per group of tombs inexpensive (from the kiosk near the crossroads)

TOMBS OF THE NOBLES: INSIDE INFO

Top tips A visit involves walking and climbing stairs, so avoid the midday heat.
• Tombs are divided into four groups, each requiring a separate ticket. It takes an hour to visit all the tombs, but most visitors limit themselves to the best of each group, or just one group. Signposting is poor but the tombs are close together and local children or villagers are always eager to show you the way.
• Guards will light up tombs the traditional ancient way, using a mirror to reflect sunlight, in return for *baksheesh*. Be sure to refuse their services on arrival if you don't want them.

Ones to miss The tombs of Khonsu, Userhet and Benia are the least impressive.

Hidden gem Many visitors skip Sennofer's tomb as it requires a good climb, but it's delightful and colourful, reflecting Sennofer's eternal love for his beautiful wife.

At Your Leisure

2 Luxor Museum

This small museum of antiquities is an absolute gem. The choice selection of statues and objects found in local tombs and temples is well labelled in English and perfectly displayed against a dark background to bring out the best features. Among the many highlights are a strikingly beautiful statue of an eternally young King Tuthmosis III, an extraordinary statue of Amenophis III held by the crocodile god Sobek, and furniture from Tutankhamun's tomb. There are

Fine relief of King Tuthmosis III wearing the long royal beard and the 'atef' crown

also two fine heads of the rebellious Pharaoh Akhenaton and some lovely carvings taken from his temple, illustrating the bizarre physiognomy of that period. The important cache of statues, among them Ramses II and Tutankhamun found a few years ago under Luxor Temple, is also on display here in the New Hall.

➕ 202 B4 ✉ Corniche al Nil, Luxor ⊙ Daily 9–1, 4–9 in winter, 9–1, 5–10 in summer; 10–4 during Ramadan 💵 Moderate, camera permit extra

3 Mummification Museum

This interesting little museum highlights the beliefs and the historical development of mummification, and also explains the different stages of the lengthy process. Exhibits include mummification instruments and even some fine animal mummies.

➕ 202 B4 ✉ Corniche al Nil, East Bank, near the ferry terminal ⊙ Daily 9–1, 4–9 in winter, 9–1, 5–10 in summer 🚌 No public transport 💵 Inexpensive

5 Madinat Habu

The grand mortuary temple of Ramses III (1184–53 BC), modelled on the Ramesseum (➤ 100) of his ancestor Ramses II, was the last great classical pharaonic temple to be built in Egypt. Ramses III, however, was more fortunate than his namesake because this temple has survived the millennia remarkably well, but the Hypostyle Hall and Sanctuaries were severely damaged during an earthquake in the 1st century BC. The entrance to the temple complex is a lofty Syrian-style gatehouse with an upper room decorated with musicians and dancers, where Ramses III apparently entertained guests. To the right are several older chapels and what remains of the Sacred Lake, where local women still come in search of a cure for infertility. The towering First Pylon, like the Second Pylon, is decorated with scenes of battles fought by Ramses II and leads to the First Court, which features well-preserved carvings

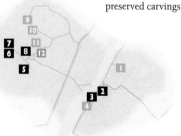

All around Medinat Habu are reminders of the Coptic settlement of Djeme

of Ramses himself making offerings to the gods.

Mudbrick remains of the Coptic town of Djeme, which covered the entire enclosure until the 19th century, can be seen above the perimeter wall.

➕ 202 B4 ✉ Kom Lola, near the ticket office ⏱ Daily 6–5 🍴 Café-restaurants opposite the entrance (£) 💰 Inexpensive

🄶 Tomb of Nefertari

The New Kingdom pharaoh Ramses II created one of the most beautiful tombs in Egypt as a shrine to the beauty of Nefertari, his wife of some 34 years. The corridors and walls in its three chambers are decorated with brightly coloured images, most famously of the stunning queen in a transparent white dress with a two-feathered golden head-dress. The ceiling is painted with bright golden stars. The tomb was reopened to a limited public in 1995 after lengthy and extensive restoration.

➕ 202 B4 ✉ Valley of the Queens, West Bank (see above right) ⏱ Daily 7:30–noon in summer, 8:30–noon in winter (visitors are only allowed in for 10 minutes) 🚫 No public transport 💰 Expensive; only 150 tickets are on sale from 6am each morning, so individual travellers should arrive early

🄷 Valley of the Queens

This is a slight misnomer as the 80 tombs belong not only to queens, but also to princes and princesses. But only four, including the tomb of Nefertari, are open to the public. The tomb of Amun-Her-Khopshef, son of Ramses III, shows beautiful scenes of the father introducing his son to the gods. Also in the tomb is the mummy of a five-month-old foetus, believed to be lost when the mother heard of the death of her nine-year-old son Amunwas. Another son of Ramses III, Prince Khaemweset, is also buried here, surrounded by similar scenes of Ramses leading him through the underworld.

➕ 202 B4 ✉ West Bank ⏱ Daily 6–5 🚫 No public transport 💰 Inexpensive; separate charge for Tomb of Nefertari

🄸 Deir al Madina

This village sheds rare light on the lives of less exalted Egyptians. The artists, masons and labourers who worked on the tombs in the Valley of the Kings (➤ 91–3) lived here with their families, segregated from the rest of the population to keep the location of the royal tombs secret. Many inhabitants were literate and a large amount of papyri records the strict organisation of their lives, as well as their complaints about hardship and working conditions. Despite this, they

Entrance to the Deir al Madina's temple

worked 8-hour days, staying in the Valley of the Kings for 10-day shifts, so there was plenty of spare time to work on their own tombs.

Near the entrance to the village are the tombs of artists Sennedjem and Ankherkha, with colourful interpretations (often parodies) of designs they worked on in the royal tombs. The tomb of Peshedu has a painting of the dead artist praying under the tree of regeneration, while Iphy's

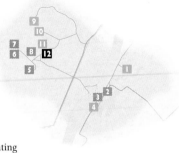

> 'I met a traveller from an antique land
> Who said: Two vast and trunkless legs of stone
> Stand in the desert…Near them on the sand,
> Half sunk, a shattered visage lies…
>
> … Nothing beside remains. Round the decay
> Of that colossal wreck, boundless and bare
> The lone and level sands stretch far away.'
> *From 'Ozymandias', Shelley*

tomb is decorated with scenes of everyday life.

A temple dedicated to the goddesses Maat and Hathor stands at the northern end of the village.

➕ 202 B4 ✉ West Bank, opposite the ticket office
🕐 Daily 6–5
💳 Inexpensive; separate ticket for Peshedu's tomb (Inexpensive)

Parts of Ramses II's colossus are scattered all over the Ramesseum

🔢 Ramesseum

Ever since the English poet Percy Bysshe Shelley (1792–1822) eternalised the broken statue of Ramses II in his poem 'Ozymandias', left, as a symbol of the vanity of transient human glory, visitors have come to the Ramesseum looking for its colossal fragments. Ramses II, who built some awe-inspiring monuments elsewhere in Egypt, intended this mortuary temple to be his eternal monument, but unfortunately chose a site that was annually flooded. It would almost certainly have been as grand as his fabulous temple at Abu Simbel (► 118–20), but it's ironic that only this one, intended to be the most important, fell to pieces.

The colossal statue, once the largest in the world at 18m high and weighing over 900 tonnes, destroyed the Second Pylon and the Second Court as it fell. You can still see its remains and marvel at the proportions. In addition to the statue itself, at the far end of the court is a smaller colossus with a more intact face.

The walls of the First and Second Pylons are decorated with scenes of Ramses' famous victories, as are the walls of the Great Hypostyle Hall, where 29 of its original 48 columns still stand. Beyond lie two smaller hypostyle halls, one with an astronomical ceiling which boasts the oldest-known 12-month calendar. The vaulted mudbrick rooms surrounding the temple were used as workshops, servants' quarters and storage houses.

🔢 202 B4 ✉ al Gurna, West Bank, Luxor 🕐 Daily 6–5 🚌 No public transport, so cycle or take a taxi
💲 Inexpensive

🔟 Abydos

Abydos is situated about 130km north of Luxor. For nearly 2,000 years

Best for Kids

- *Felucca* ride on the Nile (➤ 106)
- Horse-riding (➤ 106)
- Mummification Museum (➤ 98)
- Tombs of the Nobles (➤ 96)
- Al Aboudi bookshop (➤ 105): a huge selection of children's books on Egypt

The wall carvings at Seti I's temple in Abydos are among the finest from the New Kingdom

Abydos was Egypt's prime burial ground, as it marked the entrance to the underworld and is where Osiris's head was buried (➤ 12–13). Ancient Egyptians aspired to make a pilgrimage once in their lives and, if they weren't buried here, endeavoured to have their mummies brought here before burial elsewhere in Egypt.

The 14th-century BC Temple of Seti I is one of Egypt's finest monuments, with exquisite decoration, but the façade was finished less carefully by Seti's son, Ramses II, who also built a smaller temple here.

🔢 202 B5 ✉ Al Araba al Madfuna, 10km southwest of al Balyana 🕐 Daily 7–6 in summer, 7–5 in winter 🍴 Café opposite 🚌 Train or bus from Luxor to al Balyana, then service taxi to the site
💲 Inexpensive

Hypostyle Hall at the Temple of Hathor

style by the Ptolemies and the Romans, between 125 BC and AD 60. Hathor, wife of Horus, was the goddess of pleasure, beauty and love, often associated with the Greek Aphrodite. During the annual New Year festival, Hathor's statue was taken to the roof to be exposed to the sun-god, before being reunited with Horus at his temple in Edfu (➤ 121).

Scenes of this festival decorate the walls of the temple.

🖪 202 B5 ✉ 4km across the Nile from Qena, 64km north of Luxor ⏰ Daily 7–6 in summer, 7–5 in winter 🍴 Café (£) 🚃 Train or bus to Qena, horse-carriage to the site (check first for travel restrictions) 💲 Inexpensive

🔢 Dendera

The well-preserved Temple of Hathor was built here in the classic Egyptian

Luxor From the Air

You'll get the most spectacular view of Luxor's monuments and villages from a hot-air balloon. Each flight of about one hour is slightly different depending on the wind, but the experience is unforgettable. **Hod Hod Soliman** (tel/fax: 095-370 116) has a British pilot and offers flights with buffet breakfast at the Mövenpick Hotel, while the slightly more expensive **Balloons Over Egypt** (tel: 095-376 515) has a Virgin franchise and serves a champagne breakfast in the desert after the flight.

Where to... Stay

Prices
The prices are for a double room per night.
£ under 25LE ££ 25–60LE £££ over 60LE

EAST BANK

Emilio Hotel ££
All the rooms in this excellent hotel are equipped with private bathroom, air-conditioning, minibar, TV and a hotel video channel. There's also a small rooftop pool with relaxing chairs for sunbathing. The staff are particularly helpful and friendly. Book in advance in high season, as it can fill up with tour groups.

☐ 202 B4 ☒ Sharia Yussef Hassan
☎ 095-373 570; fax: 095-370 000

Mina Palace £
This budget hotel in a prime location offers excellent value for money. The clean, air-conditioned rooms have views of either the Nile or Luxor Temple. The service is very friendly and the terrace is a good place to meet locals.

☐ 202 B4 ☒ Corniche an Nil, near
Luxor Temple ☎ 095-372 074

Mövenpick Jolie Ville Luxor £££
The best hotel in town, the Mövenpick occupies its own island on the Nile. Accommodation is in bungalows set in a lush, well-kept garden. Rooms range from standard rooms, spartan but comfortable, to the superior and more luxurious, all with a little terrace in the garden. An excellent breakfast buffet is served outside on the Nileside terrace, weather permitting. The restaurant

food, particularly the grills and the famous ice cream, is delicious.
There's also a great pool, a small zoo and a children's playground.

☐ 202 B4 ☒ Crocodile Island, 6km
south of Luxor, near the new bridge
☎ 095-374 855; fax 374 936; email:
mpluxor@intouch.com

Sofitel Old Winter Palace £££
The Old Winter Palace, unlike its modern neighbour, has been an institution for the past century. A splendid colonial building overlooking the Nile and the Theban Hills beyond, the interior mixes colonial paraphernalia with new fabrics and objets d'art inspired by the old glory days. The large and comfortable rooms, overlooking the river or the garden, have high ceilings and are elegantly decorated, and there's a large swimming pool in well-tended gardens filled with songbirds. The main drawback is the service, which can be shambolic.

☐ 202 B4 ☒ Sharia Corniche an Nil
☎ 095-380 422; fax 095-374 087

WEST BANK

Amun al Gezira £
This delightful family-run hotel is in a modern building overlooking the Theban hills and sugarcane fields. Its simply furnished rooms (some en suite) are immaculate and comfortable. The roof terrace commands beautiful views, while breakfast and tea is served in a pretty shaded garden. Book in advance.

☐ 202 B4 ☒ Geziret al Bairat (near
the ferry ☎ 095-310912

Marsam Hotel (known as Sheikh Ali Hotel) £
This is a lovely small hotel, run by the son of Sheikh Ali Abder Rassoul, who took part in the excavations of the tomb of Seti I. Rooms are basic and clean, set in a domed mudbrick building with terraces and a courtyard. It's popular with regular visitors to Luxor, who return for the friendly service and peaceful nights.

☐ 202 B4 ☒ Opposite the Valley of
the Nobles ☎ 095-372 403

Where to...
Eat and Drink

Prices
Expect to pay per person for a meal, excluding drinks and tips.
£ up to 50LE **££** 50–100LE **£££** over 100LE

Most hotels on the East Bank have adequate restaurants serving international cuisine, while a few restaurants along the Corniche specialise in Egyptian food. Restaurants on the West Bank are basic, offering simple but fresh Egyptian stews, grilled chicken and kebabs. To sample more elaborate dishes, such as duck or stuffed pigeon, order them earlier in the day, before sightseeing.

Cafeteria Muhammad £
Friendly Muhammad takes pride in preparing simple, authentic Egyptian dishes in a cool house with a tranquil shaded terrace. The menu is small, but if you pass by in the morning, he may be able to serve a delicious *meloukhia* (stuffed pigeon) or grilled duck for lunch. The beer here's usually cold.

➕ **202 B4** ⌧ **Next to the Pharaoh's Hotel, near the ticket office, West Bank** ◉ **Daily noon–10 or later**

Horus Hotel Restaurant £
Also known as Sheikh Ali's (▲ 103), this is found on a lovely

terrace under the trees. The menu concentrates on typical Egyptian specialities such as stuffed cabbage leaves and grilled pigeon, and there's also an excellent lentil soup with lemon. Here, as elsewhere on the West Bank, you can order special dishes in advance.

➕ **202 B4** ⌧ **Opposite the Valley of the Nobles, West Bank** ☎ **095-372 165** ◉ **Daily lunch and dinner**

The Japanese Restaurant ££
As if the culture shock of being in Luxor wasn't enough, you can now sample excellent Japanese food by the banks of the Nile at the Sonesta St George Hotel. The décor is simple Asian, while the food is excellent and fresh. The sushi and grills are particularly recommended.

➕ **202 B4** ⌧ **Sonesta St George Hotel, Sharia Khalid Ibn Walid** ☎ **095-382 575; fax 095-382 571; email: sonesta@iec.egnet.net**

Kings Head Pub £–££
This popular British pub has all

the necessary trimmings from darts, billiards, and football on TV to cold beers and lagers, pub food and Brits happy to have found a home from home.

➕ **202 B4** ⌧ **Near the passport office, on Sharia Khaled Ibn el-Walid** ☎ **no phone**

La Mamma ££
In the middle of the hotel garden and beside a pond with ducks and pelicans, La Mamma is one of the most reliable restaurants in town, and is especially popular with kids. Fresh pastas, thin-crust pizzas and Italian meat dishes make a change from Egyptian fare. Even the live evening entertainment is usually a notch above the rest.

➕ **202 B4** ⌧ **Sheraton Hotel, Sharia Khalid Ibn Walid** ☎ **095-374 544** ◉ **Daily lunch and dinner**

Maratonga Café-Restaurant £
Overlooking the temple of Madinet Habu, this shady terrace is a great place to rest from sightseeing. You

can just have a cold drink (but no alcohol) and chat with the friendly staff, or test their simple but freshly prepared stews and grilled meats or sandwiches. Many guests come just for a sunset drink and end up staying for the evening.

➕ 202 B4 ⊠ Opposite Madinet Habu Temple, West Bank 🕔 Daily 8am–11pm (or until the last customer leaves)

Mövenpick Garden Terrace ££

This beautiful garden terrace overlooking the Nile is perfect for a treat at lunchtime. The menu offers good sandwiches, including a copious grilled *kofta* sandwich, excellent salads and delicious fresh pastas. But for many people the greatest attraction are the desserts, which include huge scoops of the best ice-cream in town.

➕ 202 B4 ⊠ Crocodile Island, 6km south of Luxor, near the new bridge 📞 095-374 855; fax 095-374 936 🕔 Daily breakfast (in fine weather) and lunch

Peace Abouzeid Restaurant £–££

This pleasant terrace restaurant beside the Nile serves good, traditional Egyptian dishes. As it's near Karnak, the buffet gets crowded with tourist groups at lunchtime, but at night the mood is calmer. House specialities include grilled pigeon and excellent seafood dishes.

➕ 202 B4 ⊠ Corniche an Nil, near Karnak Temple 📞 095-372 419 🕔 Daily lunch and dinner

Tutankhamun £

Muhammad, enthusiastic chef and owner, worked in an upmarket Luxor hotel until he set up on his own on the West Bank. He serves simple Egyptian dishes, house speciality being chicken with rosemary served with sweet oriental rice. The cosy indoor room is good for winter evenings, and the terrace overlooking the Nile is spacious.

➕ 202 B4 ⊠ 200m south of the West Bank ferry terminal 🕔 Daily lunch and dinner

Where to...
Shop

Luxor Town, particularly around the temple, is one big tourist bazaar with hundreds of stalls selling cheap souvenirs, from small statues and colourful skullcaps to carpets and painted papyri. It's hard to avoid them, as vendors know every trick to lure innocent-looking tourists. Few have fixed prices, so the rule here, as elsewhere in Egypt, is to bargain hard, and you might well find some evocative souvenirs. The little statues of ancient Egyptian gods are a good choice, as are scarves (watch out for synthetic ones) and hand-woven cotton tablecloths from Akhmim. Another great buy is traditional clay cooking pots, sold at two stalls beside the police station. They can be used in the oven or on a hob, but need treating

with a mixture of oil and molasses at a low heat for half an hour before use. If cooking is your thing, look out for cheap spices like cumin, chilli and black pepper. The bazaar is open in the morning until 1pm, and again from 5 to 9pm or later.

Alabaster

Alabaster is quarried 80km north of the Valley of the Kings and in workshops on the West Bank you can see how the stone is treated and polished. Several large shops sell kitsch statuettes and sphinx lamps, as well as beautiful unpolished alabaster vases or bowls in simple shapes, similar to those in the Egyptian Museum.

Bookshops

Luxor has some excellent bookshops stocking a wide selection of titles on Egypt, Arab culture and the Middle East, in several European languages. **Al Aboudi** (tel: 095-373 390) in the tourist bazaar, next to the Winter Palace has an excellent children's section and well-priced books on Egypt. It sells postcards too. Also next to the Winter Palace is **Gaddis** (tel: 095-372 142), with books on modern and ancient Egypt, as well as postcards, Egyptian papyrus stationery and good-quality souvenirs.

Quality Crafts

Fine fabrics have been hand-woven in Akhmim for centuries, and the best selection of fabrics and table-cloths from there is available at the Winter Akhmim Gallery in the arcade of the **Old Winter Palace Hotel**. **Egypt Crafts Centre Luxor** (tel: 095-381 723) in Sharia Manshia, Luxor Town, is an excellent shop with a selection of crafts that have come from various women's projects throughout Egypt, all of whom share in the profit. It sells hand-woven rugs from the Western Desert, Nubian baskets and plenty of other high quality souvenirs, all at fixed prices.

Where to...
Be Entertained

Luxor has so many monuments to visit that the only entertainment most tourists want at the end of the day is a dive in the pool, a cool drink, a good dinner and a soft bed. And that's just as well because there isn't really much else to do. But if you do still have the energy, you'll find listings of special events and exhibitions in the monthly magazine *Egypt Today*, available from bookshops.

Feluccas and Boats

Here, as elsewhere on the Nile, taking a *felucca* is a great way to wind down, once you've negotiated the price. The most popular destination is Banana Island, 4km upriver, where souvenir stalls await unwary tourists (so you might want to avoid it). Instead, take a boat for a few hours and just sail up the Nile, enjoying the beauty of the river and the landscape. It's particularly lovely around sunset. If there's no wind, you will be rowed – or it's an opportunity, perhaps, to take one of the small motorboats.

Horse-riding

Another way to relax is to rent a horse or camel from one of the stables. Try the **Arabian Horse Stable**, behind the Mobil petrol station on the West Bank (tel: 095-310 024). An hour-long circuit will take you through some lush countryside and then back along the

Nile. You can even visit some sights, such as Madinet Habu Temple and the Colossi of Memnon, by horse.

Swimming

Nearly all hotels will open their pools to non-residents, either for an entrance fee or for a minimum charge on drinks and snacks.

Nightlife

Luxor has a few discos in the hotels, but don't expect the latest dance music or a laser show. The liveliest discos are at the **Etap Hotel**, and aboard the Lotus boat at the **Novotel**. The **Mövenpick Hotel** has a good belly dance and folkloric show in its Fellah's Tent.

Sightseeing by Night

An excellent **Sound and Light Show** happens daily, in different languages, at Karnak Temple (▲ 84–7). Luxor Temple (▲ 88–90), dramatically floodlit at night and open until 10pm, makes for an unusual evening stroll.

Upper Egypt and Nubia

Getting Your Bearings

During the 19th century, as more and more archaeological discoveries were made, it became fashionable to spend the winter in Upper Egypt. Wealthy Europeans would rent a private *dahabiyya* (sailing houseboat) and set off on the river from Cairo, stopping to explore ruins and monuments.

Today the best and most relaxing way to visit the sights of Upper Egypt is still by boat. Luxury craft run three- to five-day cruises between Luxor and Aswan that stop at the temples, but leave you plenty of time to idle around on deck and take in the serene and beautiful Nile and life on its banks. If you're feeling more adventurous, you can get a lot closer to the river on a three- or four-day *felucca* ride, sleeping under the stars. Several cruisers now offer an even more relaxing

Right: There seem to be temples and necropoles everywhere in Aswan

four-day trip on Lake Nasser, taking in rescued Nubian monuments. You can also fish for huge Nile perch and try to spot elusive crocodiles.

Note that at present visitors can only travel in a private vehicle from Luxor to Aswan in an armed police convoy, which leaves two or three times a day from both places, but doesn't stop at any sights. Security concerns have also made it impossible to travel by road from Aswan to Abu Simbel.

South of Luxor the landscape changes and the desert closes in on the Nile. The people change too, as many Nubian families who lost their land when the area was flooded after the Aswan Dam was built moved north to Aswan and beyond.

By the time you reach Aswan you know you've left the Mediterranean and the Middle East behind and entered a more exotic, more African environment. Aswan has fewer important monuments than Luxor, and is therefore the perfect place to slow down and relax while enjoying views on the river and the islands.

Previous page and above: Sailing by *felucca* between Luxor and Aswan is an idyllic way to experience the temples

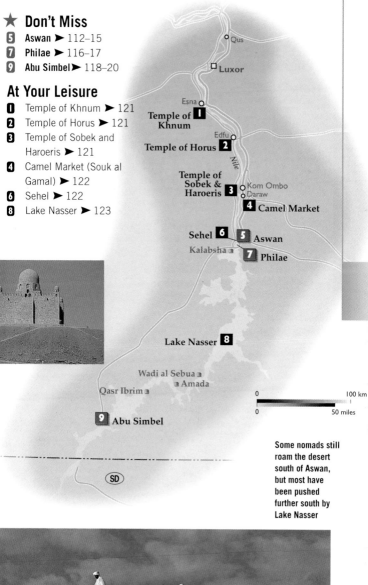

Qus

□ **Luxor**

Esna
Temple of **1**
Khnum

Edfu
Temple of Horus **2**

Nile

Temple of
Sobek & **3** Kom Ombo
Haroeris   Daraw
          4 **Camel Market**

Sehel **6** **5** **Aswan**
Kalabsha ▪ **7** **Philae**

Lake Nasser **8**

Wadi al Sebua ▪
        ▪ Amada
Qasr Ibrim ▪

9 **Abu Simbel**

SD

0		100 km
0		50 miles

Some nomads still roam the desert south of Aswan, but most have been pushed further south by Lake Nasser

Enjoy the peaceful pace of Aswan and Lake Nasser, taking in the sites partly by taxi but mostly by motorboat or *felucca*. The light in the early morning and late afternoon is stunning, and the singing voices of Nubian children on the river before sunset are unforgettable.

Upper Egypt and Nubia in Three Days

Day One

Morning

Start early and hire a private taxi for a half day. Leave **Aswan** (➤ 112) along the road past the **Fatimid Cemetery** (➤ 114) and the **Unfinished Obelisk** (➤ 114) on the outskirts of the town. Continue via the Old Aswan Dam to the Philae dock in Shallal to buy a ticket to the site and take a boat to the island (➤ 116). Spend about 90 minutes here, then drive on for a look at the **Aswan High Dam** (➤ 115) and return to Aswan via the Old Dam. Have a late lunch at the Aswan Moon restaurant (➤ 125).

Afternoon

From the terminal opposite the Egypt Air office, take a ferry out to Elephantine Island on the Nile to visit the **Aswan Antiquities Museum** and its peaceful garden for an hour or so (➤ 112). Stroll to the north of the island through the palm groves and Nubian villages. Back at the ferry landing, you can take a *felucca* around the islands. Have the *felucca* wait while you walk through the botanical garden on **Kitchener's Island** (➤ 115) and then sail around the islands, past the **Aga Khan's Mausoleum** on the West Bank (➤ 115).

Evening

Finish the day with the Oriental show at the **Nubian Restaurant** (➤ 126).

Day Two

Morning
Take a taxi for a round trip south to **Kalabsha Temple** on Lake Nasser (below left, ➤ 123). Depending on the height of the lake you may have to take a boat from the harbour. Boatmen usually allow for an hour's visit, which is enough. Return to Aswan for lunch in one of the places along the Corniche (➤ 125–6).

Afternoon
Stock up on water and good sun protection and take a *felucca* on a two-hour round trip to **Sehel Island** (left, ➤ 122). After returning to Aswan, walk over to the **Nubian Museum** (➤ 112–14) for a late afternoon visit. Stroll back to the Old Cataract Hotel for an early evening drink on the terrace and dinner at the beautifully restored Moorish restaurant (➤ 126).

Day Three

Morning
Having booked your return plane tickets in advance with a travel agent or Egypt Air, take a half-day excursion to the temples of **Abu Simbel** (right, ➤ 118), a flight of around 30–45 minutes. Head back to Aswan for lunch in the Aswan Moon or one of the other riverside cafés.

Afternoon
Relax by one of the hotel swimming pools (➤ 127) until late afternoon then stroll over to the *souks* for some souvenir shopping and to take in the atmosphere as the sun goes down.

Evening
Take a cab to Philae for the *son et lumière* show (➤ 128, check with the tourist office for times or online at www.sound-light.egypt.com/pyr).

5

Aswan

Aswan's setting on the Nile is both dramatic and idyllic. Here the river is squeezed in between the Eastern Desert and the Sahara. Its cool sparkling blue waters contrast starkly with the hot, golden desert sands, the pink granite boulders it flows around and the lush green islands in its stream. But the views over Aswan and the Nile are the real spectacle, particularly in the late afternoon.

The town of Aswan has been a frontier since ancient times, as Egypt's southernmost city and the gateway to Nubia and Africa. It has a sweet, exotic smell and its tall, dark Nubian population has more in common with the Sudanese than with other Egyptians. The climate is fabulous in winter – hot and dry – and the atmosphere is totally laid back. Aswan has fewer spectacular sights than Luxor or Cairo, so there's more time to hang out in the riverside cafés watching the sun set and the *feluccas* sail by, and to stroll in its quirky *souk*.

Nilometers
These instruments were used to record the annual flooding of the Nile, until it was controlled by the Aswan Dam. It was vital to know the accurate level of the Nile, as it formed the basis of tax calculations: the higher the waters rose, the bigger the harvest and therefore the higher the taxes.

Modern Aswan
Aswan is a relaxed and easy town to explore, and its attractive Corniche is lined with pleasant waterfront café-terraces. Sharia al Souk, the main market street, still retains an exotic air even though it's become increasingly touristy. At the southern end of the Corniche are the Ferial Gardens, a tranquil place to sit and watch the sunset if you can't get on the terrace of the Old Cataract Hotel (► 126).

Behind the hotel grounds is the **Nubian Museum**, a tribute

Feluccas sail gently and peacefully around the small islands on the Nile in Aswan

---

✚ 202 C3
✉ West Bank, 215km south of Luxor
☎ 097-312 811 (tourist office)

Aswan Museum/Nilometer/Ruins of Yebu
✉ Southern tip of Elephantine Island
🕐 Daily 8:30–5 in winter, 8:30–6 in summer
🚢 Ferry from opposite the Egypt Air office
💵 Inexpensive

Fatimid Cemetery/Unfinished Obelisk
✉ 1.5km south of Aswan 🕐 Obelisk daily 7–5 💵 Moderate

Nubian Museum
✉ Sharia Abtal al Tahrir, between the Old Cataract and Basma hotels 🕐 Daily 9–1,

5–9 in winter, 9–1, 6–10 in summer
🚶 Walk or private taxi 💵 Moderate

Botanical Garden
✉ Kitchener's Island 🕐 Daily 7am–dusk
🍴 Cafeteria (£) 🚢 Ferry from west side of Elephantine Island or rented boat or *felucca*
💵 Moderate

Tombs of the Nobles
✉ West Bank, Aswan 🕐 Daily 7–5
🚢 Ferry from northern end of Corniche, then hike uphill 💵 Inexpensive

High Dam Pavilion
✉ A few kilometres south of Aswan
🕐 Daily 7–5 💵 Officially free, but tip the guardian to open it

to the culture and art of the people whose lands were flooded
when the dams were constructed to create Lake Nasser. The
museum's impressive collection, well displayed and labelled in
English, traces the history of Nubia from prehistoric times.

About 1.5km south of Aswan is the vast **Fatimid Cemetery**,
with domed mudbrick tombs from the 9th century, and the
gigantic **Unfinished Obelisk** that was abandoned after a flaw
was discovered. It's thought that it was intended to stand in
Tuthmosis III's temple at Karnak (➤ 85–7).

Upriver from the First Cataract (➤ 122) is the Old Dam
built in 1902, and further on the High Dam, completed in 1971.

The *souk* in
Aswan is very
much an
African affair –
look out for
charms, textiles
and exotic
spices

Ancient Aswan

In ancient times the main town and temple area were on
Elephantine Island, mid-river opposite modern Aswan, mainly
on its southern tip which was known as Yebu (meaning 'ivory'
and 'elephant'). The fortress of Yebu, protected by the turbulent
waters of the Nile, was a perfect base for Egyptian expeditions
into Nubia, Sudan and Ethiopia and an important cult place
dedicated to Khnum – the god who controlled the Nile's level –
his wife Satis and their daughter Anukis. During the Islamic
period Yebu became an important trading post for the caravans
of camels and elephants laden with ivory, gold, spices and
slaves. Excavations of the extensive ruins of ancient Yebu are
still underway, but so far you can see a small early Old
Kingdom step pyramid, a gateway on which Alexander II is
shown worshipping Khnum, and the 30th-Dynasty Temple of
Khnum. Further north there's a Nilometer with Greek, Roman,
pharaonic and Arabic numerals.

Both the Nilometer and the ruins of Yebu now form part of
the **Aswan Antiquities Museum**, which is housed in the villa
of Sir William Willcocks, the British engineer who designed the
Old Aswan Dam. The villa contains a huge collection of artefacts found on Elephantine, but it's a rather musty display of
Middle and New Kingdom pottery, jewellery and sculpture and

Aswan Dams: Vital Statistics
- The Old Dam was the world's largest when built by the British in 1898–1902 and was later raised twice.
- It's 50m high, 2km long, 30m wide at the base and has 180 sluice gates.
- The High Dam is 111m high, 3.8km long and 980m wide at the base.
- Lake Nasser, the world's largest reservoir, covers 6,000sq km.
- It's forbidden to take photos of the Aswan Dam.

a beautiful gilded statue of Khnum. If you've already been to the large museums in Cairo or Luxor, you might prefer to stroll through the Nubian villages on Elephantine, set amid lush, scented gardens.

The West Bank

The most visible landmark opposite Aswan on the Nile's west bank is the **Aga Khan's Mausoleum** (now closed to the public) where Aga Khan III, and recently also his wife the Begum, are buried. Further north, the tombs of the Princes of Elephantine Island, cut into the rock, are floodlit at night and command excellent views.

Café terraces along the Nile, particularly the **Aswan Moon** (➤ 125), serve delicious fresh juices and good, simple Egyptian food. Alternatively, the terrace of the **Old Cataract Hotel** (➤ 126) is the traditional place for an English tea and to watch the sunset, but it's closed to non-residents during busy periods.

Watch the sunset from the terrace of the colonial Old Cataract Hotel

ASWAN: INSIDE INFO

Top tips Take at least one *felucca* ride around the islands as there's nothing more relaxing, particularly around sunset when local children go out on their home-made boats and sing Nubian songs.
- Visit the sweet-smelling **Botanical Garden** on Kitchener Island, where General Kitchener planted shrubs imported from all over the world.

Hidden gems There's a good if tiring 30-minute walk across the desert from the tombs of Elephantine's nobles to the beautiful ruins of 7th-century St Simeon Monastery (open daily 7–5; admission moderate). A guardian will open the basilica and show you the place where St Simeon's beard was tied to the ceiling to stop him falling asleep during his prayers.

One to miss You can skip the tombs of Elephantine Island if you've been to the West Bank in Luxor.

7

Philae

The splendid Temple of Isis, set on an island surrounded by
the blue waters of Lake Nasser, is one of Egypt's most romantic sights, especially as you arrive by boat. For more than 800
years, until AD 550, this temple to Isis and Osiris was one of
the most important Egyptian cult centres.

Ptolemaic and Roman rulers, keen to identify themselves with
this powerful ancient Egyptian cult, all added their mark,
making for an interesting blend of styles. The worship of Isis
as the Mother of the Gods eventually spread all over the
Roman Empire, and early Coptic art clearly associates the Virgin
Mary and baby Jesus with Isis suckling her infant son Horus.

Originally the Temple of Isis was built on the island of
Philae (the 'Island from the Time of Re') facing Bigah Island,
which was believed to be one of the burial sites of Osiris. But
Bigah was only accessible to
priests, so all the religious
festivities took place on
Philae. With the building of
the first Aswan Dam the
temple was submerged for
half the year. In the 1970s,
when the High Dam
threatened to submerge it
completely, UNESCO and the
Egyptian Antiquities
Organisation painstakingly
moved the entire complex to
nearby Agilkia Island, which
had been landscaped to
resemble Philae.

*Before Philae
Temple was
moved to the
island of
Agilkia, visitors
toured it by
rowing boat*

Temple Highlights

Boats land near the oldest structure on the island, the
Vestibule of **Nectanebo I**, beyond which lies a large court
flanked by two elegant colonnades and the impressive **First
Pylon** of the Temple of Isis. The small door to the left leads
into a 3rd-century BC **Birth House**, whose
outside back wall shows some lovely

*Below: Some
carvings are
remarkably well
preserved*

✚ 202 C3
✉ Agilkia Island, between the Old Dam
and the High Dam, 9km south of Aswan
🕐 Daily 7–5 in summer, 7–4 in winter and
Ramadan
🍴 Small cafeteria (££)
🚕 Taxi to Shallal dock for a boat to the island
💵 Moderate

scenes of Isis nursing Horus in the marshes. The main gate, with two granite lions, leads to the **Second Pylon**, opening up to a **Hypostyle Hall**. The inner temple lost most of its decoration when it was converted into a church around AD 553, but the **Sanctuary** still contains Isis's sacred *barque*.

The lofty Kiosk of Trajan supported by 14 columns is locally known as the 'Pharaoh's Bed'

Near by, the **Temple of Hathor**, the cow goddess of music (among other things), has a wonderful relief of the gods playing musical instruments. And an elegant monument here is the **Kiosk of Trajan** (used as a gateway to the temple in Roman times), with its superb views across the lake.

TAKING A BREAK

There are a few simple cafés at the dock, but nothing on the island, so go prepared.

PHILAE: INSIDE INFO

Top tips Check the official price list for boats at the docks before hiring one. The price allows for a one-hour visit, but pay the captain extra if you want to spend more time.
• The sound and light show at the Temple of Isis is often considered the best in Egypt (➤ 128)

Hidden gem The Osiris Room on the upper floor, where Osirian mysteries were enacted, has interesting reliefs illustrating the story of Isis and Osiris. It's usually closed, but the guards will open the doors for some *baksheesh*.

9

Abu Simbel

The 13th-century BC rock-hewn Temple of Ramses II at Abu Simbel is the most impressive monument in Nubia, perfectly expressing the imperial ambition and audacity of the New Kingdom period. The four 21m-high seated figures of Ramses II that guard the temple's façade are among the largest sculptures in Egypt, and seem designed to warn the Nubians of Egypt's mighty power.

No modern Europeans had seen the temple until the Swiss explorer Jean Louis Burckhardt sailed past it in 1813. But by then the massive statues were buried up to their necks in sand and it took 20 days of digging in 1817 to clear the entrance, then under some 15m of sand. In the 1960s a different operation was underway, as the international community united to raise this wonderful temple above the rising waters of Lake Nasser. The temple and the hillside into which it was cut were sawn into 1,050 blocks weighing up to 30 tonnes

🔲 202 A1   ✉ 280km south of Aswan, 40km from the Sudanese border
🕖 6am until the last plane leaves
🍴 Café (£)
🚌 Bus from Aswan (check for security restrictions)
✈ Egypt Air flights from Cairo and Aswan; a few less reliable private airlines, including Luxor Air (tel: 012-317 0464), and Pharaoh (tel: 012-316 9947). Flights from Aswan are sold as packages, including return trip and transfer to and from the site. This only leaves you about two hours to enjoy the site, which can be quite short, particularly if the outward flight is delayed
💶 Expensive including tour by a local guide

each, and reassembled on higher ground. Before the salvage operation few people visited Abu Simbel, but today it's a major tourist attraction.

A Labour of Love

It took Ramses II about 30 years to build his 'Temple of Ramses, Beloved of Amun'. He dedicated it to Ra-Herakte, Amun-Ra and Ptah, but most of all to the deified image of himself. Next door he built a smaller temple for his favourite wife Nefertari, where she is identified with the cow goddess Hathor. The original temple was perfectly oriented so that the sun's rays would illuminate the statues deep in the sanctuary on Ramses II's birthday and on the day of his coronation. The relocated temple catches the rays a day later, and at dawn on 22 February and 22 October the sun's rays reach into the inner sanctuary of the Sun Temple and illuminate the remains of the four deities.

The massive doors to the temple are opened by an *ankh* key, the symbol of life

Left and below: Colossi of Ramses II front the main temple and also the temple dedicated to Queen Nefertari

The temple's façade is dominated by magnificent colossi of Ramses II, staring eternity in the face. The statues' heads and torsos are finely sculpted (but one lost its upper half during an earthquake in 27 BC), while the feet and legs seem rather crude. Members of the royal family, including Nefertari, Ramses' mother Muttuya and several of his children, stand at his feet.

Following the classic temple design, the interior reveals a series of increasingly smaller chambers with a floor that rises noticeably. The massive rock-hewn Hypostyle Hall contains eight 10m-high statues of the king as Osiris. The walls are decorated with scenes from his military campaigns, including

the Battle of Qadesh which was fought against the Hittites, Libyans and Nubians. On the back wall he offers his captives to the gods. A smaller hall leads to a vestibule and the Sanctuary, with four statues of Ptah, Amun-Ra, the pharaoh-god Ramses II and Ra-Herakte.

The scale of the inner rooms of the Great Temple is progressively smaller as you approach the sanctuary

Queen Nefertari's Temple

To the north is the smaller temple of Nefertari, dedicated to Hathor. As with Ramses' temple, the rock was smoothed and angled to resemble a pylon, with six 10m colossi (four of Ramses and two of Nefertari) flanking the façade. Although smaller, this temple follows a similar plan, containing a hypostyle hall with carved Hathor images, a vestibule and small sanctuary.

TAKING A BREAK

There's only a small **café** on the site, with cold drinks and very little to eat, so bring a picnic to enjoy in the shade of the trees near the lake.

ABU SIMBEL: INSIDE INFO

Top tips Stay on board ship (if you're cruising) or at an Abu Simbel hotel and have the temple almost to yourself in the early morning or later afternoon. Sit on the left of the plane from Cairo or Aswan for a good view of the temple.

• There are several *son et lumière* shows daily starting at 6pm in winter and 8pm in summer (tel: 02-385 2880; www.sound-light.egypt.com).

Hidden gem Look for a small grey door next to the northernmost colossus of Ramses and take a peep at the very modern structure of the false mountain, built specially to support the temple. It's eerie, like the set of a science fiction film, and is nearly as fascinating as the temple itself.

At Your Leisure

❶ Temple of Khnum

Also known as Esna, and located 155km north of Aswan, the temple, rebuilt by Ptolemy VI (180–145 BC) on an older structure, was probably once as large as the one at Edfu (see below). Nowadays people come to see the temple's wonderful 1st-century AD Roman Hypostyle Hall – the only part that's been excavated. Here you get a true sense of what the hall was meant to represent. With 24 columns topped by various finely carved floral capitals, it really feels like a beautifully enclosed garden. The walls are decorated with carvings of various Roman emperors making offerings to Egyptian deities.

➕ 202 B4 ✉ Esna, 54km south of Luxor, 155km north of Aswan ⏲ Daily 6–5:30 in winter, 6am–6:30pm in summer 🚌 Bus or taxi from Luxor or Aswan 🚂 Trains from Luxor, Edfu or Aswan to Esna, then a *calèche* to the site 🎫 Inexpensive tickets from the riverside kiosk near the tourist bazaar

❷ Temple of Horus

The Ptolemaic temple at Edfu (105km north of Aswan), built from 257–237 BC, is the best preserved and one of the finest in Egypt. Built in classic pharaonic style, it gives a clear idea of the appearance and purpose of an Egyptian temple, as plenty of explanations are inscribed on the walls. The site was chosen because the falcon-headed god Horus fought here with Seth (► 12) for power over the world. Visitors now approach the temple from the back, but it's best to start from the First Pylon, fronted by two splendid falcons. Carvings on the inside walls record the annual Festival of the Beautiful Meeting, where the

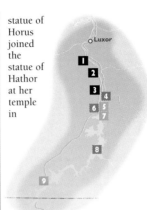

statue of Horus joined the statue of Hathor at her temple in Dendera (► 102). The annual festivals were celebrated in the Festival Hall, and recipes for incense and perfumes line the walls of a small side chamber. During the New Year festival, the statue of Horus was carried on to the roof to be revitalised by the sun. Outside the temple is the Birth House. Look at the carvings of Horus being suckled by his mother Isis.

➕ 202 C4 ✉ Edfu, 115km south of Luxor, 105km north of Aswan ⏲ Daily 7–4 in winter, 7–5 in summer 🍴 Café (£) 🚌 Bus or service taxi from Luxor or Aswan 🚂 Trains from Luxor and Aswan 🎫 Moderate

❸ Temple of Sobek and Haroeris

The remains of this Graeco-Roman temple at Kom Ombo, unusually dedicated to two deities, still look truly imposing, particularly from the river. The temple has

Some of carvings are remarkably well preserved at the double temple of Kom Ombo

3 Great Views over the Nile
• Over the First Cataract from the top of the Eastern Hill on Sehel Island (right)
• Over the islands from the tombs of the princes on Elephantine Island (► 114)
• Sunset on the Nile from the Old Cataract Hotel terrace (► 126)

two identical halves: the eastern part is devoted to the crocodile god Sobek, and the western to Haroeris, or Horus the Elder, the 'Good Doctor', who attracted thousands of sick pilgrims hoping to find a cure for their illnesses. Its spectacular location on a bend of the river was responsible for the pylon and the forecourt eventually disappearing into the water, but much of the inner temple remains. The Chapel of Hathor near the entrance housed mummified crocodiles, while live ones swam in the well. A double entrance leads into the inner Hypostyle Hall, with elegant floral columns and two ceremonial paths leading into the symmetrical sanctuaries. Behind are seven chapels whose outer walls reveal a fascinating display of sophisticated instruments that were used to perform brain surgery.

✚ 202 C3 ✉ Kom Ombo, 45km north of Aswan ⊙ Daily 7–5:45 🍴 Stall with cold drinks (£) 🚌 Bus or taxi from Aswan 🚂 Slow train from Luxor or Aswan 🎟 Inexpensive

❹ Camel Market (Souk al Gamal)

Egypt's largest camel market is a fascinating place, especially early in the morning when Sudanese traders go noisily about their business. Herdsmen walk the camels across the desert along the Forty Days Road from Sudan, to somewhere north of Abu Simbel where

they are driven to Daraw and some-times to Birqash (► 71).

✚ 202 C3 ✉ Outskirts of Daraw, 5km south of Kom Ombo – just follow the crowds ⊙ Tue 6:30–2 in winter (also Sun mornings, best before 10:30)
🍴 Cafés (£) 🚐 Service taxi from Aswan, private taxi taking in Kom Ombo

❻ Sehel

This small island commands superb views over what was the white water of the First Cataract, where the Nile is channelled through dramatic outcrops of granite. Ancient Egyptians believed this to be the source of the Nile, from where the river flowed south into Nubia and north into Egypt. The Nile gods Hapy and Khnum were thought to live in a cave under the rapids from where they controlled the annual flood. Locals made offerings on Sehel for a good harvest and travellers prayed here for a safe return, as the area remained a danger for anyone travelling south until the Aswan dams were built.

These days the waters are less stormy and the *felucca* ride is the main attraction. However, two hills made up of granite boulders reveal more than 250 roughly carved ancient Egyptian inscriptions that record expeditions upstream. The Famine Stele, on top of one of the hills, relates how King Zoser (► 22) ended a seven-year famine by building a temple on Sehel Island.

On the other side of Sehel the Nubian villages, with their lovely gardens, are also worth exploring.

✚ 202 C3 ✉ 4km upriver from Aswan
🍴 Some villagers offer tea for *baksheesh* (£)
🚤 Accessible only by *felucca* or motorboat from Aswan (► 128)

○ Luxor

1
2
3
4
6 5
7
8
9

Cruises on Lake Nasser

Several luxurious cruise boats make three-, four- or seven-day tours from Aswan to Abu Simbel, stopping at the other Nubian temples. Happily, numbers have been limited. Choose between the stylish *Eugenie* and *Qasr Ibrim* boats (tel: 02-703 7935; fax 02-703 6114), which offer a jacuzzi, swimming pools and excellent French cuisine.

8 Lake Nasser

The building of the Aswan dams buried the Nubian Nile and created this, the world's largest reservoir, stretching over 500km south of Aswan. The Nubian communities who lived along the Nile for thousands of years lost their homes, land and much of their rich culture to the dams and lake, but many of the ancient monuments were relocated to drier ground, with help from the international community. These include the little-visited Temple of Mandulis at Kalabsha. This healing temple, dedicated to the Nubian fertility god Marul (Mandulis in Greek), was mostly rebuilt during the Ptolemaic-Roman period, which is obvious from the blend of styles on the fine wall carvings. Next door is the photogenic Ptolemaic Kiosk of Kertassi and the small rock-hewn temple of Beit al Wali. This was built in honour of Ramses II, who is shown on the colourful

A cruise on Lake Nasser offers a more peaceful and more relaxing alternative to the traditional Nile cruise

reliefs in a battle with the rebellious Nubians. The interesting but more remote temple groups of Wadi al Sebua, Dakka and Amada and the fortress site of Qasr Ibrim can only be visited on a luxury cruise, although new roads are being built.

Fishing trips are increasingly popular on the blue waters of the lake, which is home to a few crocodiles, the elusive tiger fish and the Nile perch – one of the largest freshwater fish, weighing up to 100kg (► 128).

Kalabsha Temple/Beit al Wali
🚩 202 C2 ✉ Next to the High Dam
🕐 Daily 7–5 🚌 Private taxi, also rented boat from the harbour
💲 Inexpensive

Wadi al Sebua/ Amada/Qasr Ibrim
🚩 202 C2
🕐 Daily 6–6
🚌 Currently accessible by cruise boat only
💲 Inexpensive

Something for the Children

There are no attractions specifically for kids but they'll probably enjoy:
• A *felucca* ride around the islands in Aswan
• The camel market in Daraw (► 122)
• Baby crocodiles in the *souk* (► 127)

Where to... Stay

Prices
The prices are for a double room per night.
£ under 200LE ££ 200–500LE £££ over 500LE

ASWAN

Amoun Island Club ££–£££

The original royal hunting lodge and splendid gardens have been incorporated into this small hotel. The rooms are simple yet spacious and comfortable. All overlook the west bank of the Nile. The food is good, the atmosphere relaxed and the nights silent, but it's the setting that makes this the sort of hotel guests return to again and again. It's accessed by motorboats from the dock opposite the Egypt Air office.

➕ 202 C3 ☒ Amoun Island ☎ 097-313 800; fax: 097-317 193

Basma Hotel ££

A typical large resort hotel on a rise away from the Nile, the Basma caters mainly for package tourism, but it's not bad if you want to stay longer in Aswan and enjoy time beside one of its large pools. It's decorated by two Egyptian artists, and most rooms have excellent views over the Nile and its islands.

➕ 202 C3 ☒ 1km south of the centre, on the Nile ☎ 097-310 901; fax: 097-310 907

Happi £

This good budget hotel has 64 immaculate air-conditioned en-suite rooms, some with balconies and

Nile views. Guests can use the rooftop pool at the Cleopatra Hotel on Sharia al Souk at a discount.

➕ 202 C3 ☒ Sharia Abtal at Tahrir ☎ 097-314 115

Oberoi Aswan £££

Apart from its ugly tower, which dominates Aswan's skyline, the Oberoi is a comfortable hotel set in lush gardens on quiet Elephantine Island. The spacious rooms have good views of the Nile, and the riverside pool is extremely pleasant.

➕ 202 C3 🔆 **Northern tip of Elephantine Island** ☎ 097-314 666; fax: 097-313 538

Old Cataract Hotel £££

Immortalised in the film of Agatha Christie's *Death on the Nile*, this is one of Egypt's most famous and romantic hotels. The splendid 100-year-old Moorish building is set in lush gardens and most rooms command stunning views over the Nile and Elephantine Island. Some rooms are still impressive, as are the

public areas of the hotel. For real indulgence, stay in one of the amazing King Farouk or Agatha Christie suites with terraces over the river.

➕ 202 C3 ☒ Sharia Abtal at Tahrir ☎ 097-316 000; fax: 097-316 011

ABU SIMBEL

Nefertari Hotel ££

Currently the best option at Abu Simbel, the most important thing to know here is that it's air-conditioned, which is essential in the summer. The rooms are small but the swimming pool, surrounded by trees, is pleasant enough.

➕ 202 A1 ☒ 400m from the temple ☎ 097-400 508/9

Nobaleh Ramses Hotel ££

This slightly less expensive hotel in Abu Simbel town offers more spacious rooms in similarly characterless architecture, but is popular with tour groups.

➕ 202 A1 ☒ Abu Simbel ☎ 097-400 380

Where to...
Eat and Drink

Prices

Expect to pay per person for a meal, excluding drinks and tips.
£ up to 50LE ££ 50–100LE £££ over 100LE

Don't expect grand cuisine in Aswan. It seems that most tourists visiting Aswan eat on board their cruise ships. Restaurants on the Corniche serve good but basic food, such as *kefta* and vegetable stews. Eateries in the *souk* specialise in cheap snacks such as kebab, *taamiya* or *fuul* sandwiches, and *koshari*. The food in international restaurants in the hotels can be a touch bland.

1902 Restaurant £££

The date refers to the opening of the Old Aswan Dam but the décor is less historical and more pure Oriental-Moorish fantasy, where you can dine in style under a huge dome. The four-course set menu prepared by a French chef is rather pricey and not always very inspired, but with a good Oriental show and white-glove service, it makes for a memorable night out.

🚹 **202 C3** ⊠ **Old Cataract Hotel, Sharia Abtal at Tahrir** ☎ **097-316 000** 🕘 **Daily 7pm–midnight, but can be closed to non-residents when the hotel is full**

Aswan Moon £

The entrance through a mock castle gate may be alarming, but it gets a lot better after that. The restaurant has a floating extension, popular with *felucca* captains and tourists alike. There's also an attractive terrace for watching the sunset over the Nile while smoking a waterpipe. By day it's the perfect place for fresh juice, breakfast or a light lunch in the shade. But at night it gets lively and the Nubian music is turned up. The food is simple Egyptian fare, but well prepared (often in earthenware pots), and the beer's cold.

🚹 **202 C3** ⊠ **Corniche al Nil** ☎ **097-326 108** 🕘 **Daily 8am–11pm (or until the last customer leaves)**

Aswan Panorama £

The food is similar to that of the Aswan Moon, but the restaurant is a lot quieter. This is a good place for breakfast or to while away a lazy afternoon, sitting in the shade of some greenery and looking over Elephantine, with a cold drink and a delicious *roz bi laban* (milky rice pudding with a few drops of rose water). No alcohol.

🚹 **202 C3** ⊠ **Corniche al Nil, opposite the duty free shop** 🕘 **Daily 8am–11pm (or until the last customer leaves)**

Darna ££

This cosy restaurant, designed as an Egyptian house, is worth trying out. It offers a large buffet of well-prepared and sometimes more unusual Egyptian dishes, such as quails, rabbit and pigeon stuffed with rice. Make sure you keep some room for the desserts as the sweet pastries are a delight.

🚹 **202 C3** ⊠ **New Cataract Hotel, Sharia Abtal al Tahrir** ☎ **097-316 002** 🕘 **Daily 7:30pm–11**

Emy Restaurant £

This small restaurant, next door to the Aswan Moon, is located partly on a boat moored beside it. As well as the usual Nubian stews and kebabs, there is also an excellent selection of fresh juices, milkshakes and fruit cocktails.

The good views of the Nile from the terrace are supplemented by a delicious evening breeze.

✚ **202 C3** ✉ **Corniche al Nil**
🕐 **Daily 8am–11pm**

Ile Amoun Restaurant ££

Amoun Island used to belong to the royal family, and the old hunting lodge has been incorporated into a hotel run by Club Med (▶ 124). Non-residents are welcome to share Aswan's best buffet, which usually includes a vast selection of meat and fish, grilled on the spot, as well as freshly prepared salads and vegetable dishes, both Egyptian and Mediterranean. Free boats to the island run from the Egypt Air office.

✚ **202 C3** ✉ **Amoun Island Club, Amoun Island** ☎ **097-313 800**
🕐 **Daily dinner only**

Isis Hotel Italian Restaurant ££

This rather run-down hotel contains Aswan's only Italian restaurant. It offers reasonable,

fresh pasta and pizza on a shady terrace that smells of basil. This is a good choice if you're tired of hotpots and kebabs.

✚ **202 C3** ✉ **Corniche al Nil**
☎ **097-317 400** 🕐 **Daily lunch, dinner**

Al Masry Restaurant £

Go local in this simple family restaurant that's famed for serving the best grilled *koftas* and kebabs in town. The décor is loud Islamic kitsch, with brightly coloured vinyl tablecloths, plastic flowers and Swiss mountain views on the walls. But the service is friendly and the delicious kebabs come with fresh bread, *tahina* and a good salad. The front room is for men only, but women and mixed couples are welcome to eat in the family room at the back of the restaurant, which is very popular with locals. However, there is no alcohol.

✚ **202 C3** ✉ **Sharia al Matar, off Sharia al Souk** ☎ **097-302 576**
🕐 **Daily noon–11pm (or until the last customer leaves)**

Al Madina £

The Madina is a popular travellers' dive serving good-value set meals of fish, *kofta* or kebab with salad, *tahina* and rice. No alcohol is served.

✚ **202 C3** ✉ **Sharia al Souk, near the Cleopatra Hotel** 🕐 **Daily all day**

Nubian Restaurant ££

Try this for a Nubian night out. There's a three-course set menu followed by a folklore show of regional music and dance. The food is tasty – grilled meats and stews as usual – but this time done the Nubian way, which usually means with more spices. Be warned that it mostly seems to cater for tour groups.

✚ **202 C3** ✉ **Essa Island, south of Elephantine: free shuttle boat from opposite the Egypt Air office** 🕐 **Daily 7–11:30pm**

Old Cataract Terrace ££

A legendary location, this splendid terrace, shaded by traditional Egyptian tent material, is a perfect place to watch the sunset. The view over the Nile, the peaceful garden and the boulders on the tip of Elephantine Island is spectacular, and the afternoon tea (Earl Grey, cakes and sandwiches) is a real treat. It's also a lovely place to while away the evening but beware of the steep minimum charge for non-residents from 4pm to dusk.

✚ **202 C3** ✉ **Old Cataract Hotel, Sharia Abtal al Tahrir** ☎ **097-316 000**
🕐 **Daily 8am–11pm, but can be closed to non-residents when the hotel is full**

Royal Restaurant, Pub and Coffee Shop £

As you might guess from the name, this tries to cover all the angles. In fact it's a spacious, spotless café-restaurant serving cheap cold beers and passable Egyptian and international fast food; and it's also an internet café so you can check your email while looking over the Nile.

✚ **202 C3** ✉ **Corniche road, above the duty free shop** 🕐 **Daily 8am–11pm (or until the last customer leaves)**

Where to...
Shop

There's only one place to shop in this area and that's in the **Aswan souk** (market), smaller but certainly far more exotic than most Egyptian markets. During the day it may be too hot for browsing, but shops stay open late so it's more pleasant to visit later in the afternoon, or early evening. The *souk* is a feast for the senses, filled with bright colours and sweet smells, and the merchandise gives you the feeling that this really is the doorstep to Africa.

Aswan is famous for *karkadeh*, dried hibiscus flowers which are soaked in boiling water to make a delicious blood-red tea, drunk hot or cold. You can also find good-quality **henna** powder, used by local women to paint their hands and feet, and *fuul sudani*, excellent

roast peanuts from Sudan, at good prices. If buying **spices**, stick to those used locally such as cumin, coriander, black pepper and chilli, as other spices are often fake. The electric-blue powder you see in spice shops is used to bleach clothes. Spice shops also sell typical colourful flat **Nubian skullcaps** that make good wall decorations when you get home. Elsewhere, look out for the equally colourful handmade Nubian **skullcaps** that are worn by local men. Everywhere in the *souk* you can find brightly coloured, woven **scarves** that travel well but, contrary to what you'll be told, may not be silk. Also look out for cotton **woven cloths**.

Aswan also has a selection of souvenir stalls selling such items as **cotton tablecloths**, in damask or painted with pharaonic motifs, hand-painted **papyri**, **brass or copperware**, intriguing Nubian and Sudanese **charms** and **magic spells**, and **leatherbound baskets** like the ones in the Nubian museum.

Where to...
Be Entertained

Aswan is a quiet and pleasant and provincial town. Most tourists are more than occupied with sightseeing during the day, or lying by the hotel pool late afternoon. The best entertainment is probably to stroll along the Corniche and watch the parade of locals who come to do exactly the same thing, often dressed in their Sunday best. The Nile offers a shifting view at all times of the day, but is particularly spectacular at sunset or later at night when several sites are floodlit. The best place to go for a drink is one of the terraces beside the Nile.

Swimming

Aswan is often hot, and temperatures are even pleasantly warm in winter, so a dip in a pool is usually welcome. It's not advisable to swim in the Nile, not necessarily because of the crocodiles (although some have been spotted north of the High Dam), but because of the serious threat of bilharzia – a common yet chronic waterborne disease caused by parasitic flatworms.

Foreigners are not allowed in the public pool on the Corniche, so you'll have to resort to hotel pools. For a fee, non-residents can use the small rooftop pool at the **Cleopatra Hotel**, or the large but more expensive pools of the **Basma** and **Isis Island** hotels. At quiet times you might also get into the **Oberoi's** pool on Elephantine Island.

Felucca Trips

One of the best ways to enjoy Aswan and the islands on the Nile is to take a *felucca*, particularly just before sunset, when the light works its magic. Boats are moored all along the Corniche and you can just turn up and leave at once, after agreeing on a price. The usual trip sails around the islands of Elephantine and Kitchener and past the Mausoleum of the Aga Khan, but another slightly longer, and even more beautiful, trip goes to Sehel Island (▶122).

Indeed, the most romantic way to get to Luxor from Aswan is to sail there by *felucca*. It's probably also more practical than travelling by road, because you don't have to travel in an armed convoy. The journey takes four days, and you'll visit the temples of Kom Ombo, Edfu and Esna on the way, eating and sleeping on the boat.

The tourist office in Aswan lists official prices for all the different excursions and can help you arrange trips with reliable boat captains. Always take enough water and protect yourself from the sun. You'll also need to buy provisions from the food market around the railway station and Sharia al Souk.

Fishing

Fishing is an increasingly popular activity on Lake Nasser (▶123), as it contains some of the largest freshwater fish in the world. These include the Nile perch (which can weigh up to 200kg) and the hard-to-catch tiger fish. **Al Bohayrat Orascom** (PO Box 190, Aswan; tel/fax: 097-314 090) organises two-day or one-week fishing safaris with experienced guides, as well as one-day crocodile safaris. The **African Angler**, run by former Kenyan safari guide Tim Bailey, offers a range of outings, including week-long fishing safaris. You can contact them through Abercrombie & Kent, Cairo (tel: 02-393 6255) or at the Basma Hotel in Aswan (tel: 097-310 901; www.abercrombiekent.com).

Sound and Light Show at Philae

There are two or three performances of the spectacular *son et lumière* at the temple of Philae per day, when a 60-minute tour leads through the dramatically floodlit temple to the tunes of a rather melodramatic soundtrack. The tourist office has a timetable of shows in several foreign languages, or you can check online at www.sound-light.egypt.com/pyr. You can buy tickets at the Shallal dock and also get a ferry across to the site.

Music and Dance

Most live Nubian music is performed at Nubian weddings. As the singers and band are a major part of the wedding expenses, the bridegroom often invites plenty of friends and relatives, charging them about 10LE a head. Foreign guests are thought to bring good luck to the couple, so you may well be invited to join in the week-long celebrations. A similar offering of money will be more than welcome. But beware of occasional touts who invite foreigners to weddings in their village, get them drunk or stoned and then rob or cheat them.

The **Nubian Folk Troupe** performs at the austere looking building of the Palace of Culture on the Corniche daily at 9:30–11pm from October until May, and all through Ramadan. The show, which is popular with locals, includes story-telling, Nubian stick dancing and traditional wedding and harvest songs. A nightly show of live Nubian music is also held at the Nubian Restaurant (▶126).

The nightclubs at the **New Cataract Hotel** (Sharia Abtal al Tahrir, tel: 097-316 000) and the **Oberoi Hotel** (Elephantine Island, tel: 097-314 667) put on a floor show for tourists with Western and Nubian music, while the **Isis Hotel** (Corniche, tel: 097-315 000) offers a rather subdued nightly disco (except Mondays) which plays Western music.

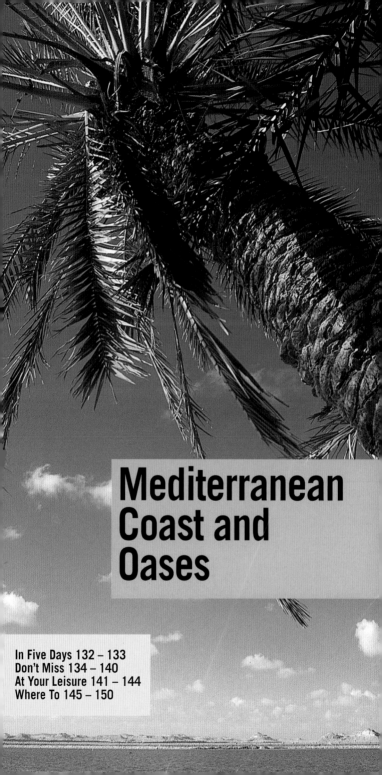

Mediterranean Coast and Oases

Getting Your Bearings

The north coast is Egypt's conduit to the Mediterranean.
Although most foreigners left at the time of the Revolution in
1952, Alexandria retains something of its cosmopolitan flair.

It may seem tired and dilapidated, but
this ancient city is still worth exploring – for the remains of its former
glory, for its unique atmosphere and
also for its excellent fish restaurants.

Because it's been inhabited continuously since antiquity, most
historic monuments have disap-
peared beneath the sea or the modern city, so the
Graeco-Roman Museum is the best place to start a visit. Other
layers will be revealed as you walk the downtown streets,
which follow the ancient pattern.

Alexandria's
market behind
Midan Tahrir
offers a fasci-
nating array of
produce

The rest of the coast seems to have rejected its links to the
Mediterranean and become 100 per cent Egyptian. What was a
pristine sandy coastline has been developed into a string of
mediocre resorts aimed at Egyptian holidaymakers. The
Western Desert oases, some of which were important agricultural centres in Roman times, have their own idiosyncratic
character because of their long isolation. Roads in the Western
Desert are relatively recent. Before them, the oases – separated
from each other by hundreds of kilometres of desert and cut off
from the Nile Valley – were only accessible by camel caravans.
Life in the oases is slow and traditions die hard. Siwa in particular has retained its very distinct character. A road was laid in
the early 20th century, but it's only in the last few years that
travellers no longer require a special permit to get there. But
with the advent of television, the growth of desert tourism and
the Egyptian government's plan to relocate people from the
crowded Nile valley to the oases, change is coming fast.

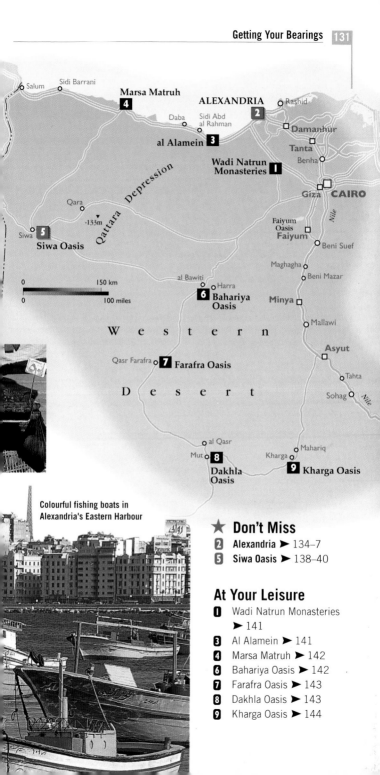

Salum
Sidi Barrani
Marsa Matruh `4`
ALEXANDRIA `2`
Rashid
Daba
Sidi Abd al Rahman
Damanhur
al Alamein `3`
Tanta
Benha
Wadi Natrun Monasteries `1`
Giza **CAIRO**
Qara
Qattara Depression
▼ -133m
Siwa `5`
Siwa Oasis
Faiyum Oasis
Faiyum
Beni Suef
Maghagha
Beni Mazar
al Bawiti
Harra
`6` **Bahariya Oasis**
Minya
Mallawi
W e s t e r n

0   150 km
0   100 miles

Asyut
Qasr Farafra `7` **Farafra Oasis**
D e s e r t
Tahta
Sohag
al Qasr
Maghariq
Mut `8`
Kharga
`9` **Kharga Oasis**
Dakhla Oasis

Colourful fishing boats in
Alexandria's Eastern Harbour

★ Don't Miss

At Your Leisure

This is a tour of two extremes. Enjoy the pleasures and delights of the ancient and modern city of Alexandria for two days, then experience the freedom of the desert and the tranquillity of the oasis of Siwa.

Mediterranean Coast and Oases in Five Days

Day One

Morning

Your first stop in **Alexandria** (► 134) must be the **Graeco-Roman Museum** (statue of Marcus Aurelius, left, ► 136) as it's only here and at the **Roman Odeon** (► 136), in the city centre, that you can really get a feel of what the city once was. Near the Odeon is Pastroudis, the pâtisserie made famous by the writer Lawrence Durrell and a perfect place for lunch.

Afternoon

Hire a taxi for three hours to visit the **Serapeum and Pompey's Pillar** (► 136) and the nearby catacombs of **Kom al Shuqqafa** (► 135). Back in downtown Alexandria stroll through the streets admiring the grand façades of 19th-century buildings or sniffing out antiques in the **Attarin junk shops** (► 149). Have a drink in the Sofitel Alexandria Cecil Hotel lounge (► 145) and walk along the Corniche to one of the fish restaurants. The dome of Abbu al Abbas Mosque is pictured below.

Day Two

Morning

Hire a *calèche* along the Corniche to **Fort Qaytbey** (► 137) and the little fishing harbour beside it. Return via the impressive new Alexandria Library, still under construction. Leave by car or taxi to **Marsa Matruh** (► 142), a journey of about three hours, and stop for a simple lunch and then a swim in the brilliantly clear sea at the small resort of Sidi Abd al Rahman.

Afternoon

Continue to Marsa Matruh and visit the little town on foot, or check out the nearby beaches of Cleopatra or Agiba before returning to Marsa Matruh for dinner at the Beausite Restaurant on the beach.

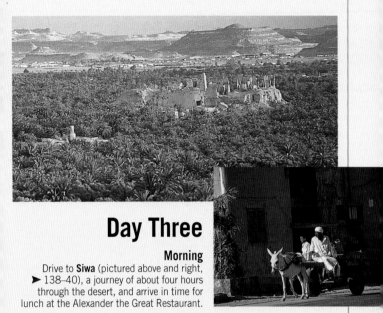

Day Three

Morning
Drive to **Siwa** (pictured above and right,
➤ 138–40), a journey of about four hours
through the desert, and arrive in time for
lunch at the Alexander the Great Restaurant.

Afternoon
A half-hour walk through splendid palm groves leads to **Aghurmi** where
Alexander the Great consulted the Oracle (➤ 140). Continue to the Temple of
Amun and Cleopatra's Bath, where you can stop for a drink at the cafeteria. A
further 10 minutes through the palms is Gebel Dakrur, with wonderful views
over Siwa. Return by foot along the first dirt road for about half an hour, and
back in town climb up to Shali (the old town) for some more superb views.

Day Four

Morning
Visit on foot the **Traditional Siwan House** (➤ 139), then take the Matruh road
out of town and continue walking for about 30 minutes to the tombs of **Gebel al
Mawta** (➤ 140). Have lunch back in town.

Afternoon
Take an organised tour into the desert around Siwa for a chance to see the sand
dunes and explore the saltwater lakes and hot-water pools.

Day Five

Take a bus or taxi back to
Alexandria (about seven
hours), stopping en route for
lunch and a swim in Marsa
Matruh.

2

Alexandria

Modern Alexandria may be a little worn, but its name still conjures up some dazzling images. Alexander the Great founded the city in AD 331; beautiful Cleopatra had her passionate love affair with Mark Antony here; the Alexandrian Library was the intellectual centre of the ancient world; while the lighthouse, the Pharos, was one of the seven wonders of the world.

The city's wealth and glory slowly vanished after the Arab conquest of AD 641, but in the 19th century Alexandria regained some of its wealth and grandeur, growing rich from trading in cotton and adopting the cosmopolitan air evoked in Lawrence Durrell's series of novels, the *Alexandria Quartet*.

But in spite of all its history and legends, modern Alexandria reveals very little of its past. Fragments of Cleopatra's Palace and the Pharos have recently been found in the Mediterranean, but for centuries rulers and archaeologists have searched in vain for Alexander the Great's tomb.

Kom al Dikka held about 800 spectators

Alexandria Tourist Office
✚ 200 A5 ✉ Midan Saad Zagloul ☎ 03-484 3380 🕐 Daily 8–6

Graeco-Roman Museum
✉ 5 Sharia al Mathaf al Romani ☎ 03-486 5820/483 6434 🕐 Sat–Thu 9–4, Fri 9–11:30, 1:30–4 💷 Moderate

Kom al Dikka (Roman Odeon)
✉ Behind Cinema Amir, Sharia Salman Yusuf
☎ 03-490 2904 🕐 Daily 9–4 💷 Inexpensive

Pompey's Pillar
✉ Sharia Amud al Sawari, Karmouz 🕐 Daily 9–4 🚌 Tram 16 from Ramla 💷 Inexpensive

Kom al Shuqqafa Catacombs
✉ Off Sharia Amud al Sawari, Karmouz
☎ 03-482 5800 ext 430 🕐 Daily 9–4
💷 Moderate

Cavafy Museum
✉ 4 Sharia Sharm al Sheikh, off Sharia Sultan Hussein, Downtown 🕐 Tue–Sun 10–3
💷 Inexpensive

Royal Jewellery Museum
✉ 21 Sharia Ahmad Yahya, Glim, behind the governor's residence ☎ 03-586 8348
🕐 Sat–Thu 9–4, Fri 9–11:30, 1:30–4 🚌 Tram 2 from Ramla to Qasr al Safa 💷 Moderate

Fort Qaytbey
✉ Western end of the Corniche ☎ 03-480 9144 🕐 Sat–Thu 9–4, Fri 9–11:30, 1:30–4; Naval Museum Sat–Thu 9–3 🚌 Tram 15 from Ramla 💷 Inexpensive; extra charge for museum (inexpensive)

The Corniche curves around the Bay of Alexandria

Watch Your Step

You may not see so much of it, but Alexandria's past is always beneath your feet, and every construction site reveals new sections of the hidden city, yielding the remains of buildings, statues and pottery. Elsewhere, holes suddenly appear in the city's roads, leading to the discovery of underground treasures. Egypt's largest Roman burial site, the eerie catacombs of **Kom al Shuqqafa**, were discovered when a donkey fell through a hole in the ground. These 2nd-century AD catacombs are decorated in a uniquely Alexandrian blend of Egyptian, Greek and Roman motifs, even including some bearded serpents, images of Medusas and the Egyptian gods Anubis and Sobek dressed as Roman legionnaires.

City Highlights

At first, Modern Alexandria, a sprawling and overpopulated town, may seem disappointing, but time spent discovering its

Could Alexandria's founder, Alexander the Great, be resting under this busy street?

Below: A gem from the Royal Jewellery Museum.
Bottom: A sphinx guards the giant granite column of Pompey

hidden splendours is rewarded. The fascinating **Graeco-Roman Museum** is the best place to start as it houses Egypt's largest collection of artefacts of the period (c331 BC–AD 300), most found in and around the city. Highlights include carved heads of Alexander the Great, some elegant Hellenistic sculptures and a superb 2nd-century AD black-granite Apis bull and statue of Serapis, the main god of Alexandria – a cross between the Greek Dionysus and the Egyptian god Osiris. The terracotta tanagra figurines (4th–2nd century BC), which were placed in tombs of women and children to celebrate their youth and beauty, are particularly pleasing.

Kom al Dikka ('Pile of Rubble'), a short walk away, has an elegant 2nd-century AD Roman Odeon with a marble seating area and the remains of a mosaic floor. Near by, a Graeco-Roman street passes late Roman ruins, 9th–10th century Muslim tombs and an 18th-century fort before disappearing beneath the modern city.

Pompey's Pillar is a 27m high pink granite column, erected around AD 295. Crusaders wrongly attributed it to Pompey, but the pillar probably supported a statue of Emperor Diocletian (AD 284–305). Two granite sphinxes and a few statues are the only other remains of the fabled Serapeum on Rhakotis, the settlement Alexander the Great developed into Alexandria. The Serapeum housed the magnificent Ptolemaic temple of Serapis and the Second Alexandrian Library, containing Cleopatra's private collection of some 200,000 manuscripts. For 400 years, until its total destruction by Christians in AD 391, this was one of the Mediterranean's most important religious and intellectual centres.

ALEXANDRIA: INSIDE INFO

Top tips Take time to explore the back streets downtown and in **Attarin** (➤ 149), to catch glimpses of history both in the monuments and the people.
• Escape the urban sprawl in the **Muntazah Gardens** east of downtown, or in the elegant **Antionadis Gardens**.

Hidden gems The **Royal Jewellery Museum** in Glim is a splendid little museum housed in the kitsch neoclassical palace of Princess Fatma al Zahraa. It contains a collection of royal jewellery from the time of Muhammad Ali to the revolution in 1952, and everything is perfectly labelled in English.

Ones to miss If time's short skip the **Naval Museum** in Qaytbey and the five very faded tombs from 250 BC in the Anfushi Necropolis.

Royal Connections

Alexander's city had two main streets – Canopic and Soma – which survive in the downtown streets of al Hurriya and Nabi Danyal. The area opposite the old-style Sofitel Alexandria Cecil Hotel (➤ 145) was the site of the Ptolemies' palaces and of the Caesareum, Cleopatra's monument to Mark Antony. Two obelisks marked the site – one now stands alongside the Thames in London, and the other is in Central Park, New York. Archaeologists have also found fragments of a royal palace in the waters of the Eastern Harbour, and there are plans to open the world's first underwater museum here, where a transparent tunnel will allow visitors to see the submerged remains. A splendid new **Alexandrian Library** is under construction on the Corniche (due to open 2001).

The **Nabi Danyal mosque** on Sharia Nabi Danyal houses the tombs of Danyal al Maridi and Lukman the Wise, and some believe Alexander's tomb is in the crypt. Near by, the former home of Greek poet Constantine Cavafy (1863–1933) has become the **Cavafy Museum**, a place of pilgrimage for his many fans. At the western end of the Corniche, 15th-century Fort Qaytbey and the Naval Museum covers the site of the 125m high Pharos, built in 279 BC by Sostratus for Ptolemy II, and destroyed by earthquakes in the 11th and 14th centuries. Underwater excavations have revealed fragments of the Pharos.

Mashrabiya windows at the Abu al Abbas Mosque on the Corniche

The garden of the Graeco-Roman Museum

TAKING A BREAK

Downtown Alexandria is a great place to stroll or hang out in one of the excellent pâtisseries or bars immortalised in Durrell's *Alexandria Quartet* and Cavafy's poems.

5

Siwa Oasis

The oasis of Siwa is one of the most remote and idyllic places in Egypt, where lush palm groves and gardens appear like a mirage from the surrounding desert of rocks and sand. Here you'll find freshwater springs and natural hot pools, salt lakes and the dangerous sand dunes of the Great Sand Sea.

In late antiquity Siwa was famous for its Oracle of Amun, whose predictions were sought by people all over the ancient world. It was important enough for the Persian emperor Cambyses to send an army of 50,000 to conquer the oasis and destroy the Oracle. The troops were subsequently lost in the desert, thus enhancing the Oracle's reputation. In 331 BC the young Alexander the Great, having conquered Egypt, travelled eight days from Alexandria to consult the Oracle, hoping to confirm his divine birth.

Splendid Isolation

Until the late 19th century Siwa was virtually cut off from the Nile valley and the rest of the world and Siwans had a reputation for extreme hostility towards non-Muslims. They had their own language, Siwi, and their own customs and rituals. Change came

✚ 198 A4
Siwa Tourist Office
✉ Opposite the Arus al Waha Hotel, Siwa Town
☎ 046-460 2883
🕐 Sat–Thu 8–2

Traditional Siwan House
✉ Siwa Town
🕐 Sat–Thu 10–noon
🎫 Inexpensive

The impressive medieval Shali, founded by a Berber tribe, still dominates Siwa town

Siwan saying: 'It is good to know the truth and speak the truth, but it is even better to know the truth and speak about palm trees'

quickly in the 1980s with a new road from Marsa Matruh and the arrival of electricity and, therefore, television. This and the advent of tourism have made dramatic changes to the villages of Siwa, and unfortunately not always for the best. Siwans now welcome foreigners, but they are proud of their traditions and keen to preserve them.

In and Around Siwa

Siwa town is still a sleepy and laid-back place, even though much of its old mudbrick architecture has been replaced by shabby breeze-block structures and hotels. The **Traditional Siwan House**, in a conventional mudbrick building, contains a beautiful collection of silver jewellery and costumes.

The new town is overshadowed by the ruins of **Shali**, the fortified hilltop town founded in 1203 and inhabited until

1926, when a heavy rainstorm caused serious damage and forced the inhabitants out. Shali's melting labyrinth of houses, storerooms and passages disintegrates more with every rainfall.

Just outside the town is **Gebel al Mawta** ('Mountain of the Dead'), a sculpted rock formation pitted with ancient Egyptian and Graeco-Roman tombs, only four of which are open to the public. To the south is **Aghurmi**, an older fortified settlement under which Siwans believe a large amount of treasure is buried. The 6th-century BC **Temple of the Oracle**, built over an older temple dedicated to Amun, is where Alexander the Great sought confirmation that he was Zeus or Amun's son, but he died before revealing what the Oracle told him.

A walk through the palm groves, past **Cleopatra's Bath**, leads to **Gebel Dakrur** where rheumatics are buried in the hot sands to help ease their condition. A few kilometres from Siwa is the edge of the **Great Sand Sea**, stretching over 800km south and with dunes up to 150m high.

TAKING A BREAK

The best restaurants in Siwa are **Abdu's** (▶ 148) and **Alexander the Great**. These are also good places to meet desert guides or to find an organised tour into the desert.

Below: Siwans waiting for hot pitta bread at the bakery and sweet shop

---

SIWA OASIS: INSIDE INFO

Top tips The oasis is still very **traditional**, so dress modestly out of respect for local customs. Women in particular should keep arms and legs covered and avoid wearing bikinis in the local baths. Also, avoid shows of affection in public.

• Don't bring **alcohol** into the oasis.

• The **best time to visit** is during spring and autumn when the climate is most pleasant. In winter the days are usually fine enough but the nights can get very chilly, while from May onwards it's just hot, hot, hot.

• Around the full moon in October there's a big **harvest festival** on Gebel Dakrur that lasts for three days.

• Friday is **market day** in the main square.

Hidden gems Most visitors stick to Siwa Town, but further afield you can discover the beautiful **Birkat Siwa** or swim in the spring of **Fatnis Island**.

In more depth The history of Siwa is recorded in the **Siwan Manuscript**, a secretly kept record of local culture based totally on oral traditions from the mid-7th century AD until the 1960s when it was discontinued.

At Your Leisure

1 Wadi Natrun Monasteries

Wadi Natrun played an important role in Egypt's Coptic Church, as for over 1,500 years its popes have invariably been elected from these monasteries. The Coptic Church is currently undergoing a monastic revival and many educated Copts have chosen to retreat here. One of Wadi Natrun's earliest monks was St Bishoi (AD 320–407), and more than 100 monks and hermits now live at his monastery. Deir al Suryani, originally inhabited by Syrian monks and formerly the home of the current Pope Shernouda III, has superb frescoes in its Church of the Virgin. Here also is St Bishoi's Cave where the saint's hair was tied to the ceiling to keep him standing. The church of the remote Deir al Baramus has a beautiful iconostasis, while Deir Abu Maqar (closed to the public) is the resting place of many Coptic popes.

✚ 200 B4 ✉ Valley off the desert road between Cairo and Alexandria ☎ Bishoi 03-591 4448; al Suryani 03-592 9658; al Baramus 03-592 2775 ☻ Phone for details; closed during the five seasons

The Wadi Natrun monasteries are often a place of retreat for highly educated men

of Fast 🍽 Wadi Natrun Resthouse on desert road (£–££) 🚍 Cairo–Alexandria bus via the desert road stop at Resthouse, then pick-ups to the monasteries 💰 Donations welcome

3 Al Alamein

This tiny coastal village was the site of the battle in 1942 that changed the course of World War II. Winston Churchill claimed 'Before Alamein we never had a

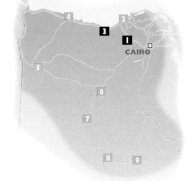

victory. After Alamein we never had a defeat.' Over 70,000 soldiers were wounded and 11,000 killed in the battle between the German Afrika Korps under Field Marshal Rommel and Field Marshal Montgomery's British Eighth Army. The Commonwealth War Cemetery, overlooking the battlefield, is an eerie and moving place containing more than 7,000 graves. The smaller German and Italian cemeteries lie further west. The War Museum houses a small collection of artillery, uniforms, maps and models related to the North Africa Campaign and the Battle of al Alamein.

🔲 198 C5 ✉ 106km west of Alexandria 🕐 Museum daily 8–6; Commonwealth War Cemetery daily 7–4:30 🍴 Alamein Resthouse (£) 🚌 Alexandria–Marsa Matruh buses stop near the War Museum, but there's no public transport to the cemeteries 🎫 Museum inexpensive, cemeteries free

❹ Marsa Matruh

Egypt's entire northern coast is being developed into an unattractive sprawl of resorts for Egyptian holidaymakers, and the once sleepy fishing village of Marsa Matruh has not escaped. During the summer its fantastic beaches are overcrowded with Egyptian families, fully dressed even in the water. And without sufficient services to cope with this influx, both beach and sea are polluted. Slightly cleaner is Rommel's Beach, where the World War Two Field Marshal known as the Desert Fox reputedly took a dip. The nearby

Rommel Museum has some of his memorabilia, including his coat. The best beaches are further out of town. Cleopatra's (or the Lovers') Beach has some interesting rock formations and, according to legend, Cleopatra's Bath is where the exiled queen took a dip with her lover Mark Antony. Agiba (Miracle) Beach seems to deserve its name for the beauty of its dazzling turquoise water.

🔲 198 B5 ✉ 290km west of Alexandria, 512km from Cairo 🕐 Tourist office: 046-493 1841 🍴 Beausite Restaurant (££) 🚌 Buses from Cairo, Alexandria and Siwa; flights from Cairo; trains from Cairo

---

Great Natural Wonders in the Oases

• Surreal sculptures in the White Desert
• Acres of palm trees and gardens in Siwa
• Sand dunes near Mut in Dakhla
• Hot springs in all the oases

---

❻ Bahariya Oasis

In ancient times Bahariya was a considerable agricultural centre, famous for its good wines, but with the decline of the Roman Empire in the 4th century AD the rich fields returned to desert. A trip into the desert, particularly to the amazing White Desert or to one of the hot desert springs, is a must – the views over the oasis and the desert are magnificent.

Several villages make up the oasis, and the main town, with 30,000 inhabitants, is al Bawiti. Its only real sight is the Oasis Heritage Museum with a display of local costumes, clay figures representing scenes of traditional village life, and a small shop selling good crafts.

Towards the Roman well of Ain Bishnu are the mudbrick houses of Bawiti's old quarter. Hot water (30°C) flows into the palm-filled gardens. Further along is the old settlement of al Qasr, which was built over the ancient capital. Noticeable here are the ruins of the Temple of Bes (664–525 BC) and a Roman triumphal arch.

In 1996 archaeologists discovered near Bahariya the largest cache of mummies ever found, with probably thousands of Graeco-Roman tombs. Excavations continue.

🔲 198 C4 ✉ 330km southwest of Cairo ☎ Tourist office 018-802 222 🕐 No fixed hours for the museum 🍴 Popular Restaurant (£) 🚌 Buses daily from Cairo; from Farafra Sat, Mon and Thu at 1:30pm 🎫 Museum free, donations welcome

🔟 Farafra Oasis

This is the most isolated of Egypt's oases. Known as the 'Land of the Cow' in ancient times, Farafra's cows look uncannily like those depicted in tomb paintings. Qasr Farafra is the only settlement in this beautiful oasis, and its only sight is Badr's Museum, a

Farmer working near Bahariya Oasis

pretty mudbrick structure built by the eponymous local artist. Farafra's main attraction is its peace and quiet, especially in the palm groves and gardens, and its location near the spectacular White Desert, with its bizarre, eroded, white rock formations, shaped like moon craters or icebergs. Ain Besai, 15km from town, has ancient rock tombs and a cold freshwater spring.

🔲 198 B3 ✉ 180km south of al Bawiti, Bahariya 🕐 Opening times of the museum vary 🍴 El Badawiyya Hotel restaurant (£–££) 🚌 Buses from Cairo, Bahariya and Dakhla daily except Wed

🔟 Dakhla Oasis

Recent excavations have shown that the lush oasis of Dakhla has been inhabited continuously since prehistoric times, when it was the site of a vast lake. Mut, the ancient and modern capital, has an old citadel, hot sulphur pools (believed to cure colds and rheumatism) and a small Ethnographic Museum with scenes of oasis life. West of Mut are the colourful ancient Muwazaka Tombs, with mummies intact, and the 1st-century AD Roman temple of Deir al Haggar.

Dakhla's medieval capital, al Qasr,

The medieval city of al Qasr at Dakhla Oasis

is a charming place lined with interesting mudbrick houses. The 12th-century mosque of Nasr al Din has an unusual mudbrick minaret. Next to the pottery factory you can see how mudbricks are still made in the ancient way.

The picturesque village of Balat, on the way to Kharga, also retains its medieval Islamic charm. Further along this road, just beyond Teneida, are strange rock formations with prehistoric rock paintings of antelopes, fish and giraffes.

🔂 198 C2 ☒ 310km southeast of Farafra ☎ Tourist office: 092-821 686/820 404 ⏰ Opening times vary but custodians are around 🍴 Ahmad Hamdy (£) 🚌 Daily buses from Cairo, Asyut, Kharga, Farafra and Baharia ✈ Two flights a week from Cairo 🖐 Mostly free or inexpensive

🟧 Kharga Oasis

Kharga Town, the capital of the New Valley, has unfortunately retained little of its original character and charm, but there are still several individual attractions. The New Valley Museum houses a small collection of well-labelled archaeological finds from local excavations. North of town is the ancient capital Hibis, its 6th-century BC temple built by the Persian emperor Darius I and

Rock formations rise from the White Desert

dedicated to Amun. The nearby Roman Temple of Nadura commands fabulous views over the oasis and the desert, while the impressive Bagawat Necropolis has finely decorated mudbrick Christian tombs dating from the 3rd to the 7th centuries. The ruins of the monastery of Deir al Kashef overlook the crossroads of two major caravan routes.

🔂 199 D2 ☒ 195km east of Dakhla ☎ Tourist office 092-921 206 ⏰ Museum daily 8–4; Bagawat Necropolis daily 8–5 🍴 Pioneers Hotel (£–££) 🚌 Daily from Cairo, other oases and Asyut, and two a week from Luxor 🚆 Third class to Luxor, trains to Paris, Qena and Safaga not yet scheduled ✈ Two flights per week from Cairo 🖐 Museum & Hibis Temple moderate

Where to... Stay

Prices

The prices are for a double room per night.
£ under 200LE **££** 200–500LE **£££** over 500LE

Alexandria has some wonderful old-style and sumptuous new hotels, but accommodation elsewhere along the coast is usually basic. Some oasis hotels are set in luscious palm groves, but most are simple. With the advent of upmarket desert travel, this may change.

ALEXANDRIA

Acropole £

Next door to the Sofitel Alexandria Cecil Hotel, this Greek family-run top-floor pension offers a spartan version of the old style. The rooms, with their old wooden furniture, have certainly seen better days, but they're spacious, clean and full of character. Some rooms even share the same views as the Cecil, but others suffer from passing trams.

➕ 200 A5 ✉ 27 Rue Chambre de Commerce ☎ 03-480 5980

Paradise Inn Metropole ££

With its art deco friezes and brass-gated lift, guests used to stay at the Metropole for a cheap and cheerful reminder of old Alexandria. Now restored, it still has its colonial atmosphere, but the large, cosy rooms have been renovated 'in the French style' (big beds, heavy curtains, wooden furniture) and sculpture adorns the public areas. Front rooms suffer from tram noise, but that's a small price to pay for a harbour view. The staff are friendly and efficient, and always happy to offer information about Alexandria. Book well in advance.

➕ 200 A5 ✉ 52 Sharia Saad Zaghloul ☎ 03-486 1465; fax: 03-486 2040

As Salamlek Palace Hotel £££

The Salamlik, a pseudo-Swiss chalet, former home of the Austrian mistress of Khedive Abbas and later a royal guesthouse, offers the most stylish accommodation in town. The large and luxurious rooms are quiet and overlook the Muntazah Gardens and the sea. There's also a lovely private beach, excellent French and Italian restaurants and the only casino in Alexandria, but you'll need your passport to get in.

➕ 200 A5 ✉ Muntazah Gardens ☎ 03-547 7999; fax 03-547 3585; email: Salamlek@sangiovanni.com

Sofitel Alexandria Cecil Hotel ££–£££

For a long time the grandest hotel in Alex and still an institution, the Cecil was immortalised by Lawrence Durrell in his *Alexandria Quartet* novels. It's no longer a celebrity hangout and the renovation was insensitive, but with all that history, the occasional old waiter to tell a story and magnificent sweeping views over the bay, it's still worth the stay. The mirrored tea-room and Monty's bar are a must, but you can give the restaurants a miss, with the selection of good restaurants near by.

➕ 200 A5 ✉ 16 Midan Saad Zaghloul ☎ 03-487 7173; fax: 03-485 5655

SIWA

Adrere Amellal £££

This splendid eco-lodge, on the edge of Siwa Lake and built in mud and salt against the White Mountain, is Egypt's answer to the boutique hotel. The rooms are simple but comfortable and stylish, decorated with local findings and lit by oil lamps (but don't worry – there is electricity in the lobby and kitchens). Drinks are supplied on the wonderful terrace and the chef serves some of the best food in Egypt, fresh from the hotel's organic farm and gardens. There are also activities on offer – for example, guests can enjoy the beautiful natural spring or go on a desert safari. Rooms must be booked in advance from the Cairo office.

198 A4 ⊠ Near the White Mountain, Birket Siwa, 18km from Siwa Town ☎ 02-736 7879/735 9976; fax 02-736 3331; email: info@eqi.com.eg

OASES AND ELSEWHERE

Al Badawiyya Hotel ££

This is the only place where you can stay in Farafra, apart from the uninviting tourist resthouse, and happily it's one of the best hotels in the oases. The friendly owners, Saad and his brothers, are very much part of the local scene. Their tastefully designed mudbrick hotel contains domed rooms, many of them split-level, with immaculate private or shared bathrooms. Make sure you book well in advance as rooms can be hard to come by.

198 B3 ⊠ Main street, Farafra ☎ 02-345 8524

Beausite ££

This is arguably the best accommodation in Marsa Matruh, but that's not saying much, given the competition. Egyptian families favour the Beausite for its clean private beach and its good, simple Greek-Mediterranean food. Insist on a room in the older part of the hotel as the new addition seems to be based on a detention block. Half-board is usually compulsory.

198 B5 ⊠ Sharia al Shati, 1.5km west along the Corniche from Marsa Matruh ☎ 046-493 4012; fax: 046-493 3319 ◷ May–Oct only

options in the oases, this modern rather uninspiring-looking, salmon-pink hotel is a comfortable base for travelling in the desert. There's a good swimming pool and the spacious air-conditioned rooms boast all mod cons, including satellite TV if you're missing your favourite programmes back home.

199 D2 ⊠ Near the temple of Hibis, Kharga ☎ 092-927 982; email: mgg@mgroup.com.eg

Al Beshmo Lodge ££

Set rather idyllically on the edge of a palm grove and the surrounding desert, Al Beshmo Lodge provides that perfect sense of actually being in an oasis. Rooms are simple but spotless, all have fans and some have private bathrooms.

198 C4 ⊠ Near the tomb of Sheikh al Bishmu, 10 minutes from the main street, al Bawiti, Bahariya ☎ 018-802 177

Mut Talata Resort ££

This small hotel, owned by the same company as the Pioneers Hotel in Kharga, contains spacious, comfortable, en-suite rooms with fans, all built around a wonderful, large, hot spring. A bigger villa, which can accommodate up to 20 people, can also be hired if you are part of a group.

198 C2 ⊠ Mut Talata, Dakhla ☎ 092-821 530

Pioneers Hotel £££

One of the few more luxurious options in the oases, this modern rather uninspiring-looking, salmon-pink hotel is a comfortable base for travelling in the desert. There's a good swimming pool and the spacious air-conditioned rooms boast all mod cons, including satellite TV if you're missing your favourite programmes back home.

199 D2 ⊠ Near the temple of Hibis, Kharga ☎ 092-927 982; email: mgg@mgroup.com.eg

Riviera Palace £–££

A good alternative for the winter when the Beausite is closed, the Riviera Palace is a modern and rather kitsch hotel in the centre of Marsa Matruh. Rooms are clean, spacious and comfortable, but unfortunately lacking something in character. However, the welcoming lounge is enlivened by an organist playing the usual evergreen tunes. No alcohol is served, either in the bar or in the rather good restaurant.

198 B5 ⊠ Sharia Iskandariya, Marsa Matruh ☎ 046-493 3045

Where to...
Eat and Drink

Prices
Expect to pay per person for a meal, excluding drinks and tips.
£ up to 50LE ££ 50–100LE £££ over 100LE

Alexandria may no longer have glamorous restaurants where the likes of the Aga Khan entertained international politicians and famous movie stars, but there are still some pleasant and fun places. Many specialise in fish and shellfish and the cuisine is generally more Greek-Mediterranean or Levantine than Egyptian. Some city bars have a typical port atmosphere with a mixed crowd of locals and visiting sailors. Food along the rest of the coast and in the oases is mostly standard Egyptian fare. In Kharga the only places to eat are in the hotels, the best of which is probably at the Pioneers Hotel (▶ 146), but even here the food is mediocre.

ALEXANDRIA

Cap d'Or £
This small but delightful art nouveau bar-restaurant is one of a kind. Cap d'Or is probably the type of bar you'd come across in a back street of Marseilles, serving cold beers and tasty, sizzling dishes of shrimps, casseroles and squid stew to the tunes of aged Euro-pop music. The patron races horses, and his clients are mostly laid-back Egyptians and ex-pat residents.
✚ 200 A5 ✉ 4 Sharia Adib, off Sharia Saad Zaghloulm ☎ 03-483 5177 ◉ Daily noon–3am

Hassan Bleik £
This is the perfect place for a cheap, uncomplicated lunch of well-crafted Lebanese food, where the old waiters and the slightly faded room in no way prepare you for the excellent cuisine. The choice of dishes is extensive but house specialities include stuffed pigeon and chicken with almonds, and excellent pastries from the Oriental sweets counter. No alcohol is served.
✚ 200 A5 ✉ Opposite 18 Sharia Saad Zaghloul ☎ 03-484 0880 ◉ Daily lunch only

Pastroudis £–££
Featured in Durrell's *Alexandria Quartet* as a stylish hang-out, Pastroudis may only be a shadow of its former self, but it's still wonderfully atmospheric. Watch the world go by on the café terrace or hide from the noisy outside world in the plush and intriguingly dark restaurant that serves good if uninspiring Franco-Mediterranean dishes.
✚ 200 A5 ✉ 39 Sharia al Hurriya ☎ 03-492 9609 ◉ Daily 9am–midnight

Samakmak ££
This charming though unpretentious place is Alexandrians' favourite fish restaurant. Once you've chosen your fish, fresh from the nearby market, it will be perfectly grilled or fried and served with delicious *mezze* (starters). It's more fun to sit outside on the breezy street terrace than indoors.
✚ 200 A5 ✉ 42 Qasr Ras at Tin, al Bahri ☎ 03-480 9523 ◉ Daily lunch and dinner

Santa Lucia ££

Awarded the 'Grand Collar' in 1980 for being one of the best restaurants in the world, Santa Lucia has slipped considerably since then. It may no longer serve the best seafood in Egypt, but the Graeco-Mediterranean menu is still enticing. The glamour has gone along with the glamorous clientele, but with the black-tie waiters trying to keep up the old standards, this offers a glimpse of Alexandria's past.

🕀 200 A5 ☒ 40 Sharia Safya Zaghloul ☎ 03-482 0332 🕐 Daily noon–4, 7–2am (bar closed Wed and Sun)

Spitfire Bar £

This popular 1970s watering hole caters mainly for a few hard-core locals, some ex-pats and visiting American marines. The walls are covered with pictures of warships, favourite customers and other memorabilia, the atmosphere is thick with smoke and the music is pure rock and roll. For an unusual Egyptian souvenir, you can buy a Spitfire T-shirt over the counter.

🕀 200 A5 ☒ 7 Sharia al Bursa al Qadima, off Sharia Saad Zaghloul ☎ 03-480 6503 🕐 Mon–Sat noon–midnight

Trianon ££

Literary souls will revel in the fact that the Greek poet Cavafy (▶ 137) worked above and often hung out in this stylish bar-pâtisserie. Others can admire the splendidly restored panelled restaurant. The excellent pâtisserie, with gilt columns and a terrace, serves a good breakfast, delicious pastries, snacks and drinks (including alcohol). The restaurant has its pretensions and cuisine to match, including flambé steaks and Oriental specialities.

🕀 200 A5 ☒ Corner of Saad Zaghloul and Midan Ramleh ☎ 03-486 0986 🕐 Daily 8am–midnight

Zephyrion ££

This popular Greek-run restaurant is packed at weekends, when Alexandrian families come to enjoy the perfectly grilled fish and seafood on the breezy, pastel-painted terrace overlooking the Mediterranean. It's like the archetypal Greek taverna on the beach, something of a rarity on the north coast of Egypt, and it's definitely worth making the journey out of town to sample it.

🕀 200 A5 ☒ 41 Sharia Khaled Ibn Walid, Abu Qir beach ☎ 03-560 1319 🕐 Daily noon–midnight

THE OASES

Abdu's £

If you're on a tight budget, this simple restaurant is the best in Siwa. It serves traditional Egyptian dishes and vegetable stews, as well as couscous and pizzas, and the yoghurt and pancakes are particularly recommended for breakfast. You might also pick up some useful tips about the oases here.

🕀 198 A4 ☒ Siwa Town 🕐 Daily breakfast, lunch and dinner

Adrere Amellal ££-£££

Most Siwan restaurants cater for backpackers, but the restaurant at the eco-lodge (▶ 145) has its sights on a different sort of visitor. It serves some excellent and innovative Mediterranean cuisine in a pleasant, candle-lit restaurant or on the shady terrace. Most of the ingredients are grown in the hotel's organic garden.

🕀 198 A4 ☒ Outside Siwa Town

Ahmad Hamdy £

Another popular travellers' meeting place, serving not only the usual roast chicken, kebabs and vegetable stews, but also delicious fresh lime juice and ice-cold beers.

🕀 198 C2 ☒ Near the Mebarez Hotel, Mut, Dakhla Oasis ☎ 092-820 767 🕐 Daily 24 hours

Al Alamein Hotel ££

The food's nothing special and the service is slow, but this is the best place you're going to find along the coast between Alexandria and

Marsa Matruh. Console yourself by heading for the white sandy beach and brilliant turquoise water.

➕ 198 C5 ☒ Sidi Abd ar Rahman, 23km west of al Alamein ☎ 03-492 1228 ☺ Daily lunch and dinner

Al Badawiyya Hotel Restaurant
£–££

By far the best option in town, the Badawiyya has a shady courtyard and serves some relatively expensive, but well-prepared standards such as pasta dishes and chicken and rice to weary desert travellers.

➕ 198 B3 ☒ Farafra ☺ Daily breakfast, lunch and dinner

Beausite Restaurant ££

The menu offers old-fashioned Graeco-Mediterranean food of the sort that once dominated Alexandrian cuisine. This beachside restaurant is spacious, a bit like a very large domestic dining room, and one member of the family of patrons is usually around to welcome newcomers, or to chat to the many returning regulars.

➕ 198 C5 ☒ Sharia al Shati (▶ 27), Marsa Matruh ☎ 03-493 4012 ☺ Daily breakfast, lunch and dinner

Pizza Gaby £

There are plenty of pizza places in Marsa Matruh, but this is the one for excellent thin-crust pizzas with a variety of toppings. The only drawback is that it's only open in summer. Other pizza places near by can be pretty unpleasant.

➕ 198 B5 ☒ Near Negresco Hotel, Corniche, Marsa Matruh ☺ Daily 11am–3am in summer

Popular Restaurant £
(also known as Bayyumi's)

The only restaurant outside the hotels in this oasis, Bayyumi serves a basic selection of meat and vegetable stews, bread, omelettes and soup, and is something of a meeting place for locals and tourists.

➕ 198 C4 ☒ Main intersection of al Bawiti, Bahariya ☺ Daily breakfast, lunch and dinner

opposite the Popular Restaurant in Bawiti, has a selection of rugs, blankets and knitwear, and the **al Badawiyya Hotel** in Farafra sells camel-hair hand-knitted socks and sweaters made by 'Mr. Socks'.

Siwa has a rich craft tradition, but most of the older pieces and family heirlooms were sold to foreign collectors long ago, so most of what's on sale is new. Siwans traditionally wear large, heavy silver jewellery, including a wedding ring worn on the middle finger, which covers half the hand. The oasis is also famous for its embroidery, with green, red, orange and black thread used on wedding dresses and shawls. Wonderful Siwan baskets are woven from palm fronds and embroidered with similar colours, cowrie shells and mother-of-pearl shells. Pottery is made of clay mixed with pigment from Gebel Dakrur. A few shops in Siwa sell these crafts – the best is the fixed-price **Siwa Original Handicrafts**, next to Abdu's restaurant.

Where to...
Shop

ALEXANDRIA

Alexandria has a small *souk* off Midan Tahrir selling cheap clothes, shoes and plastic kitchen tools. Alternatively, the **Attarin Market** has an amazing variety of antiques and junk shops, crammed into a maze of alleys. Many items were left behind by Alexandria's wealthy European families who fled after the Revolution in 1952 (▶ 27). Dealers know the value of their stock, but there's still the occasional bargain. And if not, it's an atmospheric neighbourhood to explore.

THE OASES

Most handicrafts sold in the Western oases are made of camel hair. **New Nashwa Handicrafts**,

Where to be...
Entertained

ALEXANDRIA

Alexandria tries hard to sustain a cultural life on a par with Cairo, but since the exodus and expulsion of foreigners in the mid-20th century, it's been a mere shadow of its former grand and cosmopolitan self. Most Alexandrian families now hang out in one of the city's pâtisseries for entertainment, while the men smoke water pipes, play dominoes, chat and drink coffee in one of the multitude of *ahwas* (coffee houses). One of the most atmospheric cafés is unnamed, but occupies the central courtyard of a grand building on the corner of **Midan Tahrir** and **Midan Orabi**, reached via a small passageway.

A few cinemas in town – including the newest cinema complex,

Renaissance, at Zahran Mall in Smouha – show English-language films. There's little theatre or music, but if something is happening it's usually at one of the international cultural centres or at Alexandria's opera house, the **Sayyid Darwish Theatre** (22 Sharia al Hurriya, tel: 03-482 5106). For listings of events and exhibitions check the monthly magazine *Egypt Today*.

Beyond that, nightlife is pretty minimal, although it does perk up in summer. Several hotels offer a belly dance show, the best and most lively being at the **Helnan Palestine** or the nearby **Muntazah Sheraton**. They also have discos, but don't expect the latest Western music or laser shows.

For the more active, the **Delta Hash House Harriers** organise

weekly runs and walks in the countryside around Alexandria on Fridays at 2pm from September to June. Everybody is welcome and the meeting point is at the Portuguese Cultural Centre, Sharia Kafr Abdu, Rushdi. You can get more information from Zizi Louxor (tel: 03-582 4309; email: zlouxor@yahoo.com).

THE OASES

Nights can be long in the oases, but if you're lucky you may find a cool beer on a café terrace, a water pipe to smoke in the company of locals or a light bright enough to read by. The only daytime entertainment, apart from quiet swims in the palm groves and outings to the desert, is bathing in the hot springs. But springs in town should be avoided, especially by women, as they're too public. More isolated springs are often delightful, but women are not advised to visit these alone. To get

to some springs you'll need your own transport or you can join a trip organised by local restaurants or hotels, on which you'll see some spectacular desert scenery as well. Most will also offer overnight stays in the desert, which are recommended.

If you want to see more of the desert, you'll need careful planning, an experienced desert guide and a four-wheel drive vehicle. A number of reliable and experienced guides have set up travel companies: **Amr Shannon**, has been taking small groups through the Egyptian deserts for over 20 years. He has his own four-wheel drive and camping equipment, and can also take food for the trip (tel: 02-519 6894). The brothers at the **Al Badawiyya Hotel** (▶ 149) arrange excellent treks in the Western Desert. They have offices in Farafra and Cairo (02-345 8524). **Dr Rabia's Abanub Travel**, based in Nuweiba (tel: 062-520 201; fax 062-520 206), organises wonderful desert trips in Sinai, the Red Sea mountains and the Western Desert by jeep or by camel.

Red Sea & Sinai

Getting Your Bearings

The main attractions of the Red Sea and Sinai are underwater: whatever their experience, there isn't a diver in the world who wouldn't want to explore these crystal waters. The Red Sea is home to some of the world's most amazing coral reefs, with about 1,500 different fish species and 150 types of coral. Much of the coastline of Sinai and the mainland is being developed, partly to exploit the diving possibilities, but also because of the area's year-round sunshine and beautiful beaches. Most resorts have a wide range of accommodation, and internationally accredited dive clubs.

In contrast to the hedonism along its coast, Sinai also has its spiritual side and is holy to Jews, Christians and Muslims. This was where Moses received the Ten Commandments and led the Hebrews across the parted Red Sea. The Holy Family also passed this way after fleeing Herod's wrath. For millennia Christian hermits have settled near Wadi Feiran and Muslim pilgrims have passed by on their way to Mecca.

Surrounding the deep blue waters of the Red Sea is the harsh desert and barren, rugged mountains that inspired Egypt's early Christians to build the first monasteries – St Anthony's and St Paul's. Since ancient times people have also come in search of the gold that is found around Wadi Hammamat, turquoise from mines around Serabit al Khadem and more recently phosphates, which are mined in the Eastern Desert.

The Suez Canal separates Africa and Asia and, although the canal cities have lost most of their lustre, historic Ismailiya and Port Said still make a pleasant change from the rest of the coast.

Sinai's coastline is slowly being developed, except for the wilder shores of Ras Mohamed

Previous page: St Catherine's Monastery is a haven in a harsh landscape

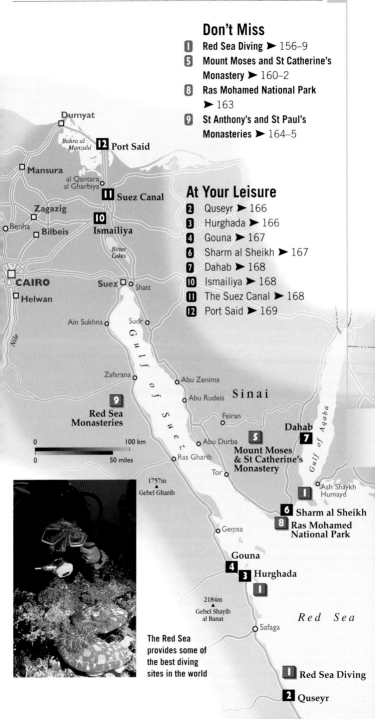

Don't Miss

- **1** Red Sea Diving ➤ 156–9
- **5** Mount Moses and St Catherine's Monastery ➤ 160–2
- **8** Ras Mohamed National Park ➤ 163
- **9** St Anthony's and St Paul's Monasteries ➤ 164–5

At Your Leisure

- **2** Quseyr ➤ 166
- **3** Hurghada ➤ 166
- **4** Gouna ➤ 167
- **6** Sharm al Sheikh ➤ 167
- **7** Dahab ➤ 168
- **10** Ismailiya ➤ 168
- **11** The Suez Canal ➤ 168
- **12** Port Said ➤ 169

Dumyat

Bahra al Manzala **12** Port Said

Mansura

al Qantara al Gharbiya

11 Suez Canal

Zagazig

Benha ☐ **Bilbeis** **10** **Ismailiya**

Bitter Lakes

CAIRO

Suez ☐ Shatt

Helwan

Ain Sukhna Sudr

Nile

Zafarana Abu Zenima

Abu Rudeis **Sinai**

9
Red Sea Monasteries

Feiran

Abu Durba **5**
Mount Moses & St Catherine's Monastery

Ras Gharib

Tor

| 0 | 100 km |
| 0 | 50 miles |

1757m ▲ Gebel Gharib

Dahab

7

Gulf of Aqaba

Ash Shaykh Humayd

6 **Sharm al Sheikh**

8 **Ras Mohamed National Park**

Gemsa

Gouna

4 **3** **Hurghada**

2184m ▲ Gebel Shayib al Banat

Red   Sea

Safaga

The Red Sea provides some of the best diving sites in the world

1 **Red Sea Diving**

2 Quseyr

Besides the wonderful diving and snorkelling opportunities, the mountains in the Sinai interior and along the Red Sea coast also have their attractions. From early Christian monasteries to a fantastic barren landscape, they form a perfect contrast to the dazzling colours of the underwater world.

The Red Sea and Sinai in Five Days

Day One

Morning
From your base in **Sharm al Sheikh** (➤ 167), hire a car or book a taxi for the day and make the 30-minute drive to **Ras Mohamed National Park** (➤ 163). Stop at the Visitors' Centre for a video show of the park's highlights. Divers can take a boat to the Shark Reefs or The Mushroom, while non-divers can snorkel at Anemone City or the Mangrove Channel. You can have lunch at the Visitors' Centre, but the park also has some great places to picnic.

Afternoon
Late afternoon, return to Naama Bay in Sharm al Sheikh (above) for a stroll along the beach walkway and then dinner at the Hilton's fish restaurant.

Day Two
Morning
Once again arrange a car and start with a 90-minute or so drive to **Dahab** (➤ 168) where you can stop for a swim or snorkel at the **Canyon** (➤ 157) a bit further up the coast. Have lunch at one of the numerous beach restaurants that line the bay of Asilah in Dahab.

Afternoon
After lunch drive inland for about two hours to the St Catherine area and start your ascent of **Mount Moses** (➤ 160, also known as Mount Sinai) at around 5pm (earlier in winter) in time to watch the spectacular sunset over the desert mountains. Take the long and easy route up the camel path (about three hours) and descend by the muscle-wrenching Steps of Repentance, which will take about 90 minutes.

Day Three

Morning

If you missed the sunset, you can see the even more spectacular sunrise by rising very early (check with the monastery for exact times). Rent a car or get a cab or bus and visit **St Catherine's Monastery** (below, ▶ 160) before midday.

Afternoon

Drive back to Sharm al Sheikh for a late lunch and a swim, then catch the 6pm ferry to Hurghada in time for dinner and an overnight stop.

Day Four

Morning

Pack a picnic for lunch and get a car or taxi for the two-hour drive into the desert to **St Paul's Monastery** (▶ 164), around 200km north. It's then another 82km to **St Anthony's Monastery** (▶ 164–5).

Afternoon

After lunch drive back towards Hurghada and stop at Gouna (about 20km north of Hurghada) for a swim and dinner later in Gouna Town before heading back to Hurghada for the night.

Day Five

Morning

Spend the morning diving in the area (▶ 156–9), or visit Hurghada's Red Sea Aquarium (▶ 166) and take a trip in the **Sindbad Submarine** (▶ 166). Have lunch in Hurghada Town, perhaps swapping stories with divers in Peanuts Bar (▶ 174).

Afternoon

After lunch it's a six-hour drive through Sinai to Cairo so that you can arrive there in time for dinner.

0

Red Sea Diving

For many divers and snorkellers the Red Sea is sheer paradise. Its easily accessible coral reefs are among the most fascinating in the world, with deep coral walls, lagoons and submerged gardens teeming with a variety of sealife. The sun shines most of the year, the sparkling waters are warm and the visibility is generally crystal clear.

The Red Sea lies along the northern section of the Great Rift Valley, which runs from the Jordan Valley, through the Dead Sea, across Kenya and Tanzania and down to Mozambique. The Red Sea is about 1,930km long and can reach a depth of 1,850m.

The Nature of Coral

The sea's tropical reefs are built from corals – primitive animals closely related to sea anemones. Each coral is made up of a mass of minute polyps that grow together in a colony. When a colony dies, another one grows on top of its skeleton, so only the outermost layer of the reef is alive. Corals grow very slowly, around 1–10cm a year, but the size of a colony can vary from a few centimetres to a few metres. Some are hundreds of years old.

The most prolific coral growths are found in shallow, well-lit waters that are warm enough (at least 18.5°C) to allow zooxanthellae (microscopic plants on which corals depend) to thrive.

Three types of reef are found in Egypt.

The following are among the better-established and more reputable diving centres.

Sharm al Sheikh

African Divers ✚ 201 F2 ✉ Naama Bay ☎ /fax: 069-660 307; email: african@sinainet.com.eg

Camel Dive Club ✚ 201 F2 ✉ Naama Bay ☎ 069-600 700; fax 069-600 601; email: reservations@cameldive.com

Red Sea Diving College ✚ 201 F2 ✉ Naama Bay ☎ 069-660 145; fax 069-600 312; email: college@sinainet.com.eg

Sinai Divers ✚ 201 F2 ✉ Ghazala Hotel ☎ 069-600 697 direct or 069-600 150 through Hotel Ghazala; fax: 069-600 158; email: info@sinaidivers.com; www.sinaidivers.com

Dahab

Nesima Diving Center ✚ 201 F3 ✉ Nesima Hotel ☎ 062-640 320; fax: 062-640 321

Hurghada

Aquanaut ✚ 201 E1 ✉ Shedwan Golden Beach Hotel ☎ 065-549 891; fax 065-547 045

Jasmin Diving ✚ 201 E1 ✉ Jasmin Village ☎ 065-446 442; fax: 065-446 455

Red Sea Diving Center ✚ 201 E1 ☎ 065-442 960; fax 065-442 234; email: wrkneip@intouch.com

Quseyr

Subex al Quseyr ✚ 199 E3 ✉ Mövenpick Hotel ☎ 065-432 124; fax: 065-432 100

Protecting the Reefs

Egypt's coral reefs have suffered both at the hands of hotel builders and the tourists, so it's extremely important to protect them:

• Don't touch the corals and certainly never stand on them.

• Avoid kicking up sand, as it smothers the corals.

• Don't fish or feed the fish.

• Don't collect or buy any shells, corals or other marine souvenirs.

Fringing reefs lie in shallow water near land. Barrier reefs, much larger, grow along the edges of islands and continental shelves and tend to be separated from the shore by a lagoon. Patch reefs are mounds of coral that grow like islands out of the sandy seabed. The area between the shore and the seaward reef, the back reef, is a mixture of sand, coral colonies and rubble.

Sinai's Top Five Diving and Snorkelling Sites

• **Blue Hole** (a few kilometres north of Dahab). This large lagoon on top of a 300m-deep vertical shaft features hard corals and a variety of fish on the outer reef. But beware that diving deep down is extremely dangerous and has claimed many lives.

• **The Canyon** (near the Blue Hole, Dahab). This narrow, extremely beautiful canyon has plenty of corals and a range of reef fish that can even be seen by new divers. But only experienced divers should attempt the deep exit out of the canyon.

• **The Islands** (near the Laguna Hotel, Dahab). A magnificent seascape covered with the most diverse and well-preserved corals in the area, with an amazing variety of fish. The added attraction here is a large amphitheatre, halfway along the reef, where schools of barracudas are common. It's also excellent for snorkelling.

• **End of the Road Reef** (north of Sharm al Sheikh). This submerged island has some of the best corals in Egypt and an abundance of fish.

• **Ras Ghozlani** (Ras Mohamed, ► 163). The most beautiful spot on the south coast features plenty of small reef species and well-preserved corals.

Top Mainland Spots for Diving and Snorkelling
• **Shaab Abu Ramada** (The Aquarium), about 15km south of Hurghada. This shallow reef is home to the tiniest reef fish, stingrays, barracuda, tuna and grey sharks.
• **Carless (Careless) Reef**, 5km north of Giftun Island. Divers from all over the world come to see the population of semi-tame moray eels, untamed sharks and jacks.
• **Green Hole**, 59km north of Quseyr. Excellent for both snorkelling and diving, this stunning coral growth is home to dolphins and blue-eagle rays.
• **Beit Goha**, 20km north of Quseyr. An exceptional and very shallow coral labyrinth harbours elaborate canyons and exquisite coral gardens.
• **Sirena Beach Home Reef**, Mövenpick Quseir Hotel, Quseyr. Off the hotel's jetty is a fantastic reef with a variety of corals and fish (➤ 171).

Spectacular Sealife
Even on the patchiest corals you might find small gobi, snappers, triggerfish, emperors and sea urchins, as well as bottom-dwelling species burrowing in the sand. In protected lagoons you might see wonderful varieties of seaweed and seagrasses. Most divers head straight for the reef fronts, with their spectacular features and variety of marine life. The top 20m attracts many of the brightest-coloured species, including damselfish, butterflyfish, clownfish and snappers. Even sharks are known to thrive here.

Try a Dive
Most hotels in Sinai and along the coast have a diving centre (or arrangements with one), with boats, equipment and experienced instructors (➤ 156) and snorkelling equipment for rent or to buy. Egypt's diving centres are a relatively inexpensive way to learn open-water diving and earn a PADI (Professional Association of Diving Instructors) or CMAS (Confédération Mondiale des Activités Subaquatiques / World Underwater Federation) certificate, which enables you to dive anywhere in the world. Around Sharm al Sheikh and along most of the mainland coast diving is done offshore from a boat. But beyond Dahab and Nuweiba you can easily swim out to the reefs, and Sinai in particular offers some interesting snorkelling opportunities along almost the entire coast. In Hurghada, most snorkelling and diving sites are only accessible by boat. The most popular day trip is to Giftun Island with snorkelling before and after lunch.

RED SEA DIVING: INSIDE INFO

Top tip The best time to dive is spring or autumn. In summer, temperatures below the surface are pleasant, but out of the water it can be unbearably hot. From March to June there is the *khamsin*, a hot desert wind bringing dust and sand. During the winter the water can be too cold for snorkelling without a wetsuit.

Hidden gems The hundreds of kilometres of coast south of Hurghada, particularly past Quseyr, are still mostly untouched, with spectacular unpolluted reefs.

TAKING A BREAK

Ras Mohamed National Park has some good spots for a picnic, and Hurghada and Dahab have plenty of eating places and watering holes.

Left: Royal angelfish.
Below: A large shoal of anthias

5

Mount Moses and St Catherine's Monastery

For centuries pilgrims have climbed Gebel Musa (Mount Moses or Mount Sinai) to visit the site where Moses is believed to have received the Ten Commandments. Some make the ascent for the spectacular mountain views, while others search for a more spiritual experience.

Mount Moses rises 2,285m above sea level and can be climbed via two routes. The easiest (and longest) follows a camel path and takes about three hours. The other route, known as Sikkat Sayyidna Musa (Path of our Lord Moses), takes 90 minutes but is far more exhausting because it leads up the 3,750 steep Steps of Repentance, hewn by monks.

The monks of St Catherine hold closed services in the small Greek Orthodox chapel on top of Mount Moses

Deir Santa Katerina (St Catherine's Monastery)

At the foot of Mount Moses is the remarkable 6th-century Greek Orthodox monastery of Christian martyr St Catherine of Alexandria, built on the supposed site of the Burning Bush. In AD 337 the Byzantine Empress Helena built a chapel over the Burning Bush, which had already attracted many pilgrims and hermits. Emperor Justinian then enlarged and fortified it in the 6th century. About 20 monks, mostly from Mount Athos in Greece, now live at the monastery. However, the rapid expansion of tourism along the coast and the many day trippers threaten the peace of the monastery.

The entrance to the monastery is a small gate in the massive granite walls, near Kléber's Tower. To the right is Moses' Well,

---

✚ 201 E3
✉ Sinai interior, 450km from Cairo, 140km west of Dahab
☎ 062-470 341/3; fax 062-470 033 (head office of St Catherine Protectorate)
🕐 Mon–Thu and Sat 9–12; closed public holidays; phone in advance to check
🍴 Café/restaurant (£)
🚌 Buses from Cairo, Sharm al Sheikh, Dahab and Nuweiba to St Catherine village (al Milga), 2km from the monastery
✈ Air Sinai flights to St Catherine from Cairo 🖐 Free

The Ten Commandments

According to the scriptures (Exodus 3), God revealed himself to Moses as a flame of fire in the Burning Bush (also associated with Sinai), and told the prophet to lead the people of Israel out of Egypt to escape hardship under the pharoah. The people fled to Sinai and Moses spent 40 days on the mountain, where God communicated the Ten Commandments to him, which were written on two stone tablets. Sinai is sacred to Jews, Christians and Muslims because the Ten Commandments became the basis of Christian and Jewish religion, and the incident is also recounted in the Quran.

where the prophet met his future wife Zippora, while a left turn leads to an enclosure with a thorny bush, a cutting from the Burning Bush – the original is inside the chapel.

The granite Basilica of St Catherine, entered through beautiful original cedar-wood doors, has 12 magnificent pillars for each month of the year, each decorated with an icon of a saint.

A Christian Martyr

Born in AD 294 to an Alexandrian family, St Catherine was tortured for her faith on a spiked wheel, which broke and beheaded her. This later inspired the Catherine wheel firework and heraldry symbol. Her remains are said to have been taken to Sinai by angels.

The basilica of St Catherine dominates the monastery compound

The iconostasis (altar screen) is 17th century, but the sanctuary beyond it houses the Mosaic of the Transfiguration (AD 550–600), a masterpiece of Byzantine art. The icon collection is unique and covers 1,400 years, including the period between 746 and 842 when the monks in this isolated monastery were unaware of the injunction banning Byzantine Christians from painting the Holy Family or saints. The monastery also has a precious collection of rare and early manuscripts, not on public display.

A 6th-century Byzantine mosaic of the Transfiguration

TAKING A BREAK

Bedouins often sell tea at the top of the mountain (pictured right), but don't count on it – take your own food and drink. Al Milga village has restaurants and little shops where you can stock up for a picnic. Simple meals are included if you're staying at the monastery's hostel.

MOUNT MOSES & ST CATHERINE'S MONASTERY: INSIDE INFO

Top tips The climb up Mount Moses is spectacular, both at dawn and dusk, and you can take in both by bringing a sleeping bag and staying outdoors in Elijah's Basin, near the summit. You can leave your luggage in the monastery's storeroom.
• Take lots of water for the intense heat, but also come prepared with suitable gear, as it can snow here in winter and temperatures drop dramatically at night, even in summer.
• Dress modestly when visiting the monastery.

In more depth You need special permission to see the Chapel of the Burning Bush.
• The St Catherine Protectorate publishes a good guide to the monastery, as well as some excellent walking guides to the surrounding area.
• Visitors to the mountains must be accompanied by a Bedouin guide, which can be organised from al Milga tourist office.

⑧

Ras Mohamed National Park

Egypt's first national park was created in 1988. Only 12 per cent of it is open to the public, and it can get crowded with day trippers from nearby Sharm al Sheikh. Nevertheless, so far the project has been extremely successful in protecting the area's outstanding ecosystem.

The park's underwater area has some of the Red Sea's most remarkable coral reefs, including the rich growth of spectacular Anemone City. On land too there's a lot of wildlife, including foxes, gazelles and ibexes, and the mangroves are a valuable breeding ground for migratory birds. Children love the warm shallow waters of Mangrove Channel and the Crevice Pools. The Visitors' Centre has free telescopes, wildlife videos and information on the park trails.

The modern entrance to Ras Mohamed National Park

➕ 201 F2
✉ 30km northwest of Sharm al Sheikh 🕐 Daily dawn–dusk
🍴 Restaurant at Visitors' Centre (£–££)
🛏 Inexpensive, camping permits available from the Visitors' Centre

RAS MOHAMED NATIONAL PARK: INSIDE INFO

Top tips Take your passport to go through the **UN checkpoints**; Israelis and foreigners without a full Egyptian visa (only the Sinai visa) should expect delays.
• You can rent **diving equipment** at Ras Mohamed, but it's safer to get it from a diving centre in Sharm al Sheikh.

9

St Anthony's and St Paul's Monasteries

The monasteries of Deir Anba Antunius and Deir Anba Bula (St Anthony and St Paul), hidden in the barren Red Sea mountains, are the oldest Christian monasteries in Egypt, perhaps in the world. Monastic rituals were more or less invented here, where the daily life of the Coptic monks has barely changed in 1,600 years. The hermit St Anthony found refuge here in the silence of the desert, but silence can be hard to find when the tours arrive from Hurghada.

St Anthony's Monastery

St Anthony (► 24) moved to the desert in AD 294, settling first in a spot with palm trees. But when things became too crowded he moved to a cave in the mountain, where he lived for 25 years until his death at the age of 105. The monastery dedicated to him was founded around AD 361 by his disciples, who lived an ascetic life in a community. Surrounded by 12m-high walls, the monastery compound is dramatically located beneath a ridge of cliffs in the Wadi Araba, at the foot of St Anthony's Cave, covered in centuries of graffiti and supplications left by pilgrims. The views from the top are fantastic, and well worth the steep climb up 1,200 steps. The monastery itself is home to about 65 monks and looks similar to an Egyptian village, with houses, churches and gardens. The oldest building is the Church of St Anthony, with contains the saint's tomb and beautiful 13th-century murals.

Top right: St Anthony's monastery contains some beautiful stained glass windows. Right: The peaceful Monastery of St Anthony was at the foot of the mountain where the saint went into retreat

St Paul's Monastery

St Paul the Ascetic (not to be confused with the apostle) is called Egypt's first hermit, settling here before St Anthony, living in his cave for 90 years until his death at the glorious age of 113. He met St Anthony at the end of his life and

➕ 201 D3 ✉ St Anthony's: 50km west of Zafarana; St Paul's: 40km south of Zafarana ☎ St Anthony's 02-590 6025; St Paul's 02-590 0218 🕐 Daily 9–5. Closed Lent and Coptic Christmas (7 Jan) 🚌 Join a tour from Hurghada or Cairo or take a taxi. Buses from Suez to Hurghada stop 26km south of Zafarana; then walk 13km to St Anthony's. To get to St Paul's stop on the turn off on the Suez–Hurghada road, near the Zafarana lighthouse, then walk for 14km

recognised his spiritual superiority. The rather dilapidated monastery, built around his cave by St Paul's followers, has always been overshadowed by its larger neighbour. The wonderful Church of St Paul, filled with candles and murals, encloses the saint's cave. The 17th-century Church of St Michael has an icon of the Virgin attributed to St Luke (AD 40).

TAKING A BREAK

Both monasteries have cafés and St Paul's also has a grocery, but consider taking a picnic.

ST ANTHONY'S AND ST PAUL'S MONASTERIES: INSIDE INFO

Top tips The easiest, although perhaps not the most satisfying, way to visit both monasteries is by taking an organised tour from Cairo or Hurghada.
• To stay the night at St Paul's guesthouse you need written permission from the monastery's office in Cairo (26 Sharia al Kanisa al Morcosia, Kolet Beck, Cairo; tel: 02-590 0218).
• Take plenty of water while visiting the monasteries and the mountains.

In more depth Fit and experienced walkers can hike along a trail in the hills between the two monasteries in about two days. Maps are available from St Anthony's.

At Your Leisure

2 Quseyr

You can enjoy some of the best snorkelling along the coast at this sleepy fishing town. The beaches here are beautiful, and the peace and quiet make this an agreeable alternative to Hurghada.Until the 10th century Quseyr was the largest port on the coast and even in the 19th century there was regular traffic. The remains of a 16th-century fort, built by Sultan Selim, are a reminder of the town's former significance.

🚹 199 E3 ✉ 80km south of Hurghada
🍴 Mövenpick Quseir (£££) 🚌 No public transport, taxi from Hurghada

3 Hurghada

Since about 1980 al Ghardaka (Hurghada) has grown from a tiny fishing village into Egypt's largest resort, and it's still expanding along the coast. The sprawling town and *souk* have little character, but the offshore reefs are a diver's delight and the beaches, with a warm sea for most of the year, offer all manner of watersports. The Sindbad Submarine

The splendid beaches of Mamhya Island, off the Hurghada Coast

(tel: 065-444 688 to book) and the small Red Sea Aquarium (6 Sharia al Corniche, next to the Three Corners Hotel) give an enjoyable insight into reef life.

🚹 201 E1 ✉ 529km southeast of Cairo, 299km northeast of Luxor
☎ 065-444 420 (tourist office)
🍴 Several 🚌 Regular buses from Cairo, Luxor, Aswan and Suez ✈ Flights daily from Cairo, three per week from

Bedouin Life

The Bedouin of Sinai used to be split into tribes, each of which roamed its own patch of territory to graze its herds. But as Sinai's coastline is developed, the dwindling Bedouin community is being settled into windswept concrete villages inland. Very few Bedouin remain semi-nomadic – many work in tourism, as builders or taxi drivers. The largest Bedouin settlement is in al Arish in northern Sinai, which has an interesting market on Thursdays.

Luxor, and weekly from Sharm al Sheikh and St Catherine ⛴ Ferry from Sharm al Sheikh several times a week (tel: 065-444 003/546 282)

🛈 Gouna

The mainland's most upmarket resort is built on a series of islands and lagoons. Wealthy Cairenes own villas here, while tourists stay at the beautiful luxury hotels. The complex also includes an 18-hole golf course, a private airport (➤ 37), aquarium and a small museum with replicas of ancient Egyptian treasures.

🔢 201 E1 ✉ 30km north of Hurghada 🍴 Kiki's Café (££) 🚌 Taxis from Hurghada ✈ Flights from Cairo with Orascom (tel: 02-301 5632)

Sharm al Sheikh has developed from a tiny fishing hamlet into a world class beach resort in just a few years

🛈 Sharm al Sheikh

The Israelis developed Sharm al Sheikh during their occupation of Sinai (1967–82), both for military purposes and as a holiday resort. But since the Egyptians returned, things have changed dramatically, and Sharm has lost its military associations to become one of the Red Sea's most popular and upmarket resorts. The highest concentration of hotels and restaurants is at Naama Bay, which is known for its excellent watersports facilities, but hotels have now also spread into the neighbouring bays. On the cliff north of Naama Bay is Sharm's residential area, with villas and condominiums mostly inhabited by staff working at the hotels. Here also is the first Ritz hotel in Africa. Most of Sharm's treasures are under water – the only sight on land is Ras Kennedy, a rock vaguely resembling the face of former US president John F Kennedy.

🔢 201 F2 ✉ 470km from Cairo 🍴 Several 🚌 Buses from Cairo, Dahab, Nuweiba, Suez and Taba ✈ Domestic flights from Cairo, Luxor and Hurghada ⛴ Ferry from Hurghada several times a week (tel: 062-660 765)

5 Things for the Kids

• See the corals and fish from the **Sindbad submarine** in Hurghada.
• **Red Sea Aquarium**, Hurghada, with colourful local fish and corals.
• **Camel rides** in Naama Bay, Gouna or Hurghada beach.
• **Fun Town Amusement Park**, Naama Bay (tel: 069-602 556).
• Children between 8 and 11 years old can **learn to dive** in swimming pools. From the age of 10, they can do an open-water diving course at the Red Sea scuba schools in Hurghada and Sharm al Sheikh (tel in the UK: 0870 2201 777; website: www.regal-diving.co.uk).

🟦 Dahab

Dahab, which means 'gold' in Arabic, has superb beaches and some of Sinai's best dive sites near by (► 157), although the town itself is a bit of a mess. It's divided into three distinct parts: the Bedouin settlement of Asilah; the hotel area of al Mashraba; and Al Masbat, which is made up of cheap campsites and hotels, where old hippies and young backpackers rave and hang out. The strip of seafront bars and restaurants serve typical backpacker staples such as spaghetti, milkshakes and banana pancakes. Young Egyptians associate Dahab with drug culture but,

The traditional main street in Dahab's Bedouin village

although things may appear relaxed, the Egyptian police are taking a tougher line and penalties are severe. The real attractions here as elsewhere along the coast are underwater, particularly the dangerous Blue Hole, the Canyon and other nearby reefs. Alternatively, Bedouin organise fascinating camel treks into the spectacular desert interior.

🟦 201 F3 ⊠ 100km northwest of Sharm al Sheikh 🍴 Bars, restaurants in the bay of Asilah (££) 🚌 Buses from Sharm al Sheikh, Taba, Nuweiba, Cairo and St Catherine

🔟 Ismailiya

Ismailiya's renovated and tree-shaded old town, built at the same time as the Suez Canal, makes for a pleasant walk. Start on Muhammad Ali Quay at the Swiss-style house of Ferdinand de Lesseps, the canal's French architect. Near by is the Ismailiya Museum's collection of ancient artefacts. Around Lake Timsah (Crocodile Lake) are several good beaches and restaurants. One of the best views of the canal is from Nemra Setta, a lovely garden suburb with colonial villas.

🟦 201 D4 ⊠ 120km east of Cairo, 85km from Port Said ☎ 064-321 072 (tourist office in Sharia Saleh Salem) ⚫ Ismailiya Museum Sat–Thu 9:30–4, Fri 9:30–2; to visit de Lesseps House check with the tourist office 🍴 Several 🚌 Buses from Cairo, Hurghada and Port Said

🔟 Suez Canal

Before the 167km-long Suez Canal opened in 1869, linking the Mediterranean to the Red Sea, European ships had to sail around

Port Said's harbour at the entrance of the Suez Canal

southern Africa to reach the East, so it halved the distance between Europe and Asia.

The concept wasn't new. The idea of a canal cutting through the desert had already occurred to the 7th-century BC pharaoh Necho II, but an oracle dissuaded him from completing the project. A century later the Persians dug a small canal, but it fell out of use over the centuries.

Work on the Suez Canal began in 1859, under the supervision of Frenchman Ferdinand de Lesseps. It took 10 years and 25,000 workers to finish and is still one of the world's greatest feats of engineering. When President Nasser (➤ 27) nationalised the Suez Canal in 1956 in response to the West's refusal to help finance the Aswan High Dam, Britain, France and Israel retaliated by bombing the area. The canal cities suffered further damage during the Arab-Israel wars (1948 to 1973), when the canal was closed and the city of Suez more or less levelled (it has yet to recover).

Since the Suez Canal reopened in 1975, it has been Egypt's second-largest source of revenue, after tourism.

🔲 201 D5 ✉ Between Bur Said (Port Said) and Ismailiya 🚌 Buses from Cairo, Hurghada, Port Said and Ismailiya

🔲 Port Said

Brothels and hashish dens have long disappeared from the free port of Bur Said (Port Said), once dubbed 'the wickedest town in the East', but a hint of its former seedy atmosphere lingers in the back streets. This relaxed town is a popular, cheap shopping destination for Egyptians as its bazaar sells international brands. It's also a stopover for Mediterranean cruise liners, but there are few sights apart from the Suez Canal, which is best viewed from the free ferry across to Port Fuad. The Military Museum (Sharia 23 July) illustrates the Suez Canal's troubled history, while the National Museum (Sharia Filastine) has a small collection of antiquities from the canal's inauguration.

🔲 201 D5 ✉ 225km from Cairo, 85km north of Ismailiya ☎ 066-235 289 (tourist office) 🕐 Port Said National Museum: Sat–Thu 9–5, Fri 9–11, 2–4; Military Museum Sat–Thu 9–2 (also 6–10pm in summer) 🍴 Al Borg, from Nora's Floating Restaurant (£–££) 🚌 Buses from Cairo, Suez, Ismailiya and Hurghada

The Statue of Liberty

New York's most famous landmark was originally intended to stand at the entrance to the Suez Canal, at Port Said. Inspired by the colossi of Ramses II (➤ 100), the French sculptor Bartholdi (1834–1904) designed a huge woman representing 'Egypt carrying the light of Asia'. Khedive Ismail (viceroy of Egypt 1863–79) loved this grand idea, but later decided it was too expensive, so the statue was presented to the USA.

Where to... Stay

Prices
The prices are for a double room per night.
£ under 200LE **££** 200–500LE **£££** over 500LE

Since the 1980s Sinai's coast has developed rapidly. Sharm al Sheikh in particular has seen a boom in hotels, most resembling small villages and part of international chains for package tourists. Budget options are rare, but there's a range of inexpensive hotels up the coast in Dahab.

SHARM AL SHEIKH

Amar Sinai ££
Away from the Naama Bay hubbub, the Amar overlooks the turquoise sea and pink mountains and is designed to look like an Egyptian village. Rooms are pleasant and comfortable, often covered with a dome, and always stylishly decorated. The hotel's owner (and designer) lives on site and ensures service with a smile. The Amar Sinai has a great pool, gym and Jacuzzi as well as a farm and an Oriental café with water pipes.

✛ 201 F2 ✉ **Ras Umm al Sid**
☎ **069-662 222; fax 069-662 233**

Pigeon House £
The only viable budget option in Naama Bay, accommodation ranges from simple huts with fans to 'superior' air-conditioned en-suite rooms.

It's in a quiet area, but across the road from the beach.

✛ 201 F2 ✉ **Northern edge of Naama Bay** ☎ **069-600 996; fax 069-600 995**

Ritz-Carlton £££
The first Ritz-Carlton in Africa is in a quiet part of Sharm and offers the most luxurious accommodation in Egypt. The foyer is based on an ancient temple, while sumptuous rooms overlooking the sea or the mountains have mod cons and huge marble bathrooms. The garden contains two large pools and there's also a private beach. Divers can explore a 12th-century shipwreck or the Amphora Reef opposite the hotel, and golfers can use the 18-hole golf course. The beauty centre offers Cleopatra's Milk Bath, among other treatments, and the hotel boasts one of Egypt's best restaurants.

✛ 201 F2 ✉ **Umm al Sid, 10 minutes from Naama Bay**
☎ **069-661 919; fax: 069-661 920; www.ritzcarlton.com**

Sanafir ££
One of the older hotels in town, the Sanafir has white domed rooms, decorated in traditional Egyptian style, set on several levels around a lagoon-shaped pool. There's also a waterfall and several lounge terraces with Bedouin sofas. Service is particularly friendly, attracting a young crowd of independent travellers and wealthy Cairenes. The Sanafir's diving centre is renowned, as are its nightspots.

✛ 201 F2 ✉ **Naama Bay** ☎ **069-600 197; fax: 069-600196; email: sanafir@sinainet.com.eg**

DAHAB

Nesima ££
This stylish and wonderfully relaxed hotel is one of the few in Sinai to be specifically aimed at the individual traveller. The very comfortable, well-designed domed rooms overlook a beautiful swimming pool. The hotel is popular with divers of all levels and has an

excellent diving centre offering equipment and tuition.

+ 201 F3 ⊠ Al Mashraba ☎ 062-640 320; fax: 062-640 321; email: nesima@intouch.com; www.nesima-resort.com

Auberge St Catherine £–££

The obvious place to stay in St Catherine is this refurbished hostel at the monastery, which offers 150 beds in single, double or triple accommodation, on a half-board basis. Rooms overlook an orchard just below the monastery. You can leave your luggage here while you climb Mount Moses.

+ 201 E3 ⊠ St Catherine's Monastery ☎ /fax 062-470 353

Basata £

Further north on Sinai's eastern coast is a place like no other in Egypt. Basata is extremely popular with Europeans, Egyptians and Israelis who come to enjoy a relaxed and peaceful stay in this camp of simple beach huts and

bungalows. Facilities are generally basic, but there is a desalination plant. The owner cares about the environment, so the preservation of the coral reef is a much-discussed topic at the simple, healthy communal meals. Drugs, alcohol and loud music are not allowed.

+ 201 F3 ⊠ Ras al Burg on the Taba–Nuweiba road, 42km south of Taba ☎ 062-500 481; fax 062-500 481

Mercure Fursan Island ££

The most luxurious accommodation in Ismailiya (part of the French-owned chain) is on Fursan Island in the middle of the lake. The hotel is popular with families who come at weekends, attracted by a private beach and the promise of quiet nights. Rooms are comfortable though uninspiring, and have all modern amenities. Some have lake views. A variety of watersports is available.

+ 201 D4 ⊠ Fursan Island, north-east of Ismailiya ☎ 064-338 040/041/042; fax 064-338 043

Dawar al Omda ££

The Dawar al Omda (Mayor's House), built on a man-made island in a lagoon, is an inventive mix of modern architecture and traditional Egyptian features. The stylish interior is simply decorated with regional antiques and locally made furniture, creating the atmosphere of a large Egyptian house. The pool is small but there's good swimming near by in the lagoons and the sea.

+ 201 E1 ⊠ Kafr al Gouna, Gouna ☎ 065-545 060; fax 065-545 061

Miramar Sheraton £££

A very luxurious American-designed hotel, the Miramar is a pastel, post-modern mirage covering several islands. The spacious rooms, overlooking either the sea or a lagoon, are decorated along a Mediterranean theme, some with domes and balconies. All watersports facilities are available, as well as a golf course.

+ 201 E1 ⊠ Gouna ☎ 065-545 606; fax 065-545 608; www.sheraton.com

Al Giftun Village ££

One of the oldest resorts in town, Giftun is still popular with divers and windsurfers for its excellent facilities, extremely friendly staff and whitewashed beach chalets. At the lively bar divers exchange the tall stories of the day.

+ 201 E1 ⊠ Hurghada ☎ 065-442 665; fax 065-442 666

Mövenpick Quseir £££

Inspired by traditional village architecture, the simple, comfortable domed rooms are in a pleasant garden. This resort is perfect for a peaceful holiday, with excellent service, good food and a large pool. It also has some of Egypt's best snorkelling and diving from its private beach and a dive centre.

+ 199 E3 ⊠ al Quadim Bay, Quseyr ☎ 065-332 100; fax 065-332 128; email: resort@movenpickquseir.com.eg

Where to...
Eat and Drink

Prices

Expect to pay per person for a meal, excluding drinks and tips.
£ up to 50LE ££ 50–100LE £££ over 100LE

ST CATHERINE

Places to eat in St Catherine are rare, but the best option is probably the **Auberge St Catherine**. In the nearest village of al Milga there are a few basic eateries, including **Katrien Rest House** and **Ihlas**. Your best bet is to visit the bakery and local shops and enjoy a picnic in this wonderful landscape.

SHARM AL SHEIKH

Sharm al Sheikh, and particularly Naama Bay have no shortage of restaurants and bars, but most are in hotels, so food is expensive. However, in Sharm itself you can find cheaper places popular with Egyptians. As the majority of tourists in Sharm al Sheikh are Italian, you should have no problem finding good pizza or excellent pasta, although you can just about eat your way around the world here now. Even the Hard Rock Café has arrived, as have McDonalds, KFC and Pizza Hut.

Bua Khao £££

This Thai restaurant offers traditional Thai dishes with varying degrees of spicyness. The seafood specialities are particularly well done, the service is authentically Thai in its efficiency and friendliness, while the simple Asian décor makes for a nice change from the many Italian eateries in town.

➕ 201 F2 ✉ Sharm Hotel, Naama Bay ☎ 069-601 391 🕐 Daily lunch and dinner

Bus Stop Bar and Disco £-££

By far the liveliest and best bar in town, attracting young Egyptians and foreigners. The Bus Stop, decorated to look a little like the inside of a bus, is a bar in the early evening, but turns into a disco later on, with the latest Western music, sound systems and psychedelic light effects.

➕ 201 F2 ✉ Sanafir Hotel, Naama Bay ☎ 069-600 197 🕐 Daily 24 hours

Café Bedouin £

Romantically lit by lanterns, the cafe sits on several terraces cut into the cliff face and has sweeping views over the sea and Naama Bay. There are some wacky details too, including caged monkeys and a Chinese pagoda. It's the perfect place to catch (or shoot) the breeze on a hot night.

➕ 201 F2 ✉ Sharm Panorama, Naama Bay 🕐 Daily dinner only

Café al Fishawi £

This Egyptian-style *ahwa* (coffee house) may have little to do with its 18th-century namesake at the Khan al Khalili bazaar in Cairo (▲ 75), but it's pleasant enough. Located in a modern 'bazaar' and set around a fountain, it's a popular place to smoke a water pipe with *touffah* (sweet apple tobacco) and drink refreshing mint tea.

➕ 201 F2 ✉ Sharm Mall opposite the Sanafir Hotel, Naama Bay 🕐 Daily 24 hours

Dananeer ££

For a restaurant to do well in Sharm, it needs to cover several bases. Dananeer is decorated in

New Egyptian style and serves well-prepared traditional Egyptian dishes such as lentil soup, *meloukhia* with rabbit and pigeon stuffed with *fereek*. It's also one of the best places in town for seafood.

🕇 201 F2 ⊠ Main Street, Naama Bay ☎ 062-600 321 ⓒ Daily lunch and dinner

Fish Restaurant ££–£££

One of the older restaurants in Sharm and just off the beach, it serves a good selection of fresh fish and seafood from its shrimp pond. The restaurant occupies a covered terrace, with nets and marine paraphernalia draped over pillars and walls. The cooking is excellent, but the service can be painfully slow.

🕇 201 F2 ⊠ Next door to Hilton Fayrouz ☎ 069-600 136 ⓒ Daily lunch and dinner

La Luna £££

Voted the best restaurant in Sinai and also one of the best in Egypt. Chef Marco Aveta flies in the best ingredients from Italy to prepare fantastic and inventive Italian dishes. Fresh pastas, steaks soft as butter, grilled fish and *osso bucco* are his signature dishes. As you would expect of a restaurant in the Ritz Carlton, the courteous and faultless service perfectly complements the meal.

🕇 201 F2 ⊠ Ritz Carlton, 0m as Sid ☎ 062-661919 ⓒ Daily dinner only

Pirates Bar ££

One of the oldest drinking haunts in town, Pirates still draws the crowds, particularly divers. The terrace is set in a kitsch but charming garden, lit by fairy lights at night, with bridges over little ponds.

🕇 201 F2 ⊠ Hilton Fayrouz, Naama Bay ☎ 069-660 136 ⓒ Daily from 2pm

Safsafa £–££

Family-run Safsafa has only eight tables, so make sure you arrive early. It attracts a mixed crowd of Egyptian families and tired divers, who come for arguably the freshest seafood in town. No alcohol.

🕇 201 F2 ⊠ Old Sharm Asia Mall ☎ 069-660 474 ⓒ Daily lunch and dinner

Sinai Star £–££

This simple eaterie serves the best-value seafood in Sharm. The place is popular with Egyptians working in Naama Bay, so the majority of customers are men. The décor is spartan, but the atmosphere is real.

🕇 201 F2 ⊠ Shopping arcade behind bus station, Sharm al Sheikh ☎ 069-600 623 ⓒ Daily lunch and dinner

Which Way £–££

This al fresco restaurant overlooking the hotel pool and beautifully lit garden offers some of the best-value food in town. The beers are ice cold and taste even better when accompanied by a selection of *mezze* and salads. Avoid the pizzas.

🕇 201 F2 ⊠ Hotel Kahramana, Naama Bay ☎ 069-601 071/72/73 ⓒ Daily lunch and dinner

ISMAILIYA

George's ££

Cairenes have been known to cross the desert just to eat at this pleasant Greek-run fish restaurant. The atmosphere is agreeable and intimate, while the owner's fresh seafood is famous.

🕇 201 D4 ⊠ Sharia Sultan Hussein ☎ 064-337 327 ⓒ Daily lunch and dinner

PORT SAID

Al Borg £–££

This excellent simple restaurant is a Suez Canal institution. Some fans claim it serves the best and freshest fish in Egypt. The speciality is delicious seafood soup, a mixture of all that swims and crawls along the Egyptian coast. Sea bass and red mullet are sublimely grilled with a slice of lemon. There's no alcohol, but you can bring your own.

🕇 201 D5 ⊠ Near the beach (ask anyone) ⓒ Daily lunch and dinner

Nora's Floating Restaurant ££

One of the only ways to cruise along the Suez Canal is by taking a 75-minute tour on the *Nora*. You can just have a drink, or a full lunch or dinner on board. Decent seafood is usually on the menu.

✚ 201 D5 ☒ Sharia Filastine, opposite the National Museum, Port Said ☎ 066-326 804 ⊙ Sailings at 3pm and 8.30pm

GOUNA

Kiki's Café ££

The most popular hang-out in Gouna has good food, friendly service, funky music and a relaxed atmosphere. Delicious home-made pastas and copious salads are served on two small open-air terraces with views over the town and lagoons.

✚ 201 E1 ☒ Above the museum in Kafr al Gouna ⊙ Daily dinner only

Sayadeen Fish Restaurant ££

Fresh seafood is an obvious speciality of this beach restaurant in a pavilion built over the sea. The menu focuses on a different national cuisine each month, so you can have your fish simply grilled or cooked the way it's done somewhere else in the world.

✚ 201 E1 ☒ Mövenpick Hotel, beach ☎ 065-545 160 ⊙ Daily lunch and dinner

Zeytouna Beach Bar £–££

The designers put some effort into this beautiful beach bar, which has become Gouna's trendy hang-out, serving snacks and drinks to the latest sounds, and overlooking its private beach. You can get to it by water taxi from the Gouna Museum.

✚ 201 E1 ☒ On the small island south of the Sheraton Miramar Hotel ⊙ 24 hours

HURGHADA

Felfella £–££

Part of the popular Cairene chain (▶ 75), this atmospheric restaurant overlooks the Red Sea and harbour. It serves Egyptian dishes, from a variety of *mezze* to delicious roast pigeon stuffed with fenugreek.

✚ 201 E1 ☒ Sharia Sheraton ☎ 065-442410 ⊙ Daily lunch and dinner

Italian Restaurant ££–£££

An excellent and inventive menu offers delicate home-made pastas, a good selection of vegetable dishes and some delicious, well-prepared Italian classics. Food is served on a starry, romantic garden terrace or inside the more intimate restaurant.

✚ 201 E1 ☒ InterContinental Hurghada Hotel ☎ 065-443911 ⊙ Daily dinner

Peanuts Bar £

This is the most popular bar in town, with reasonably priced beers, including German beer on tap, and an unlimited supply of Egyptian peanuts. The décor is nondescript but the divers, who make up most of the crowd here, don't seem to care.

✚ 201 E1 ☒ Market place near Three Corners Hotel ⊙ Daily 24 hours

Portofino ££

Fresh Italian fish and seafood dishes are a speciality and the fresh home-made pasta is the best in town. The fondues are also popular. There's an enjoyable atmosphere because the décor is simple and the service friendly: the owner likes to chat to guests in the evening.

✚ 201 E1 ☒ General Hospital Street, al Dahar ☎ 065-546 250 ⊙ Daily lunch and dinner

Al Sakia ££

Characterful Sakia is set in a large garden and also has a private beach. It's a little hard to find, which may be one reason why it's popular among wealthy Egyptians and foreign residents. The laid-back atmosphere is another reason. Here you can sample some of the best local fish and seafood, chosen from their small pond, and it's also good for a cold beer.

✚ 201 E1 ☒ On the beach in Sigala ☎ 065-442 497 ⊙ Daily lunch and dinner

Where to... Shop

Most resorts on the Red Sea and in Sinai were tiny fishing hamlets or Bedouin settlements until recently, so there are no authentic *souks* or *bazaars*. The American-style shopping malls here have no local flavour. Most shops sell cheap tourist souvenirs but a minority sell better quality produce such as Bedouin embroidery, local weaving and pottery.

An alarming sight are corals, shells, starfish and even stuffed sharks. Avoid buying these as it's damaging to the coral reefs.

The Red Sea Coast

The sprawling bazaar area in **Hurghada's al Dahar** has hundreds of shops and stalls selling the usual tourist tat. In general the quality of merchandise is quite poor, but prices are reasonable enough if you're prepared to haggle. As Hurghada has become popular with Russian and Eastern European tourists, you may also find products from these countries.

Tax-free goods are available at the **Egypt Free Shop** opposite the Egypt Air office or at the pyramid-shaped shopping mall in Sigala.

Gouna has several upmarket shops. One of the most interesting and unique is **Zaki Sherif's Shop** in the town's main shopping mall. Zaki Sherif sells replicas of Ottoman and ancient Egyptian objects and furniture, as well as items featuring his own funky designs, with which he has decorated bars in Cairo, hotels in Gouna and even establishments as far afield as New York.

Sinai

Sharm al Sheikh's ever-expanding bazaar area sells the usual tourist souvenirs that you find all over Egypt, including silver jewellery, papyri, copies of ancient statues and cotton T-shirts printed with Red Sea fish.

One shop that stands out a little is **Aladin** at the al Diar Hotel in Naama Bay (tel: 069-600 826), which sells Bedouin textiles and embroidery, small antiques, beads and scarabs and lovely Egyptian glass. **Beduin** at the Mövenpick Jolie Ville in Naama Bay sells good Bedouin jewellery and other crafts.

Every Thursday a **Bedouin market** is held in the old part of al Arish on the north coast of Sinai, where veiled Bedouin women sell their beadwork, silver jewellery and traditionally embroidered dresses. The market is geared towards tourism, as their best pieces probably go directly to the shops in Cairo, but it's still a colourful sight.

Most hotels have their own shopping malls. The best places for casual wear in Egyptian cotton are **Mobaco** at the Sanafir, **Hilton Fayrouz** in Naama Bay, and **Pyramisa Hotel** at Shark Bay in Sharm al Sheikh; the **Shirt Shop** (Mövenpick Jolie Ville) has excellent men's shirts, as has the franchised **New Man** (Sanafir and Pyramisa hotels).

One of the best dive shops in Sharm is the **Maison de la Mer** at the Red Sea Diving College.

Suez Canal

Port Said is a duty free port and therefore very popular with Egyptians looking for a bargain. Since the government liberalised the economy in the mid-1990s you can buy almost anything here. Most of the shops selling brand names, cheap electronics and designer jeans are along and around Sharia al Gumhuriya.

Other towns along the canal have little in the way of shopping.

Where to...
Be Entertained

Listings of what's on in Sinai are in the free magazine *The Peninsula*, the monthly *Sinai Today* and *Egypt Today*. For the Red Sea there's *Egypt Today* and the *Red Sea Coast Today*.

Scuba-diving/Snorkelling

All Red Sea and Sinai resorts have excellent dive centres offering equipment rental, boat excursions and diving courses (▶ 156–9).

Glass-bottom Boats/Submarines

Most resorts, both in Sinai and along the Red Sea coast, offer daily trips by glass-bottom boats that give non-swimmers the chance to explore the wonders of the coral reefs. For reservations contact

Sindbad Submarines (tel: 065-443 261 or 065-444 688) in Hurghada; **Aquascope** is at the al Kheima Resort in Sharm al Moya (tel: 065-443 710); in Sharm al Sheikh try **The Wave** (tel: 069-663 800).

Nightlife

Sharm al Sheikh can be quite lively at night around the bars and discos of hotels, especially **Bus Stop** at the Sanafir Hotel (▶ 170) and **Salsa** at the Cataract Hotel. **Pirates Bar** is popular in the early evening when there's a happy hour. Naama Bay has a **Hard Rock Café** (tel: 069-602 664), with the usual rock 'n' roll memorabilia. The **Black House Discotheque** at the Rosetta Hotel in Naama Bay (tel: 069-601 888) gets crowded later on, and the music's a real mish-mash of Euro-pop. In

high season several music bars along the beach can also be good for a dance. In Hurghada, **Peanuts** (▶ 174) and **Papa's Bar** next to Rossi Pizza in Sigala are popular meeting places for locals and divers. The most popular discos are the **Regina** at the Sindbad Beach Resort and the more upmarket **The Dome** at the Intercontinental in Hurghada. The trendy **Zeytouna Beach Bar** at Gouna (▶ 174) often has an open-air disco on summer weekends when the weather is good.

Alternatively, you can try your luck at the **Casino Royale** in the Movenpick Jolie Ville in Naama Bay (tel: 069-601 731). The **InterContinental** in Hurhada has a casino for late-night gambling.

Sports

All the resorts on the Red Sea offer watersports, including sailing lessons, banana boats, windsurfing and parasailing. The best windsurfing places in Hurghada are **Three Corners**, **Giftun** and **Jasmin**

Village. In Sinai, **Moon Beach Hotel** (▶ 174) is renowned for its windsurfing facilities.

Most resorts also offer horse-riding in the desert, camel rides on the beach or longer trips into the mountains with Bedouin guides.

Hot-air Balloons

German-run **Cast Ballooning** in Hurghada organises spectacular one-hour trips over the desert, returning by four-wheel drive. There's also breakfast at a Bedouin camp (for more information tel: 065-444 929).

Jeep Safaris in the Desert

Both the Red Sea Mountains and Sinai offer spectacular landscapes to explore, as well as Bedouin camps where life seems pretty much unaffected by the modern world. In Sinai there are trips from Dahab, Nuweiba and St Catherine's Monastery to colourful and picturesque wadis like the Coloured Canyon and Ras Abu Galtum.

Walks & Tours

1 MEDIEVAL CAIRO

Walk

The only way to discover the splendours of Cairo's medieval city is to walk its streets and alleys, lined with stunning mosques, amazing palaces and intriguing *wikalas*. Many ancient monuments are still intact, but others have collapsed . The backdrop seems medieval, but the modern world is just around the corner.

DISTANCE 4km **TIME** 3 hours to look at buildings, but easily a day to visit all the major sights
START POINT Ibn Tulun Mosque, Sharia Saliba (minibus 54 from Midan Tahrir to Sayyida Zeinab, but a taxi is easier) ⊞ 197 D3
END POINT Sharia al Azhar ⊞ 197 E4

Early morning or late afternoon is the best time to go. On Sundays the bazaar is closed and things are much quieter, so it's a good time to take a closer look at the architecture.

1–2

Turn left out of the mosque of **Ibn Tulun** (▲ 68) towards the main street. Sharia Saliba, then turn right. Sharia Saliba follows the medieval main street known as the Qasaba, lined with palaces and mosques that are currently being restored (the area was shaken by earthquakes in the 1990s). On the left is the 15th-century late Mameluke mosque-*madrasa* of **Amir Tagri Bardi**, followed by the very ornate but lovely 19th-century *sabil* (public fountain) of **Umm Abbas**. Further on, facing each other, are the tall walls of a *khanqah* (Sufi convent) to the right and a mosque to the left, both built by **Amir Shaykhu** in the 14th century. Note the unusual pharaonic cornice above the entrance gate and the beautiful ceiling of the sanctuary *iwan*. Outside turn right and walk about

The Aqsunqur Mosque is also called the Blue Mosque

Bab al Futuh
Qaytbey Wikala
Bab al Nasr

Sultan Baybars Khanqah
Amir Qarasunqur Madrasa
Oda Bashi Sabil-Kuttab

7

Gamal ad Din al Ustadar Mosque-Madrasa

SHARIA HABS AL RAHABA

Ahmad Pasha Sabil-Kuttab

AL MUIZZ LI DIN ALLAH

al Husayn Mosque

MIDAN AL HUSAYN

Khan al Khalili

6

SHARIA AL AZHAR

al Azhar Mosque

al Ghuri Wikala

8

SHARIA AL AZHAR

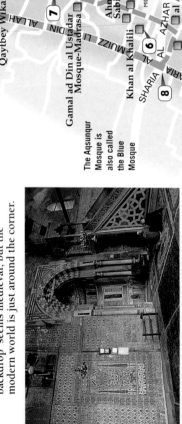

It's easy to pass the unassuming window of the **Khan Misr Touloun** (▶ 77; tel: 02-365 2227, Mon–Fri), opposite the Ibn Tulun Mosque. But inside is a spacious shop selling some of the best crafts in Egypt. Prices are fixed and the staff are friendly.

150m to the impressive Mameluke *sabil-kuttab* (fountain-Quranic school) of **Sultan Qaytbay** with an extremely handsome red, white and black entrance portal. At the fork take the street to the left past one of Cairo's most notorious prisons before arriving on Midan Salah al Din, a large square overlooked by the **Citadel** (▶ 68), and the mosques of **Sultan Hasan** (▶ 69) and **al Rifai**.

2–3

Cross the square towards the striped 16th-century mosque of **Mahmud Pasha**, a governor of Cairo who was

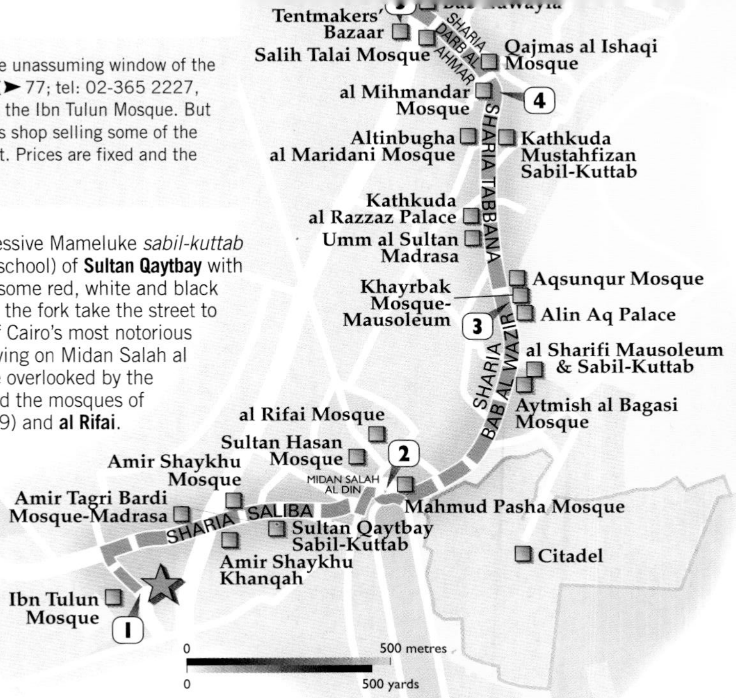

King Farouk is buried in the Mosque of al Rifai

assassinated because of his cruel ways. Just past the mosque walk left along the citadel walls and turn off at the tree-shaded Bab al Wazir, the third street on the left. A further 250m to the right is the 14th-century mosque of **Aytmish al Bagasi**, and just north of it are the

Map labels

Tentmakers' Bazaar
Salih Talai Mosque
Qajmas al Ishaqi Mosque
SHARIA BAB AL AHMAR
al Mihmandar Mosque
Kathkuda Mustahfizan Sabil-Kuttab
Altinbugha al Maridani Mosque
Kathkuda al Razzaz Palace
Umm al Sultan Madrasa
Aqsunqur Mosque
Alin Aq Palace
SHARIA TABBANA
Khayrbak Mosque-Mausoleum
al Sharifi Mausoleum & Sabil-Kuttab
SHARIA BAB AL WAZIR
Aytmish al Bagasi Mosque
al Rifai Mosque
Sultan Hasan Mosque
MIDAN SALAH AL DIN
Sultan Qaytbay Sabil-Kuttab
Mahmud Pasha Mosque
Citadel
SHARIA SALIBA
Amir Shaykhu Mosque
Amir Shaykhu Khanqah
Amir Tagri Bardi Mosque-Madrasa
Ibn Tulun Mosque

0   500 metres
0   500 yards

remains of the mausoleum and *sabil-kuttab* of **Tarabay al Sharifi** from the late Mameluke period. Further along Sharia Bab al Wazir on the right is the entrance to the ruins of the once-impressive **palace of Alin Aq** and the early 14th-century mosque-mausoleum built for **Khayrbak**, a Mameluke *amir* who became the first Ottoman viceroy of Egypt.

3–4

Further on the right is the mosque of **Aqsunqur**, which is also known as the **Blue Mosque** because of the beautiful turquoise Iznik (that is, ancient Nicaea, in northwest Turkey) tiles lining its interior. The street here is known as Sharia Tabbana. About 70m further along on the left is the grand entrance to the 14th-century *madrasa* **Umm al Sultan**, and next door the huge but rambling 15th-century palace of **Kathkuda al Razzaz**. Further along the street on the left is one of the very finest monuments in the area, the 14th-century mosque of **Altinbugha al Maridani** – with a beautifully carved *qibla* (showing the direction of Mecca) behind a stunning *mashrabiya* (wooden lattice) screen. Still on the left is the 14th-century mosque of **al Mihmandar**, decorated with lovely calligraphic verses of the Quran, which adjoins a much later Ottoman *sabil-kuttab* of Kathkuda Mustahfizan.

The traditional tentmakers now also apply their skills to more decorative wall hangings

4–5

Where the street bends, its name changes to Darb al Ahmar. At the intersection the outstanding mosque of **Qajmas al Ishaqi** has fine marble decoration. On the left, just before Bab Zuwayla is the late Fatimid mosque of **Salih Talai** and beyond it the covered **Tentmakers' Bazaar** (al Khiyamiya ▶ 77).

5–6

Walk through the gate of **Bab Zuwayla** and along the market street of **Sharia al Muizz li Din Allah** (▶ 56–8) until you reach Sharia al Azhar. Turn right and keep right along the fabric stalls to find the **Wikala al Ghuri**, a beautifully restored caravanserai now used as a cultural centre and, further along, the **al Azhar Mosque** (▶ 70). Use the underpass to Midan al Husayn and at the mosque of the same name take the small alley to the left into **Khan al Khalili** (▶ 70). The first alley left again brings you to **al Fishawi Café** (▶ 75).

6–7

After a stroll in the bazaar return to the mosque of **al Husayn** (closed to non-Muslims), and turn left along its western wall into a street lined with

various states of decay, along the street. Most are commercial centres for spices and coffee, but a few of them are still lived in.

7–8

Just before you reach the gate of Bab al Nasr, on your left is the large *wikala of Qaytbey*, built in 1481, with the typical plan of a large central courtyard surrounded by shops and storerooms on the ground floor and rooms for the traders upstairs. **Bab al Nasr** (Gate of Victory) with the two square towers is part of the Fatimid fortifications. Walk outside the gate left to **Bab al Futuh** (▶ 58) and walk back through the gate along Sharia al Muizz li Din Allah to Sharia al Azhar where you can pick up a taxi.

Taking a Break

Stop in Khan al Khalili (▶ 70) and smoke a water pipe or have a drink at the café al Fishawi (▶ 75), or in the Naguib Mahfouz Café (▶ 76) on the main street of the bazaar. The restaurant part of the Naguib Mahfouz also serves good *mezze* and Oriental dishes. There are also several cafés along Sharia Bab al Wazir.

mosque-*madrasa* of **Gamal ad Din al Ustadar**, built at great cost by the powerful prince who gave his name to this area, al Gamaliya. On the opposite corner stands the handsome 17th-century *sabil-kuttab* of **Oda Bashi** with lovely tiled panels, and next door is his *wikala* (merchant's hostel) which was one of Cairo's main trade centres for coffee and spices in the 18th century. Further to the right is the *madrasa* of **Amir Qarasunqur** who was polo master to Sultan Qalawun; two polo mallets can be seen above the window of the mausoleum. On the next corner is Cairo's oldest surviving *khanqah*, built in 1306 by Sultan Baybars II. It has superb marble panelling in the mausoleum and a typical early Mameluke minaret. There are several more *wikalas*, in

Never a dull moment in Cairo's bustling Khan al Khalili Bazaar

stalls selling prayer beads and incense. To the left is the 19th-century **Sabil-Kuttab of Ahmad Pasha**, now partly occupied by a sweet vendor. Turn left where the street bends, then immediately right and continue along Sharia Habs al Rahaba. To the left is the 15th-century

2 AROUND THE THEBAN NECROPOLIS

Cycling Tour

DISTANCE 16km

TIME 1 day (start early, particularly in summer when it's too hot to ride in the midday sun)

START POINT/END POINT Ferry terminal on the West Bank, Luxor (either ride round and cross over the bridge south of Luxor, or put the bike on the local ferry opposite Luxor Temple)

✚ 202 B4

Cycling is the best way to explore the amazing tombs and mortuary temples of the Theban necropolis and you'll also get a stronger sense of the Egyptian countryside. This tour passes beautiful villages where life is still traditional, many of the houses painted with motifs marking a pilgrimage to Mecca. you'll see people working in the field or children going to school, who might wave or give you a big smile. Take it easy and enjoy a rhythm very much in tune with the region.

You can rent bikes from several shops along Sharia al Mahatta (Station Street) on the East Bank, but better, more expensive ones are available from hotels, including the Sheraton, Etap and Windsor. Make sure you check the bike before renting it and always insist on a pump as the standards of the roads and tracks aren't always high.

In summer it might be too hot to do this tour, but even in winter you need a hat and good sunscreen. It's particularly important to drink lots of water to avoid dehydration.

The Colossi of Memnon are locally known as 'Timthileen'

1–2

Once on the West Bank cycle straight ahead for 10–15 minutes to the ticket booth on the crossroads before Deir al Madina. On the way, immediately past the al Fadliya canal to the right, note the village of **New Gurna**. This beautiful village, built by the Egyptian architect Hasan Fathy, was a failed attempt to relocate the villagers from Old Gurna, whose houses sit on top of the ancient tombs. Further to the right are the **Memnon Colossi** staring across the sugar-cane fields. These gigantic 14th-century BC statues of Amenotepis III are all that's left of his mortuary temple. At the ticket kiosk, just left at the crossroads, buy tickets for all the places you intend to visit.

2–3

Return towards the colossi, take the first road to the right along a little canal, then right again to the entrance of the vast **Temple of Madinat Habu** (▶ 98).

3–4

Turn left on leaving the temple and, after 100m, continue along the dirt track towards the ticket office and main crossroads. Follow the signpost for **Deir al Madina** (▶ 99).

4–5

Cycle back to the crossroads and turn left to visit the **Tombs of the Nobles** (▶ 96). Leave the bike in the site's car-park, opposite the Ramesseum. Walk back across the road towards the **Ramesseum** (▶ 100), where you can relax and picnic under the trees, or have a simple Egyptian lunch at the Marsam Hotel, just past the temple.

5–6

Turn right (north) on to the road and then take the first road on the left towards the **Deir al Bahari** (▶ 94).

6–7

Back on the main road, take a left to the next crossroads then turn right. The domed house on top of the hill belonged to Howard Carter who found the treasures of Tutankhamun. Temple enthusiasts can stop at the mortuary temple of Seti I, which has exquisite wall carvings, or take a look at the peaceful cemetery across the road. Continue along the same road until the canal then turn right. At the New Gurna crossroads turn left back to the ferry.

Luxor

▢ Luxor Temple

Taking a Break

Stop for a drink at the Maratonga café opposite Madinat Habu temple, or at the café near the Tombs of the Nobles.

The now-abandoned market area at New Gurna, designed by Egyptian architect Hasan Fathy

3 DESERT DRIVE IN SINAI

Tour

DISTANCE About 492km
TIME Preferably two days to stop over at St Catherine's Monastery to see the sunrise at Mount Moses **START POINT/END POINT** Sharm al Sheikh, but you could also start in Dahab or Nuweiba
201 F2

The road across the mountains of the Sinai peninsula is one of the most beautiful in Egypt, perhaps even in Africa. There are plenty of tours from Sharm al Sheikh, but they tend to be rushed and don't allow you to stop where you like, to take in a view or walk in the desert. It's a long drive, best done over two days, and a highlight of any trip to Egypt.

Although this tour follows a regularly used route, you are crossing a desert so make sure you have enough petrol and water. Be careful when leaving the main road, as there are still thousands of unexploded mines in Sinai, a legacy of the Arab-Israeli wars – do not enter any fenced-off areas. Watch out for camels that sometimes wander across the road.

Renting a car can be something of a lottery, so inspect it thoroughly before you agree to take it and make sure you know who to call if you have a problem.

The gentle way up to Mount Moses, via the camel path

1–2

Leave Sharm al Sheikh by the road, heading north to the airport and Dahab. After about 8km the road splits; take the left-hand fork to Dahab. From here the road then cuts further into the mountains, which are coloured in many places with veins of minerals. The desert here is mostly rock and scrub, the defining features being the bare mountains and the valleys and plains in between. Apart from the occasional car or bus, the chances are you will have the place to yourself, although, depending on the season, you might see Bedouin camps. The road drops down to the coast again as you come to a police post (87km). From here you can drive into Dahab (8km) for a swim and a drink, or keep going north into the desert towards Nuweiba. At the major junction, about 130km from Sharm al Sheikh, take the left turn towards St Catherine's Monastery.

2–3

The drive through the Sinai desert to St Catherine's Monastery (122km) follows a good road through beautiful if stark landscape. The driving is generally easy and there are plenty of places to stop and admire the great *wadis* (dry riverbeds) that cut through the peninsula. Wadi Ghazala, some 10km after the Dahab police post, is accessible and if you feel adventurous you could follow it some way, though your

Taking a Break

Sharm al Sheikh, Dahab and the St Catherine area all have plenty of options for eating and drinking and you'll also find refreshments at Wadi Feiran.

car probably wouldn't like it. Also on this road is the MFO checkpoint, the multinational force that observes the peace between Egypt and Israel.

There are several places to visit near St Catherine, starting with the monastery (▶ 160). The climb up to Mount Moses, where Moses is said to have obtained the Ten Commandments from God, is strenuous but worthwhile for its atmosphere and spectacular views over the mountains. The area around St Catherine is a protectorate where several excellent walking trails have been laid out. The official office (beside the monastery car-park) has details.

3–4

The road out of St Catherine continues through broad *wadis* for some 45km, where the mountains close in again. This is the beginning of the palm-lined Wadi Feiran. Early Christians identified this with the exodus of Moses and it

became sufficiently important to warrant a bishop. The ruins of the cathedral and ancient settlement are being excavated at the oasis of Feiran. You can visit the small convent near by (ask if it's open at St Catherine's Monastery, or just ring the doorbell), and the mountains are dotted with the caves and shelters of hermits.

4–5

Having crossed the desert, about 45km beyond Feiran is a junction with the west Sinai coast road. Turn left here, following signs for Tor, along the road back to Sharm al Sheikh, some 160km away. Heading south, the road cuts through a wide, barren plain with 2,000m-high mountains to your left. Some 57km from the junction a road leads right, through a small oasis, to the **Hammam Sayyidna Musa** ('Bath of Our Lord Moses'), a hot spring that's long been used for its healing properties. The farm here produces food for St Catherine's Monastery.

The main roads in Sinai are well kept and accessible to all vehicles

Further on is the town of Tor, once the gulf's main port and quarantine station for pilgrims returning from Mecca. **Ras Mohamed National Park** (▶ 163) is another 87km, and Sharm al Sheikh is 27km from there.

For more detailed itineraries in Sinai look for *The Red Sea Coasts of Egypt*, by Jenny Jobbins (AUC, available in Egypt).

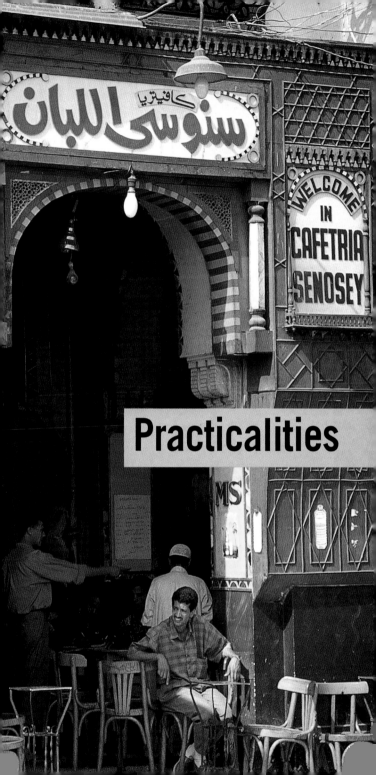

Practicalities

Websites

● www.tourism.egnet.net
A directory of hotels,
attractions, agents etc.

● http://ce.eng.usf.edu/
pharos Egypt web index

of everything from arts to
women.

● www.yallabina.com
What's on in Cairo,
including entertainment,
restaurants and nightlife.

In the UK and Ireland
Egyptian House
170 Piccadilly
London W1
☎ 020 7493 5283
Fax: 020 7408 0295

BEFORE YOU GO

WHAT YOU NEED

● Required
○ Suggested
▲ Not required
△ Not applicable

	UK	Germany	USA	Canada	Australia	Ireland	Netherlands	Spain
Passport/National Identity Card	●	●	●	●	●	●	●	●
Visa (tourist visa – available from airport on arrival)	●	●	●	●	●	●	●	●
Onward or Return Ticket	▲	▲	▲	▲	▲	▲	▲	▲
Health Inoculations (tetanus and polio)	○	○	○	○	○	○	○	○
Health Documentation	▲	▲	▲	▲	▲	▲	▲	▲
Travel Insurance	○	○	○	○	○	○	○	○
Driver's Licence (national)	●	●	●	●	●	●	●	●
Car Insurance Certificate (if own car)	●	●	●	●	●	●	●	●

WHEN TO GO

Cairo

☐ High season   ☐ Low season

JAN	FEB	MAR	APR	MAY	JUN	JUL	AUG	SEP	OCT	NOV	DEC
18°C	21°C	23°C	27°C	32°C	34°C	35°C	35°C	32°C	30°C	23°C	18°C

☀ Sun   ⛅ Sun/Showers

Temperatures are the **average daily maximum** for each month but differ greatly
between night and day, and over the country. The Mediterranean coast is always
cooler, while Cairo is extremely hot from June to September. The air becomes
drier towards the south, but although Upper Egypt is always hot, the nights can
be cold. March and April can bring the *khamseen*, a strong, hot wind that
carries sand from the Sahara. The winter months can be quite cold, often with
rain around Christmas. The tourist season is from November to February but
Cairo and Luxor are chilly then, and hotels are overbooked. The best time to
visit is May, or in October or November after the long, hot summer has ended.

In New York
630 Fifth Avenue
Suite 1706
New York NY 10111
☎ 212/332-2570
Fax: 212/956-6439

In Los Angeles
8383 Wiltshire Blvd
Suite 215
Beverly Hills CA 90211
☎ 323/653-8815
Fax:323/653-8961

In Canada
1253 McGill College Av,
Suite 250, Montreal
Quebec H3B 2Y5
☎ 014/861-4420
Fax: 014/861-8071

GETTING THERE

By air There are direct scheduled flights to Cairo from New York and Los Angeles, and from many European capitals. You can also fly there from the Middle East and most of the adjacent African countries (except Libya). Some international scheduled flights also land in Luxor, Alexandria and Aswan. Charter flights are available to Luxor, Hurghada and Sinai. When leaving Egypt, remember to reconfirm your flight 48 hours beforehand.

By sea Since Adriatic Lines stopped running regular ferries from Venice to Alexandria, cheaper but more erratic ferries from Istanbul in Turkey to Alexandria via Piraeus (in Greece) are the only option. Tickets can only be purchased in Istanbul, Athens and Piraeus. Daily ferries also run between Aqaba in Jordan and Nuweiba in Sinai.

By bus There are regular buses from Tel Aviv, Jerusalem and Eilat in Israel to Sinai and Cairo, crossing the border at Rafah or Taba, where Israeli departure tax and Egyptian entry fees have to be paid. Frequent buses also connect Cairo with Tripoli and Benghazi in Libya. Note that you cannot obtain a visa at the Egyptian border if you enter by land, and there are likely to be long delays at border crossings.

By car Complicated bureaucracy means that entering Egypt by car is one of the least popular options. You should be allowed to bring a car into Egypt for three months if you can show an *international triptyque* or a *carnet de passage de douane* issued by the auto-mobile club in the country where the car is registered. An extension of three months can be given to the driver in person by the Automobile and Touring Club of Egypt, 10 Sharia Qasr al Nil, downtown Cairo; tel: 02-574 3355.

TIME

Egypt is 2 hours ahead of GMT, or 3 hours ahead from the start of May to the start of October. But remember that time is a loose concept in Egypt.

CURRENCY AND FOREIGN EXCHANGE

Currency The basic unit of currency is the Egyptian pound (LE, *guineh* in Arabic). This is divided into 100 piastres (PT, *irsh* in Arabic). There are **notes** for 25 and 50 piastres and 1, 5, 10, 20, 50, and 100 pounds, as well as **coins** of 5 and 10 piastres. Small denominations are useful for *baksheesh*. Egypt is still generally a cash economy, so ensure that you carry sufficient money for your needs.

Travellers' cheques, preferably in US$, can be changed in all banks and exchange bureaux but it can be complicated and there is a transaction charge.

Credit cards are widely accepted at banks, hotels and upmarket restaurants, but it is wise to check first. Smaller establishments and shops are likely to prefer cash. More and more five-star hotels and banks in tourist resorts have automatic cash dispensing machines.

Exchange Independent exchange offices are quicker than banks and often offer a better rate. Always keep the receipts as you need them to buy an airline ticket or to pay the bill in a luxury hotel in Egyptian pounds.

TIME DIFFERENCES

GMT
12 noon

Egypt
2pm

USA (East)
7am

USA (West)
4am

Europe
1pm

Australia
(East) 10pm

WHEN YOU ARE THERE

CLOTHING SIZES

UK	International	USA	
36	46	36	
38	48	38	
40	50	40	
42	52	42	Suits
44	54	44	
46	56	46	
7	41	8	
7.5	42	8.5	
8.5	43	9.5	
9.5	44	10.5	Shoes
10.5	45	11.5	
11	46	12	
14.5	37	14.5	
15	38	15	
15.5	39/40	15.5	
16	41	16	Shirts
16.5	42	16.5	
17	43	17	
8	34	6	
10	36	8	
12	38	10	
14	40	12	Dresses
16	42	14	
18	44	16	
4.5	38	6	
5	38	6.5	
5.5	39	7	
6	39	7.5	Shoes
6.5	40	8	
7	41	8.5	

NATIONAL HOLIDAYS

1 Jan	New Year's Day
April	Sham al Nessim
25 Apr	Liberation Day
1 May	Labour Day
23 Jul	Revolution Day
6 Oct	Armed Forces Day
23 Oct	Suez Day
23 Dec	Victory Day

Egypt also observes Muslim feast days and the month of fasting, Ramadan. Dates follow the lunar calendar and move back by 11 days a year.

OPENING HOURS

- ○ Shops
- ● Offices
- ● Banks
- ● Post Offices
- ● Museums/Monuments
- ● Pharmacies

8am 9am 10am noon 1pm 2pm 4pm 5pm 7pm

□ Day   ■ Midday   □ Evening

All times given may vary. In tourist areas shops tend to remain open all day until late at night, especially in high season. Banks in tourist areas often stay open all day until late at night. Banks at Cairo airport and the Marriott and Nile Hilton hotels in Cairo are open 24 hours. Museums and monuments close between 11 and 1 on Friday for prayers. Post offices are open from Saturday until Thursday. Pharmacies are often open until 9pm or later.

During Ramadan, everything tends to open an hour later and close an hour or two earlier, but shops and some offices reopen from 8 to 10pm.

POLICE 122

TOURIST POLICE 126

FIRE 180

AMBULANCE 123

ANGLO-AMERICAN HOSPITAL IN CAIRO 02-735 6162

PERSONAL SAFETY

Petty crime is rare in Egypt but like everywhere else you should watch your belongings in busy tourist areas and on full buses.

- Leave valuables in the hotel safe. Carry only what you need.
- There is a crackdown on drugs, with fines for possession, and life imprisonment or hanging for anyone convicted of dealing or smuggling.
- Foreigners travelling between cities in Middle and Upper Egypt usually have to move in a police-protected convoy.

Tourist Police assistance:
☎ 126

TELEPHONES

Until recently, international calls could only be made from specified Telephone and Telegraph offices but Egypt now has an extensive network of payphones, operated by Menatel and Nile Communications. These can be used for local, national and international calls. Phonecards, available in values of LE5, 10, 20 and 40, can be bought from telephone exchanges as well as shops and kiosks displaying stickers with the Menatel logo. It is still possible to make local calls from coin-operated phone boxes, shops, hotels and kiosks, but these tend to be more expensive than calls made on Menatel phones.

POST

Buy stamps at post offices, souvenir shops and hotel newsagents. Airmail letters take about a week to arrive: post them at your hotel or at a post office; avoid street letterboxes. Cairo's main post office (open 24 hours) is on Midan al Ataba.

ELECTRICITY

The power supply is 220 volts. Sockets take two-round-pin plugs. British and US visitors will need an adaptor. North American visitors should check whether appliances need a voltage transformer.

TIPS/GRATUITIES

Tips are expected and may be a person's sole or main source of income. As a general guide:

Restaurants	✓	8–10% (if no service included)
Cafés / Bars	✓	10%
Tour guides	✓	LE5–10
Car parking	✓	LE1–2
Taxis	✓	Agree price first, 5–10%
Hotel workers	✓	LE5–10
Toilets	✓	LE2–3

CONSULATES and EMBASSIES

UK	**USA**	**Ireland**	**Australia**	**New Zealand**
☎ 02–794 0850	☎ 02-735 6437	☎ 02-736 8547	☎ 02-735 0444	☎ 02-795 9360

HEALTH

 Insurance Egypt has well-qualified doctors and good hospitals, particularly in Cairo and Alexandria. Taking out travel insurance which covers medical care is a must. Keep all receipts and medical bills for a refund back home.

 Dental Services In an emergency contact your embassy for a list of English-speaking dentists. Make sure you are covered by medical insurance. English-speaking dentist in Cairo: Maher Labib Barsoum, Sharia 26th July, Downtown; tel: 02-593 2532/591 5069.

 Weather Use a high factor sunscreen or sunblock, cover up with light cotton clothes, and wear sunglasses and hat when in the sun. Coffee and alcohol are dehydrating; instead drink at least 3 litres of water a day.

 Drugs Pharmacists (*saydaliya* in Arabic) usually speak English and can recommend treatment for minor ailments. A wide range of drugs is available over the counter and they are cheap. Check the expiry date and the leaflet to see if it is what you need. Most main cities or resorts have an all-night pharmacy.

 Water It is fairly safe to drink tap water in cities but buy bottles of mineral water elsewhere. Avoid ice cubes in drinks.

CONCESSIONS

Students and Youths
Museums and sights offer a 50 per cent reduction on tickets and there are also reductions on rail and airline tickets for students who have an official student card. An ISIC Student Card can be issued at the Egyptian Scientific Centre, 103 Mathaf al Manyal, Roda Island, Cairo (tel: 02-363 8815), or at the Ismailiya House. You need to bring one passport photo and proof that you are a student.

Senior Citizens
There are no concessions for senior citizens.

TRAVELLING WITH A DISABILITY

There are no special facilities for visitors with disabilities, although Egyptians accept disabilities as God's will and are always ready to help. Nevertheless, visiting the major sights can be quite a challenge, but if arrangements are made in advance, the experience will be rewarding.

CHILDREN

Children are welcome everywhere, and often attract a great deal of admiring attention. Some of the better hotels organise high chairs, cots and babysitters. but don't expect much in the way of baby-changing facilties.

TOILETS

Public toilets vary between sitting, squatting and standing up types, but they are often filthy. Instead of toilet paper, a bucket of water or squirter is provided. For a more comfortable experience, use toilets in upmarket hotels and restaurants.

WILDLIFE SOUVENIRS

Importing wildlife souvenirs sourced from rare or endangered species may be illegal or require a special permit. Before purchase you should check your home country's customs regulations.

SURVIVAL PHRASES

The official language in Egypt is Arabic, but English is taught in schools. People are always happy, and proud, to practise their foreign languages, but even if you only speak a few words in Arabic you will generally meet with an enthusiastic response. The following is a phonetic transliteration from the Arabic script. Words or letters in brackets indicate the different form that is required when addressing, or speaking as, a woman.

GREETINGS AND COMMON WORDS

Yes **Aywa, naam**
No **Laa**
Please **Min fadlak (fadlik)**
Thank you **Shukran**
You're welcome **Afwan**
Hello *to Muslims* **As salaamu alaykum**
Response **Wa alaykum as salaam**
Hello *to Copts* **Saeeda**
Welcome **Ahlan wa sahlan**
Response **Ahlan bik(i)**
Goodbye **Ma'a salaama**
Good morning **Sabaah al kheer**
Response **Sabaah en nur**
Good evening **Masaa al kheer**
Response **Masaa en nur**
How are you? **Izzayak (Izzayik)**
Fine, thank you **Kwayyis(a) il hamdulillaah**
God Willing **Inshallah**
No problem **Ma feesh mushkila**
Sorry **Ana aasif (asfa)**
Excuse me **An iznak (iznik)**
My name is... **Ismee...**
Do you speak English? **Bititkallim(i) ingileezi**
I don't understand **Ana mish faahem (fahma)**
I understand **Faahem (Fahma)**
I don't speak Arabic **Ana mish aarif (arfa) arabi**

NUMBERS

0	sifr	14	**arbahtaashar**
1	**wahid**	15	**khamastaashar**
2	**itnayn**	16	**sittaashar**
3	**talaata**	17	**sabahtaashar**
4	**arbah**	18	**tamantaashar**
5	**khamsa**	19	**tisahtaashar**
6	**sitta**	20	**ashreen**
7	**sabaa**	21	**wahd wa-**
8	**tamanya**		**ashreen**
9	**tesah**	30	**talaateen**
10	**ashara**	40	**arbaeen**
11	**hidaashar**	50	**khamseen**
12	**itnaashar**	100	**miyya**
13	**talataashar**	1000	**alf**

EMERGENCY! Taari!

Help! **Il haooni!**
Thief! **Haraami!**
Police **Shurta; bulees**
Fire **Hareea**
Hospital **Mustashfa**
Go away **Imshee**
Leave me alone! **Bass kifaaya!**
Where is the toilet? **Feyn it twalet?**
I'm sick **Ana ayyaan(a)**
We want a doctor **Ayzeen duktoor**

SHOPPING

Shop **dukkan**
I would like... **Ayyiz (Ayza)**
I'm just looking **Bi itfarag bass**
How much...? **Bi kaam?**
That's my last offer **Aakhir kalaam**
That's too expensive **Da kateer awi**
I'll take this one **Aakhud da**
Good / bad **Kwayyis / mish kwayyis**
Cheap **Rakhees**
Big / small **Kabeer(a) / sughayyar**
Open / closed **Maftooh / mooglak**

DIRECTIONS AND TRAVELLING

I'm lost **Mush aarif ana feen**
Where is...? **Feyn...?**
Airport **Mataar**
Boat **Madeeya**

DAYS

Today	**innaharda**
Tomorrow	**bukra**
Yesterday	**imbaarih**
Tonight	**innaharda bileel**
Morning	**issubh**
Evening	**massa**
Later	**bahdeen**
Monday	**youm al itnayn**
Tuesday	**youm at talaat**
Wednesday	**youm al arbah**
Thursday	**youm al khamees**
Friday	**youm al gumah**
Saturday	**youm is sabt**
Sunday	**youm al hadd**

Bus station **Mahattat al autubees**	
Church **Kineesa**	
Embassy **Sifaara**	
Market **Souk**	
Mosque **Gaama; masgid**	
Museum **Mathaf**	
Square **Midaan**	
Street **Shaari**	
Taxi rank **Mahattat at taxiyat**	
Train station **Mahattat al atr**	
Is it near / far? **Da urayyib / baeed?**	
How many kilometres? **Kaam keelu?**	
Here / there **Hinna / hinnaak**	
Left / right **Shimaal / yimeen**	
Straight on **Ala toul**	
When does the bus leave / arrive?	
Al autubees yisaafir emta / yawsal?	
I want a taxi **Ayyiz / ayza taks**	
Stop here **Hina kwayyis**	
Return ticket **Tazkara** *dhahab*	
Passport **Jawaz**	
Bus **Autubees**	
Car **Sayara**	
Train **Tren / ATR**	

RESTAURANT: Al matam

I would like to eat… **Ana biddeh aakal…**
What's this? **Eeh da (di)?**
Alcohol / beer **Khamra / beera**
Bread **Aysh**
Coffee / tea **Qahwa / shay**
Meat **Laama**
Mineral water **Mayya madaniya**
Milk **Halib laban**
Salt and pepper **Mih wa filfil**
Wine red / white **Nabit ahmar / abyad**
Breakfast **Fitaar**
Lunch **Ghada**
Dinner **Asha**
Table **Tarabeeza**
Waiter **Raees**
Menu **Cart / menu**
Bill **Al hisab**
Bon appetit **Bi l hana wa sh shiffa**

MONEY: Floos

Where is the bank? **Feen al bank?**
Egyptian pound **Guineh masri**
Half a pound **Nuss guineh**
Piastre **Irsh**
Small change **Fakka**
Post office **Bosta**
Mail **Barid**
Cheque **Cheque**
Travellers' cheque **Travellers' cheque**
Credit card **cart**

GLOSSARY TO THE TEXT

Ahwa café, coffee house
Amir military leader of the Mamelukes
Baksheesh alms, tip or bribe
Barque a ship with three masts
Beejou estate car service taxi
Cartouche a group of hieroglyphs representing the name of a leader, often carved into a wall or tablet
Calèche horse-drawn carriage
Caliph leader during the Islamic Fatimid Dynasty (10th-12th centuries)
Caravanserai lodgings for travellers and animals, around a courtyard
Corniche coastal road
Faience ceramic glaze, sometimes on a minaret
Falafel deep-fried, spiced, mashed chickpeas
Felucca sailing boat
Fuul ubiquitous bean stew
Hypostyle a building with a roof that is supported by pillars
Iwan vaulted space around a court-yard of a mosque or *madrasa*
Khanqah Sufi monastery
Khedive the viceroy of Egypt under 19th-century Turkish rule
Kuswari spicy mix of pulses, pasta and rice
Kuttab Quranic school for boys
Madrasa Quranic school
Mamelukes soldiers descended from slaves who established a Muslim dynasty from 13th–16th centuries
Maristan (Islamic) hospital
Mastaba grave, burial place
Mezze small plates of food, appetisers
Midan square
Mina ferry terminal
Moulid religious festival, often on the anniversary of a prophet's birth
Ptolomies rulers of Egypt, 304–330 BC
Pylon temple gateway formed by two truncated pyramidal towers
Sabil public water fountain
Sahn courtyard
Sharia street
Shawarma meat roasted on a spit
Sheesha water pipe i.e. pipe for smoking (flavoured) tobacco that draws smoke over water to cool it
Souk market
Tarboush fez, a traditional red, coni-cal flat-topped hat with a black tassel, worn by some Islamic men
Vizier governor

Atlas

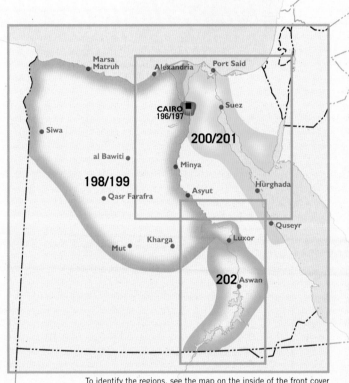

To identify the regions, see the map on the inside of the front cover

Regional Maps

—··— International boundary	□	City
═══ Major divided highway	▫	Major town
━━━ Main road	○	Large town
─── Other road	○	Town, village
Built-up area	▪	Place of interest
Cultivated area	✈	Airport

City Plan

─·─ Riverbus	*i*	Information
─── Rail line	●	Metro station
═══ City wall	▨	Important building
	◪	Featured place of interest

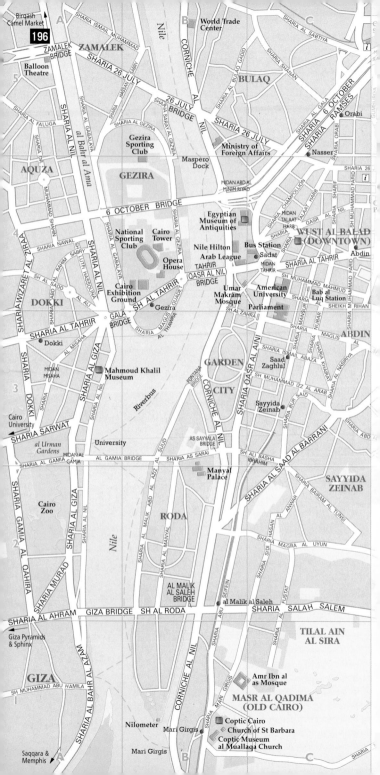

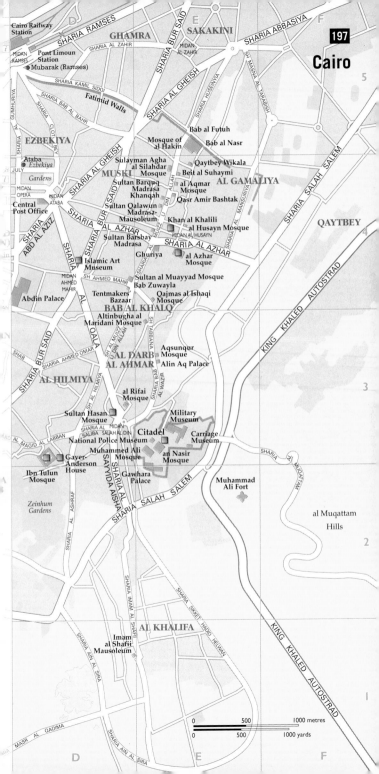

Cairo

Cairo Railway Station
GHAMRA
SAKAKINI
SHARIA RAMSES
D
E
SHARIA ABBASIYA
SHARIA BUR SAID
F
5

MIDAN RAMSES
Pont Limoun Station
Mubarak (Ramses)
SHARIA AL ZAHIR
SHARIA AL ZAHIR
SHARIA AL GHEISH
SHARIA HUSEINIYA
SHARIA AL MASNA AL TARABISI

SHARIA KAMIL SIDQI
Fatimid Walls
SHARIA BAB AL BAHR

EZBEKIYA
Bab al Futuh
Mosque of al Hakin
Bab al Nasr

Ataba
Ezbekiya
Gardens
SHARIA AL GHEISH
Sulayman Agha al Silahdar
MUSKI
Qaytbey Wikala
Beit al Suhaymi
al Aqmar Mosque
Qasr Amir Bashtak
AL GAMALIYA

MIDAN OPERA
Central Post Office
MIDAN ATABA
SHARIA AL AZHAR
SHARIA BUR SAID
Sultan Barquq Madrasa Khanqah
SHARIA AL MUIZZ LI DIN ALLAH
Sultan Qalawun Madrasa-Mausoleum
Khan al Khalili
al Husayn Mosque
SHARIA AL MANSURIYA

QAYTBEY
4

SHARIA ABD AL AZIZ
SHARIA AL AZHAR
Sultan Barsbay Madrasa
Ghuriya
MIDAN AL HUSAYN
SHARIA AL AZHAR
al Azhar Mosque
SHARIA SALAH SALEM

Islamic Art Museum
SH. AHMED MAHIR
MIDAN AHMED MAHIR
Sultan al Muayyad Mosque
Bab Zuwayla

Abdin Palace
SHARIA AL QALA
Tentmakers' Bazaar
Qajmas al Ishaqi Mosque

BAB AL KHALQ
Altinbugha al Maridani Mosque
SH. TABBANA
SH. AL MUIZZ LI DIN ALLAH

SHAB
SHARIA AHMED OMAR
AL DARB AL AHMAR
Aqsunqur Mosque
Alin Aq Palace
SHARIA BAB AL WAZIR
KING KHALED AUTOSTRAD
3

AL HILMIYA
SH. AL HILMIYA
al Rifai Mosque

AL QALA
SH. AL MAGID AL LABBAN
Sultan Hasan Mosque
MIDAN SALAH AL DIN
SHARIA AL SALIBA
Citadel
Military Museum
Carriage Museum
SHARIA AL MUQATTAM

National Police Museum
Muhammad Ali Mosque
an Nasir Mosque

Gayer-Anderson House
Ibn Tulun Mosque
SHARIA AL SAYYIDA AISHA
Gawhara Palace
Muhammad Ali Fort

Zeinhum Gardens
SHARIA AL ASHRAF
SHARIA SALAH SALEM
al Muqattam Hills
2

AL KHALIFA
SHARIA IMAM AL SHAFI
SHARIA SIKKET HADIQ HELWAN
KING KHALED AUTOSTRAD

SHARIA AIN AL SIRA
Imam al Shafi Mausoleum
1

MASR AL QADIMA
SHARIA AIN AL SIRA
0   500   1000 metres
0   500   1000 yards
D
E
F

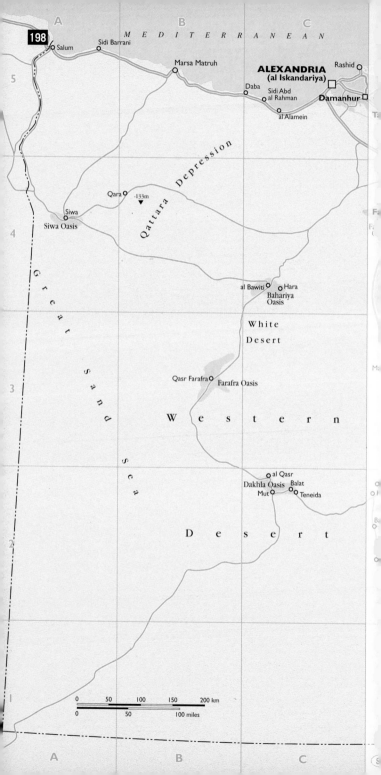

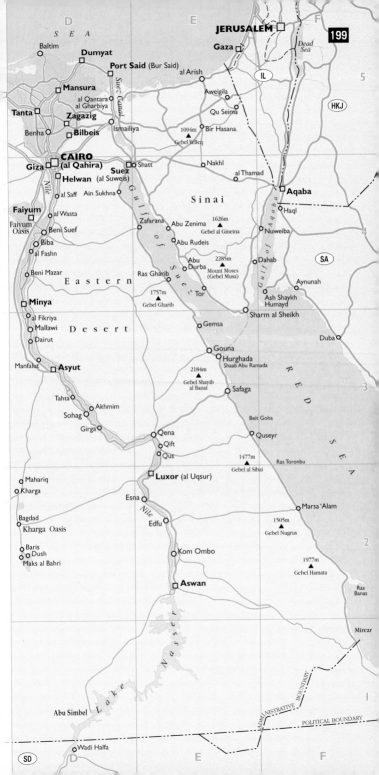

SEA

Baltim

Dumyat

Port Said (Bur Said)

al Arish

JERUSALEM

Gaza

Dead Sea

IL

5

Mansura

al Qantara
al Gharbiya

Aweigila

Qu Seima

HKJ

Tanta

Zagazig

Ismailiya

Bir Hasana

Benha

Bilbeis

1094m ▲
Gebel Yelleg

Nakhl

CAIRO
(al Qahira)

Giza

Shatt

Helwan

Suez (al Suweis)

al Thamad

Aqaba

Faiyum

al Saff

Ain Sukhna

S i n a i

Haql

SA

Faiyum
Oasis

al Wasta

Beni Suef

Zafarana

Abu Zenima

1626m ▲
Gebel al Gineina

Nuweiba

4

Biba

al Fashn

Abu Rudeis

Dahab

Beni Mazar

Ras Gharib

Abu
Durba

2285m ▲
Mount Moses
(Gebel Musa)

Aynunah

E a s t e r n

1757m ▲
Gebel Gharib

Tor

Ash Shaykh
Humayd

Minya

al Fikriya

Mallawi

D e s e r t

Gemsa

Sharm al Sheikh

Duba

Dairut

Gouna

Hurghada

Shaab Abu Ramada

Manfalut

Asyut

2184m ▲
Gebel Shayib
al Banat

R
E
D

Tahta

Akhmim

Safaga

Sohag

Girga

Beit Goha

S
E
A

Qena

Quseyr

Qift

Qus

1477m ▲
Gebel al Sibai

Ras Toronbu

Mahariq

Luxor (al Uqsur)

Kharga

Esna

Bagdad

Edfu

1505m ▲
Gebel Nugrus

Marsa 'Alam

2

Kharga Oasis

Baris

Dush

Maks al Bahri

Kom Ombo

1977m ▲
Gebel Hamata

Ras
Banas

Aswan

Mirear

Lake Nasser

ADMINISTRATIVE BOUNDARY

Abu Simbel

POLITICAL BOUNDARY

1

SD

Wadi Halfa

D

E

F

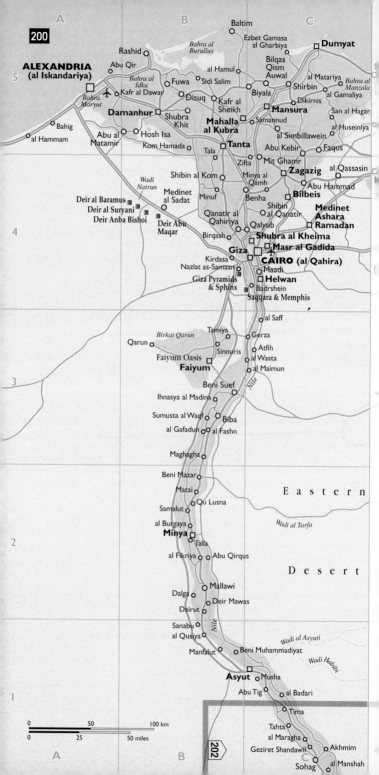

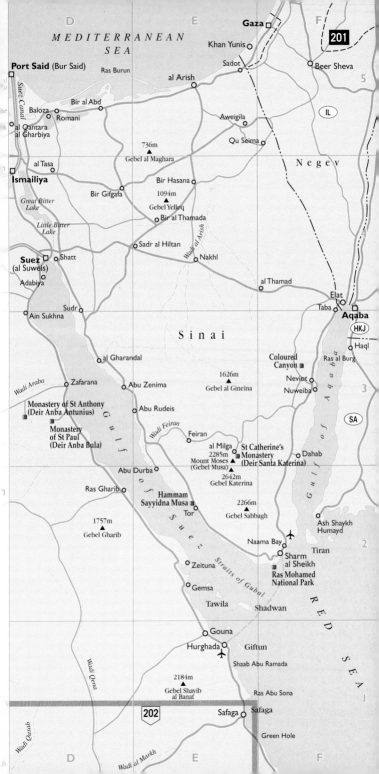

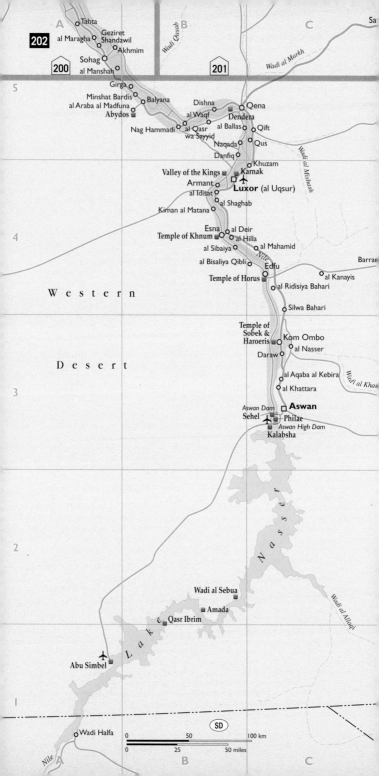

A

B

C

Sa

Tahta

al Maragha

Geziret Shandawil

Akhmim

Sohag

al Manshah

Wadi Qassab

Wadi al Markh

5

Girga

Minshat Bardis

al Araba al Madfuna

Balyana

Abydos

Dishna

al Waqf

Nag Hammadi

al Qasr wa Sayyid

al Ballas

Qena

Dendera

Qift

Naqada

Qus

Danfiq

Wadi al Mishash

Khuzam

Valley of the Kings

Karnak

Luxor (al Uqsur)

Armant

al Idisat

al Shaghab

Kiman al Matana

Esna

al Deir

Temple of Khnum

al Hilla

al Sibaiya

al Mahamid

al Bisaliya Qibli

Nile

Edfu

Temple of Horus

Barra

al Ridisiya Bahari

al Kanayis

4

W e s t e r n

Silwa Bahari

Temple of Sobek & Haroeris

Kom Ombo

D e s e r t

Daraw

al Nasser

al Aqaba al Kebira

Wadi al Kha

3

al Khattara

Aswan Dam

Aswan

Sehel

Philae

Aswan High Dam

Kalabsha

L a k e

N a s s e r

Wadi al Allaqi

2

Wadi al Sebua

Amada

Qasr Ibrim

Abu Simbel

I

Wadi Halfa

(SD)

Nile

A

B

C

0		50		100 km
0	25		50 miles	

Picture credits

Abbreviations for terms appearing below: (t) top; (b) bottom; (l) left; (r) right; (c) centre.

The Automobile Association wishes to thank the following photographers and libraries for their assistance with the preparation of this book.

Front and back cover: (t) Corbis UK Ltd/Kevin Fleming; (ct) AA Photo Library/Rick Strange; (cb) AA Photo Library/Chris Coe; (b) AA Photo Library/Chris Coe; Spine, AA Photo Library/Rick Strange.

AKG, LONDON 13cr (Erich Lessing), 25t, 26b, 27cl (Tony Vaccaro); THE ARTARCHIVE 23t, (Fine Art Museum Bilbao/Dagli Orti), 26t (Dagli Orti); ART DIRECTORS AND TRIP PHOTO LIBRARY 28/9, 29b, 71, 191t; AXIOM PHOTOGRAPHIC AGENCY 16/7 (J Morris), 56/7 (J Morris), 57 (J Morris), 67b (J Morris), 97 (J Morris), 132t (J Morris), 138/9 (J Morris), 139t (J Morris), 180 (J Morris); BRIDGEMAN ART LIBRARY, LONDON 14c Statue of the Cult of Osiris. Louvre, Paris, France/Giraudon, 25b Carpet Bazaar, Cairo, 1887 by Charles Robertson (1844–91) Christie's Images, London, UK; BRUCE COLEMAN COLLECTION 109b, 158, 160; JOHN ELK III 3(ii), 48b, 63b, 129, 130/1b, 135; MARY EVANS PICTURE LIBRARY 22t, 23b, 24t; EYE UBIQUITOUS 7b, 133t, 140, 152, 158/9, 178; GETTYONE/STONE 2(iii), 9t, 11t, 45, 64/5, 88, 89, 102t, 118/9, 143b; PATRICK GODEAU 164; RONALD GRANT ARCHIVE 15t, 15b; ROBERT HARDING PICTURE LIBRARY 8b, 10, 12b, 49t, 63t, 144; TERRY HARRIS/JUST SEAGRACE PHOTO LIBRARY 166; JIM HENDERSON AMPA ARPS 54t, 83b, 96; ROBERT HOLMES PHOTOGRAPHY 111l (Markham Johnson); HULTON GETTY 26/7 (Bettmann), 27t; THE HUTCHISON LIBRARY 12t (Juliet Hight Brimah), 20/1 (Mary Jeliffe); IMAGES COLOUR LIBRARY 14t, 59, 153, 156/7; PICTOR INTERNATIONAL, LONDON 86t; PICTURES COLOUR LIBRARY 113b, 114, 168; POWERSTOCK/ZEFA 111tr; REX FEATURES LTD 27b, 31; FRANK SPOONER PICTURES 13t (Aynos/Gamma); 13ct, 84t, 92/3, 102b; TRAVEL STOCK 163 (Tim O'Keefe); TRAVEL INK 2(ii) (Stephen Ballidas), 13b (Abbie Enock), 33 (Stephen Ballidas), 60t (Abbie Enock), 82b (Simon Reddy), 110 (Peter Kingsford); NIK WHEELER 50, 137b; PETER WILSON 52t, 53, 62/3, 139b; WORLD PICTURES LTD 2(i), 3(i), 5, 9b, 84b, 87, 107, 117, 179.
Every effort has been made to obtain the rights to use the photograph on page 32. The remaining photographs are held in the Association's own photo library (AA Photo Library) and were taken by the following photographers:
HUGH ALEXANDER 7t, 28l, 30t, 30l, 65, 90; CHRIS COE 3(iv), 6/7 b/ground, 6/7, 12/3 b/ground, 14/5 b/ground, 14b, 18tl, 18ct, 18tr, 19ct, 19b, 22tl, 28, 29r, 48t, 49b, 51b, 52c, 60b, 61, 67t, 68b, 80, 81, 82t, 93, 99t, 100, 111b, 116b, 118, 123, 131t, 132b, 133b, 134, 136t, 136c, 136b, 137t, 143t, 162t, 162b, 165t, 177, 182, 183, 185, 191bl, 191br; STEVE DAY 8/9t; RICK STRANGE 2(iv), 3(iii), 3(v), 6t, 8t, 11b, 19tl, 19tr, 22/3, 24b, 29t, 30b, 46t, 46b, 51t, 51c, 52b, 54b, 58, 66, 68t, 69, 70t, 70b, 79, 83t, 85, 86b, 91, 94/5, 98, 99b, 101, 108, 109t, 115, 116t, 119t, 120, 121, 130, 133c, 138, 141, 142t, 151, 154, 155t, 155b, 161, 165b, 167, 169, 181, 184, 186, 187.

SPIRAL GUIDES

Questionnaire

Dear Traveler

Your comments, opinions and recommendations are very important to us. So please help us to improve our travel guides by taking a few minutes to complete this simple questionnaire.

Send to: Spiral Guides, MailStop 66, 1000 AAA Drive, Heathrow, FL 32746–5063

Your recommendations...
We always encourage readers' recommendations for restaurants, nightlife or shopping – if your recommendation is added to the next edition of the guide, we will send you a FREE AAA Spiral Guide of your choice. Please state below the establishment name, location and your reasons for recommending it.

_____

_____

_____

_____

_____

Please send me AAA Spiral_____
(see list of titles inside the back cover)

About this guide...
Which title did you buy?

_____ **AAA Spiral**

Where did you buy it? _____

When? m m / y y

Why did you choose a AAA Spiral Guide? _____

_____

_____

_____

Did this guide meet your expectations?

Exceeded ☐ Met all ☐ Met most ☐ Fell below ☐

Please give your reasons _____

_____

_____

_____

continued on next page...

Were there any aspects of this guide that you particularly liked?

Is there anything we could have done better?

About you...

Name (Mr/Mrs/Ms)

Address

Zip

Daytime tel nos.

Which age group are you in?

Under 25 ☐   25–34 ☐   35–44 ☐   45–54 ☐   55–64 ☐   65+ ☐

How many trips do you make a year?

Less than one ☐   One ☐   Two ☐   Three or more ☐

Are you a AAA member? Yes ☐   No ☐

Name of AAA club

About your trip...

When did you book? m m / y y   When did you travel? m m / y y

How long did you stay?

Was it for business or leisure?

Did you buy any other travel guides for your trip?   ☐ Yes   ☐ No

If yes, which ones?

Thank you for taking the time to complete this questionnaire.

All information is for AAA internal use only and will NOT be distributed outside the organization to any third parties.